THE COMPLETE HANDBOOK OF
HOME EXTERIOR REPAIR & MAINTENANCE

Other TAB books by the author:

No. 898 *The How-To Book of Interior Walls*
No. 998 *The How-To Book of Floors & Ceilings*
No. 1244 *The Welder's Bible*
No. 1269 *How To Design & Build Your Own Workspace—with plans*
No. 1326 *The Compleat Outdoorsman*

THE COMPLETE HANDBOOK OF HOME EXTERIOR REPAIR & MAINTENANCE

BY DON GEARY

TAB BOOKS Inc.
BLUE RIDGE SUMMIT, PA. 17214

FIRST EDITION

FIRST PRINTING

Copyright © 1982 by TAB BOOKS Inc.

Printed in the United States of America

Reproduction or publication of the content in any manner, without express permission of the publisher, is prohibited. No liability is assumed with respect to the use of the information herein.

Library of Congress Cataloging in Publication Data

Geary, Don.
    The complete handbook of home exterior repair & maintenance.

    Includes index.
    1. Dwellings—Maintenance and repair—Amateurs' manuals. I. Title.
TH4817.3.G4   643.7   81-18329
ISBN 0-8306-0066-3   AACR2
ISBN 0-8306-1382-X (pbk.)

Contents

	Introduction	vii
1	**Roofing**	1
	Roof Construction—Inspecting Your Roof—Re-roofing with Asphalt Shingles	
2	**Gutters and Downspouts**	65
	Maintenance—Installation—Splash Blocks, Rain Barrels, and Dry Wells	
3	**Painting**	91
	Selecting Paint—Painting Equipment—Surface Preparation—Exterior Painting—Painting Metal—Painting Concrete—Maintaining Painted Surfaces	
4	**Plugging Leaks and Drafts**	169
	Caulking—Weather Stripping—Where to Apply Caulking and Weather Stripping—Application Tips	
5	**Masonry Repairs and Maintenance**	205
	Tools—Maintaining Concrete Surfaces—How to Patch Concrete Surfaces—Large Repairs to Concrete	
6	**Insulation and Ventilation**	239
	Condensation—Ventilators—Insulation—Ice Dams	
7	**Building Materials**	265
	Lumber—Plywood—Hardboard—Fastenings—Concrete—Siding	
8	**Siding**	275
	Siding Styles—Accessories—Tools Required—Equipment—Estimating Material—Saving Energy—Surface Preparation—Furring and Insulation Techniques—Base Chalk Line—Inside Corner Posts—Outside Corner Posts—Starter Strip—Window and Door Trim—Window and Door Trim; Gable-end Trim—Cutting Procedures—Installing the Siding—Nailing Pointers—Individual Corner Caps—Panels at Windows and Doors—Fitting at Gable Ends—Fitting Under Eaves—Insulated Siding—Vertical Siding—Caulking and Cleanup—Special Situations	
	Glossary	320
	Index	341

Introduction

Your home probably represents the largest single investment you will ever make. Consider that the average current price of a modern home is approximately $65,000—with many houses selling for above that price—and you begin to see just how large the investment can be. But purchase price is not the only cost of owning a home. You will need electricity and you must create a livable climate inside the house. Heating costs will probably account for 30 percent of your annual household expenses.

If you own a house that was built within the last five years or so, chances are that it will have sufficient insulation in walls and ceilings. If your home is more than five years old, chances are very good that it is underinsulated, and therefore inefficient in terms of heat retention capability. This inefficiency has a few other side effects that you might never have even considered. These include a shorter life for exterior coatings of paint, deterioration of siding, roof framing, and sheathing, and a roof covering (shingles) that does not last as long as it should.

A moisture problem is one of the surest signs that your home is energy inefficient. Usually the first signals noticed are peeling paint or dark spots on attic ceilings. The average American home, during the heating season, produces gallons of water vapor each day. During the colder months, when windows and doors are normally closed, moisture from cooking, bathing, washing dishes, and just plain living (we all give off about 1 pint of moisture while we sleep) will actually pass through building materials in an effort to get outside—unless some type of vapor barrier is installed in the home.

If water vapor is unrestricted in its route, it will cause paint to peel, roofing shingles to have a shorter life, masonry to crumble, and it will drastically reduce the benefit derived from insulation. Vapor barriers will cure the problem of damage caused by water vapor, but you must also provide some means for removing moisture from your home. Ventilation is the key. You will find quite a bit of information about it in Chapter 6.

In addition to providing protection from damage caused by water vapor originating inside the home, you must also prevent the entrance of water from the outside—specifically rain and snow. A sound roof is the best defense against water damage. In Chapter 1, you can find out how to judge the condition of your existing roof to determine if you need a new roof or if it will last.

Gutter and downspout systems around your roof provide the best insurance against water damage because they catch and divert water away from the house. Chapter 2 is devoted to installing, repairing, and maintaining these systems. Information is also given for constructing a dry well to hold rain and snow runoff.

In the chapter on painting, you will learn a great deal about paints in general, surface preparation, and the techniques of applying paint. Almost every American home has some surfaces that require painting. You will also find guidelines for choosing painting tools that will help you to achieve professional-looking and enduring results with any painting project.

In each of the chapters in this book, an exterior surface is examined in detail. Information is given so that you will be able to judge the condition of a given surface and determine its present state. In every case, I offer suggestions for periodic maintenance programs (ideally every spring and fall). A small amount of semiannual work will ensure that the exterior of your home looks good and, more importantly, that it is efficient in terms of preventing water damage and reducing the amount of energy required for heating and cooling.

Chapter 1

Roofing

If there is one thing that every homeowner has it is a roof over his head. Another thing that can be said for roofs is that they are probably the most overlooked part of any home. A roof just sits there on top of a house and doesn't seem to require much attention.

The truth of the matter is that a roof does require a bit of periodic maintenance. The main task of any roof surface is to keep water—in the form of rain, snow and ice—outside where it belongs. A roof in sound condition will accomplish this quite well.

If your roof leaks, chances are that the leak started many months ago with a small hole or crack in the roofing material or around some type of roof projection such as a chimney, a dormer, a wall, or a skylight. Roof leaks don't just begin to drip water into the interior of a home. This is a gradual process where first a small amount of water enters, through an opening in the roof deck, leading the way for more water to enter, and so on.

In this chapter, I will discuss the main type of roofing material in use today: asphalt (in one form or another). You will learn how to judge the age of your roof, how to determine if a new roof is called for, how to install a new roof, and how to keep your new (or existing) roof working silently for many years (Fig. 1-1).

There are several good reasons for the popularity of asphalt shingles. They are relatively inexpensive to buy and to apply to a roof surface. They have a 15- to 30-year lifespan under normal service. The weight and thickness of shingles are two of the most important factors in governing how long a roof will last.

Fig. 1-1. The most popular roofing material in America today is asphalt roofing shingles (courtesy of Celotex Corp.).

One very appealing feature about asphalt roofing materials is that they are not easily ignited. They will not spread flames and they will not contribute to a fire hazard by creating flaming brands that would endanger adjacent buildings. Asphalt roofing materials are classified by the Underwriter's Laboratories, Inc. (UL) as A, B, or C. These ratings correspond to the capability of the material to resist flame.

Modern asphalt roofing shingles are also wind resistant. This designation simply means that, when properly installed on a roof surface, the shingles can withstand winds of up to 60 miles per hour for two hours without a single tab being lifted. This wind resistance is accomplished by a special coating on the face of each shingle that cause it to adhere to the shingle on top of it and, in effect, be bonded in place (Fig. 1-2).

Add to these features the wide range of styles, colors, and textures of modern shingles and you begin to see why asphalt shingles are so popular as a roof covering. At the present time, you can find shingles in just about every imaginable color and white or black. It is entirely possible to put on a roof that will contrast with

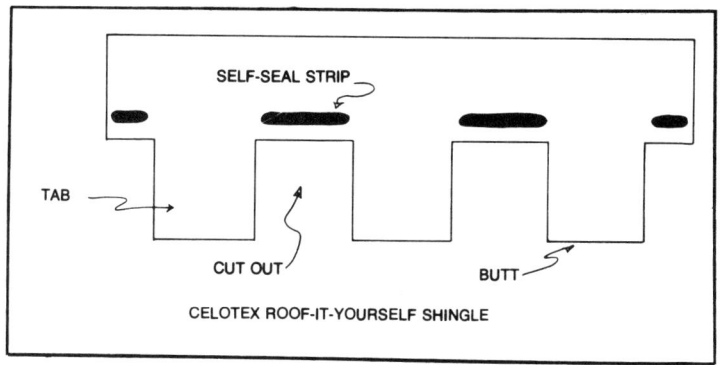

Fig. 1-2. Special self-sealing strips on modern shingles help to keep shingles down in high winds (courtesy of Celotex Corp.).

the surrounding landscape, the color of the house, and the color of the trim.

Because asphalt roofing materials are so popular, the bulk of this chapter deals specifically with them. Cedar shingles and wood shakes, slate, and tile are other types of finish roof-covering materials in use today. They are not as popular largely because of price.

Cedar shingles and shakes for roofing are the products of a distinctive natural material: the western red cedar (*Juniperus occidentalis*). This particular tree has played an important role in the building of America during the past century. The giant western red cedar grows in Washington, Oregon, Idaho, and British Columbia, and it produces a beautiful clear run of pure heartwood texture and

Fig. 1-3. Cedar shingles are attractive and they will last for approximately 25 years under normal conditions.

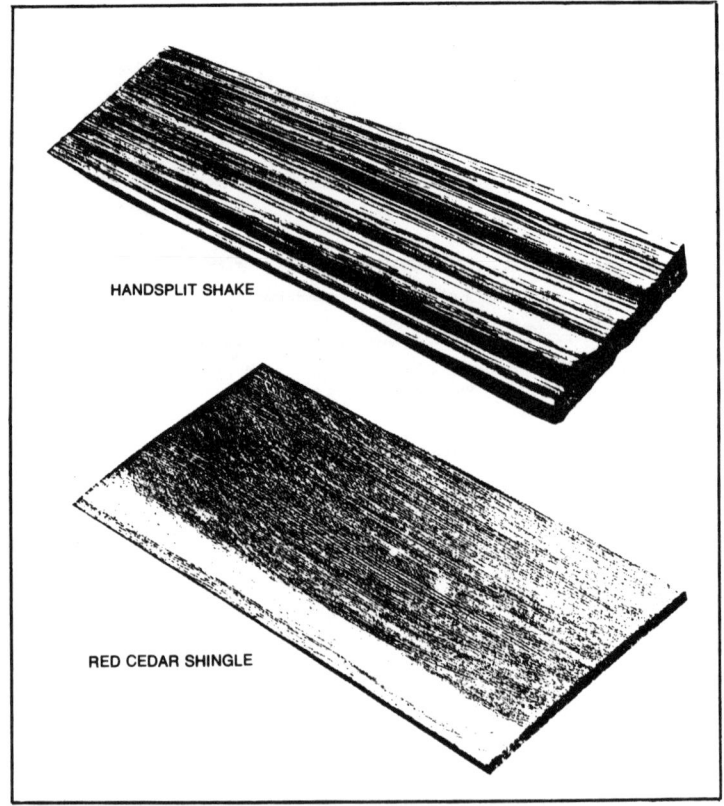

Fig. 1-4. Examples of a cedar shingle and a handsplit cedar shake.

grain that has graced the exteriors (and interiors) of thousands of homes across the land. Cedar shingles and cedar shakes are used for exterior siding and for roofing. The effect is always distinctive (Fig. 1-3).

The main difference between cedar shingles and cedar shakes is that the heavy, handsplit-and-resawn shake tends to create a strong, dominant roof while the cedar shingle, being more uniform in its lines, is more gentle in character. Generally, shakes add a rather rustic look to a roof (Fig. 1-4).

Cedar shingles and shakes are a long-life roof covering; you can reasonably expect a roof to endure the elements—wind, sun, and water—for at least 25 years. Generally, a roof covered with red cedar shingles will outlast a similar roof covered with conventional asphalt shingles. But you must pay a premium. A rough comparative estimate is that it will cost almost twice as much to install a

Fig. 1-5. Handsplit cedar shakes offer a distinctive roof pattern as well as a long-lived roof.

cedar-shingle roof or shake roof than it will to cover the same roof with asphalt roofing shingles (Fig. 1-5).

Slate roofs and tile roofs are undoubtedly the most long-lived roofs available. Slate roofs will often last approximately 100 years. As you might expect, however, a slate or tile roof is about the most expensive covering you can install. Not only must the roof structure be beefed up to hold as much as 800 pounds per 100 square feet, but slate and tile for roofing is costly in terms of materials and labor (Fig. 1-6).

Fig. 1-6. Slate roof coverings are expensive, but they are unmatched in charm or life expectancy.

Fig. 1-7. Tile roofs are very popular in certain parts of the country.

At the present time, the only active quarrying of slate in the United States is confined to the Eastern part of the country: Maine, Vermont, New York, Pennsylvania, Maryland, and Virginia. If you live very far from these states, you can expect to pay even higher prices for slate roofing tiles. While slate roofing materials are available, usually on special order, they are generally reserved for the most expensive, mansion-type houses and institutional buildings. If you own a home with a slate or tile roof, you can consider yourself fortunate. The roof will probably outlast you (unless of course it is damaged).

Roofing tiles are made in different parts of the country. The most popular type of roofing tile is terra-cotta in color and is the shape shown on the roof in Fig. 1-7. While not as expensive as roofing slate, roof tiles are more expensive than cedar shakes, cedar shingles or asphalt roofing shingles. When properly installed, roofing tiles will easily outlast the installer.

ROOF CONSTRUCTION

Before you check the condition of your roof or make any repairs, you should have some background information about how a roof is constructed. Armed with this type of information, you will not only be better equipped to handle roof repairs, but you will also better understand the underlying principles.

Basically there are two different types of roof systems in common use today: flat roofs, and pitched roofs. Flat roofs are installed over a framed structure on an almost horizontal plane. In

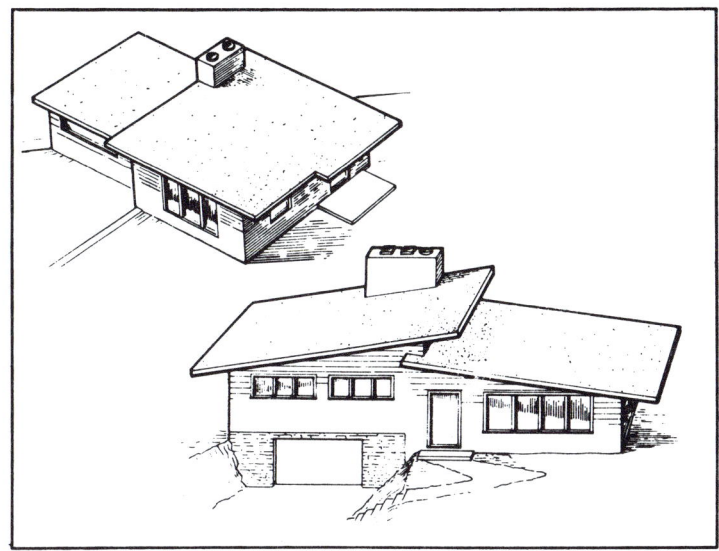

Fig. 1-8. Two examples of flat roof designs.

all cases, a *flat roof* is slightly higher on one end so that water will drain off the roof surface (Fig. 1-8).

A flat roof can be constructed of solid wooden decking (2 by 6- or 2 by 8-inch dimensional lumber, with tongue and grooved edges) or plywood sheating. In many cases, solid-wooden decking is used. This eliminates the need for joists or rafters. The decking forms the roof and a finished interior ceiling as well. With this type of structure, some type of insulating material is commonly placed over the solid decking to increase the R value of the surface (Fig. 1-9).

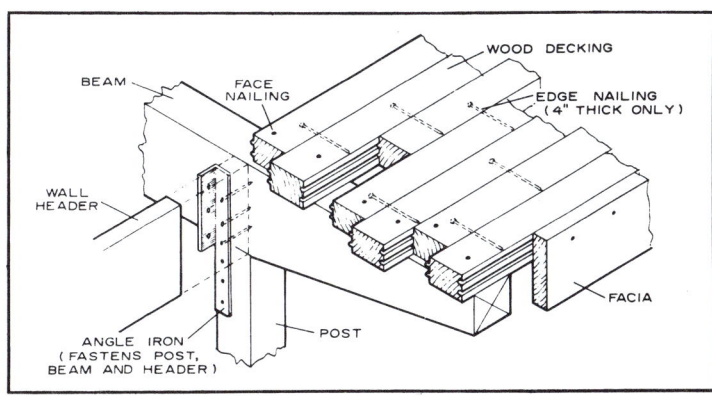

Fig. 1-9. An example of a flat-roof decking.

7

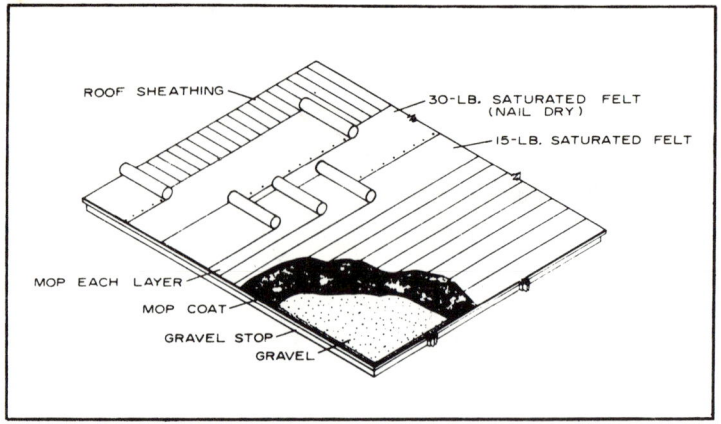

Fig. 1-10. Roll roofing on a flat roof.

When plywood sheathing is used for a flat roof deck, rafters or joists must also be used. These are most commonly spaced 16 inches apart and they are secured across the width of the structure. Then the plywood sheathing is attached to the rafters to form the roof deck.

After the roof deck is constructed—either solid wooden decking or joists and plywood—and some type of additional insulating material is added, the roof coating can be applied. This usually consists of a layer of asphalt-impregnated felt paper (commonly known as tar paper) and the finish roof coating. For flat roofs, the two most common types of finish roof coatings are roll roofing (Fig. 1-10) and hot tar and gravel.

Roll roofing is simply saturated felt paper that has been coated with a special water-resistant asphalt coating and a coating of mineral granules. The typical roll will weigh from 75 pounds to 90 pounds, and it will measure approximately 36 feet long and be 36 inches wide.

Also available are double-coverage or selvage-edged roll roofing. These rolls cover approximately one-half square of roof surface and they are meant to be installed with quite a bit of overlap. Double-coverage roll roofing is designed for flat roofs with less than 1 inch of pitch for every 12 inches of roof length.

Pitched roofs differ from flat roofs in that they require both ceiling joists (for the room below) and rafters or trusses for the roof. The simplest of all pitched roofs is called a *gable roof* (Fig. 1-11). All other types of pitched roofs are really just extensions of this simple pitched roof design.

In conventional construction, ceiling joists are nailed in place after the interior and exterior wall framing has been completed. Ceiling joists are installed across the width of the structure. Most commonly they have one end fastened to an exterior wall and the other to the top of an interior wall. In short, ceiling joists span half the width of the house. The underside of these joists will be covered with an interior finish material such as gypsum panels. The top side of these joists can be left as is or covered with plywood or other suitable material to create a floor in this attic space.

Rafters form the roof structure of the house and they are installed after the joists are secured in place. For a simple gable roof, the rafters are precut on the ground with the proper angle cut at the ridge and eaves, and with notches provided for the top plates. Rafters are erected in pairs and they are commonly spaced 16

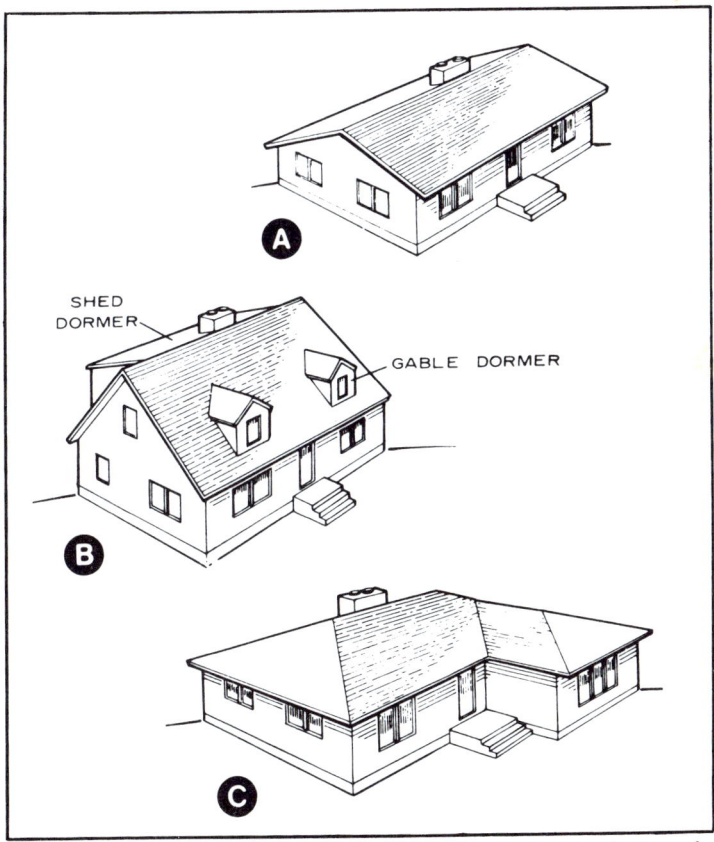

Fig. 1-11. Types of pitched roofs: (A) gable; (B) gable with dormer; (C) hip roof.

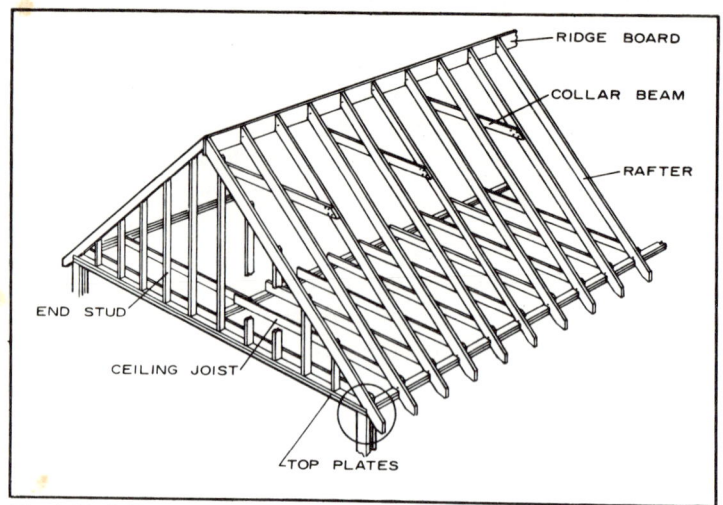

Fig. 1-12. Ceiling and roof framing on a gable roof.

inches apart. Studs for the gable-end walls are cut to fit and nailed to the end rafter and the top plate of the end wall *soleplate* (Fig. 1-12).

After all rafters have been nailed into place, at the top plate and ridge board, the roof *sheathing* can be installed. Roof sheathing can be boards—commonly 1 by 4- or 1 by 6-inch lumber with tongue and grooved edges—or plywood. Once the actual roof decking has been securely attached to the rafters, asphalt-impregnated paper is stapled or nailed into place. The next step is to install a finish roof coating. This can be either asphalt shingles, cedar shingles, cedar shakes, slate, or tile (the latter two requiring a basically heavier roof structure). See Fig. 1-13.

Roof trusses make up another type of roof structure now being used with greater frequency than the conventional joists and rafter system described above. A roof truss is an assembly of dimensional lumber that forms a rigid framework of triangular shapes that are capable of supporting loads over long spans without the need for interior load-bearing walls (from one exterior wall to another, for example). Because of this spanning characteristic, much more freedom in interior design and planning is possible.

Standard-length trusses, from 20 to 32 feet, are generally available from any lumber supply yard. Wood trusses are made in a woodworking shop and delivered to the building site. Because they are the actual roof structure, an entire roof can be installed and sheathed in a single day. Finish roofing materials are attached as described later in this chapter.

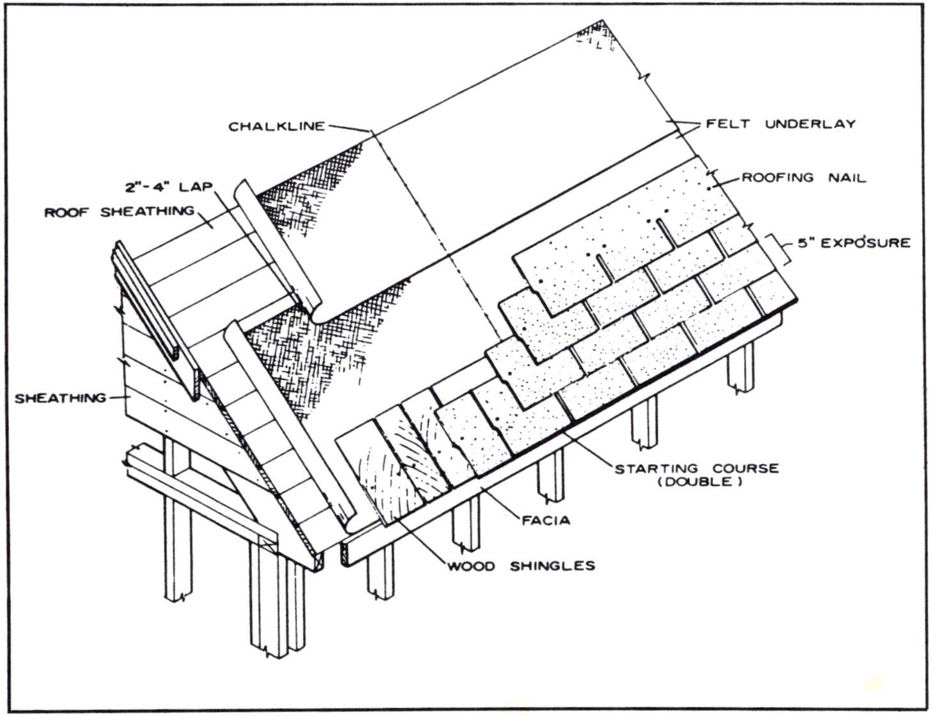

Fig. 1-13. How asphalt shingles are applied to a gable roof.

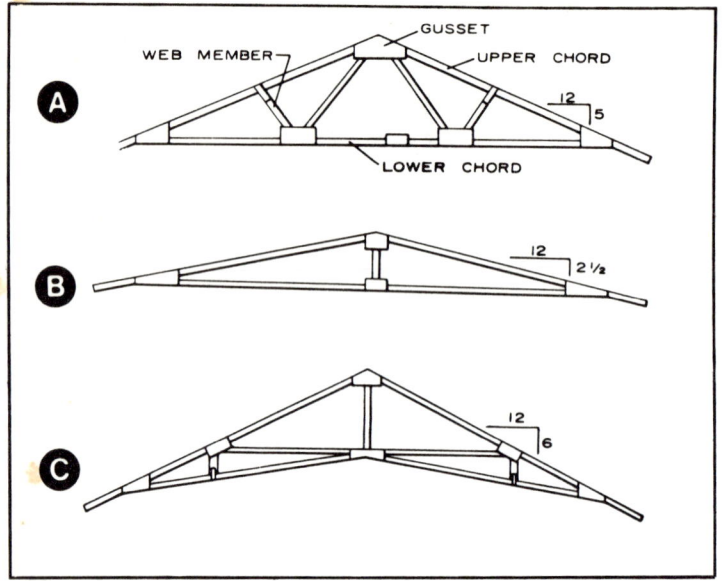

Fig. 1-14. Three examples of wood trusses: (A) W-type; (B) king-post; (C) scissors.

Two very appealing aspects of ready-made roof trusses are that they can be installed quickly, saving labor costs, and they allow almost total freedom in planning the interior of the house. Some of the more common truss designs are shown in Fig. 1-14.

INSPECTING YOUR ROOF

In this section, I will assume that you already have a roof covered with asphalt shingles. Twice a year you should spend an hour or more checking all exterior surfaces of your home. Probably the two best times of the year for these exterior checks are in the spring and fall. The spring check will indicate how your home fared through the winter months, and it will give you a good indication of the work that must be done during the warmer months. The fall check will reveal those things that must be done before cooler weather sets in once again.

The first thing to keep in mind is that many roof checks can be easily made from the ground. If your eyesight is good, you can spot roof-coating failures or signs of deterioration from the ground. If your eyes are not as good as they once were, do your checking with a pair of binoculars. While you will not be able to check your entire roof surface from the ground, you will be able to spot some problems. Then you can get out the ladder and go up for a more thorough check (Fig. 1-15).

From the ground, some of the things you should be looking for are torn or missing shingles (Fig. 1-16). These are relatively easy to spot and they are sometimes indicators of a serious problem.

Another roof deficiency you should keep an eye out for are any areas that have indentations or bulges. It is important to keep in

Fig. 1-15. You should look over your roof—from the ground if possible—at least twice a year.

Fig. 1-16. Missing shingles are easy to spot.

mind that any roof surface, flat or pitched, is supposed to be relatively flat along its plane. If sags or bulges appear, this is usually a sign that the rafters underneath the sheathing are warped. They might have to be replaced if the problem is serious. Sags on a flat roof can be more of a problem than on a pitched roof. Water will collect in these depressions. Leaks, and possibly decaying joists, can be the result of such wetness.

If you spot sags or bulges from the ground, it would be a good idea to check the attic space for other indications of the problem. Simply look at the joists or rafters. If they are black or if they are mildew covered, you have a moisture problem that needs to be corrected. In most cases, this will mean removing the old joists or rafter and replacing it with another. One alternative is to jack up the sagging rafter (a special jack can be rented for this) and to nail a section of 2 by 6 dimensional lumber to the sagging rafter. After nailing, remove the jack and the problem will have been nicely corrected. If you discover that the roof sheathing has been badly damaged by water, then you will have to replace part of the roof deck as well.

Another check that can be done from the ground is to look at the flashing. Flashing is the sheet metal-like material usually installed around any projections on the roof such as dormers. The flashing should not have any holes or missing sections.

The entire length of all roof valleys should be inspected. You will often spot debris such as leaves and twigs in valleys and these should be removed. You can do this with a strong stream from a garden hose, from the ground, or you can do a better job by going up on the roof. Roof debris is obviously more of a problem in areas surrounded by trees (Fig. 1-17).

You can also do some roof checking from inside if the building has an attic. After you are in the attic, turn off all lights in the space. Once your eyes have become accustomed to the darkness, look for spots of light coming from the outside of the roof. Some of the more obvious places to look are around chimneys, plumbing vent pipes, and any other roof projections. In most cases, these areas will have been flashed and then caulked. Nevertheless, caulking has a tendency to dry out and shrink over time.

If you spot some potential problems from the ground or from inside your attic, the next step is to get out your ladder and go up onto the roof for a more careful inspection. Before you climb up on your roof, you should keep one thing in mind. The fastest way back to the ground begins with a wrong step. Every year, especially

Fig. 1-17. Debris in valleys should be cleaned out at least twice a year.

Fig. 1-18. Always check your ladder before use.

during the warmer months when homeowners are repairing and maintaining their homes, hundreds of homeowners injure themselves while working on a ladder. In the majority of these cases, accidents could have been prevented if the homeowner had not forgotten where he or she was in the first place. To accomplish the work outlined in this book, the homeowner will have to climb up a ladder to do the various tasks: painting, roofing, and cleaning and maintaining gutters and downspouts. Obeying the following ladder safety rules will greatly reduce your chances of injury when working with a ladder.

☐ Thoroughly inspect any ladder before use. If it is in need of repair, do not use it until the problem has been corrected (Fig. 1-18).

☐ Clean the rungs of your ladder before using it and again if the rungs become dirty with mud, grease, paint or anything else.

☐ Before you climb, make certain that your ladder stands on firm ground. In some cases, this means placing a piece of plywood under the feet of the ladder—in soft dirt, for example (Fig. 1-19).

☐ When using an extension ladder, overlap so that the top section is outermost. Extend 36-foot ladders a minimum of 3 feet; 48-foot ladders at least 4 feet; and 5 feet for ladders that are 60 feet long. Make certain that the locks are securely hooked before you climb. A little oil on moving parts will keep them operating smoothly. Never attempt to extend a ladder while you are on it.

☐ Do not stand on a ladder in front of door openings unless you are absolutely certain that the door cannot be opened. One way to insure this is to place an obstacle on the inside of the door (such as a chair or a box).

☐ It is always best to extend your ladder at least 3 feet above the roof edge. You should never stand on any of the top three rungs of any ladder.

☐ When climbing up or down, always face the ladder and always use at least one hand for support.

☐ The angle of a ladder against a building is important. A good rule or thumb is that the distance from the base of the ladder to the building should be approximately one-fourth the ladder's working height.

☐ Working around electrical lines is potentially very dangerous. Try never to place your ladder around electrical lines. Be careful not to let the ladder or any part of your body come in contact with the wires.

☐ Store all ladders out of the weather (preferably hung, and in a dry, well-ventilated area).

Fig. 1-19. Use a board or a piece of plywood under ladder feet on soft or unlevel ground.

Fig. 1-20. For safety, always face a ladder when ascending or decending.

For safety's sake, you should observe these simple rules of working with a ladder. Keep in mind that they are just as important when you are using a ladder for a major project as they are for retrieving a Frisbee that someone has thrown up on your roof.

One other thing that should be taken into consideration before you climb up a ladder is the clothing and footwear you are wearing. After something like 15 years of climbing up and down ladders and being on roofs, I have come to the conclusion that the best type of footwear for this type of work is a sturdy pair of boots with a pliable rubber sole. Another choice is a pair of sneakers. Odd as it might seem, many authors recommend them because they will not mar asphalt shingles where you are working on a roof.

Fig. 1-21. Boots like these will mar asphalt shingles.

Now that you have the proper footwear on your feet and, you have set your ladder safely up against the roof, you can climb up and give the roof a thorough check. The first thing you should look at is the general condition of the shingles. A roof in good condition will have shingles that appear to lie flat. The general appearance will include lots of granular material on the surface of each shingle. If the shingles appear curled, or puffy, (they might actually crack or crumble as you walk over them) you can figure that a new roof is needed. Asphalt shingles have a life span of from 15 to 30 years. As they near the end of their usefulness, there is a general breakdown in their overall composition. The shingles will crack easily. In some parts of the country—the Southwest for example—this drying out of the shingle material can happen more rapidly than in other parts of the country where the sun is not quite as intense (Fig. 1-22).

Aside from the general appearance of the shingles, there are other areas you should check for shingle deterioration. Inspect all roof projections such as chimneys, soil vent stacks, ventilation systems, evaporative coolers, and anything else that passes through the roof. The areas directly around the projections will most often have some type of metal cover or special flashing that has been nailed down and coated with a layer of roofing tar. Check the metal and tar for signs of deterioration. With older roofs, the tar will appear cracked and dried. Usually a new layer of roofing tar (an asphalt base preparation) will add new life to the material. This

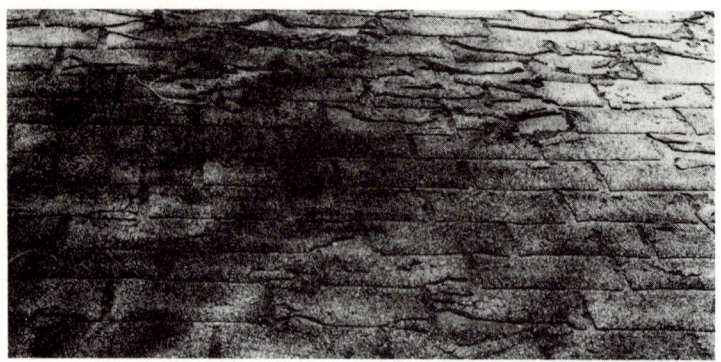

Fig. 1-22. When asphalt shingles become puffy or brittle, it is time to put on a new roof.

should be done when installing a new roof, and every fall as part of your home maintenance program (Fig. 1-23).

The next part of your roof check should be at all *ridges* on the roof. A simple gable roof will have one ridge—the very top or peak of that roof. If a dormer or other room-like projection is present, you should check these ridges as well. All ridge shingles should be flat on a roof and in good condition (**Fig. 1-24**).

Fig. 1-23. Check the cement around roof projections such as this plumbing vent pipe.

Fig. 1-24. Ridge shingles should lie flat and be in good condition.

The next check should be of the *flashing* on your roof. The most common places for metal flashing are in valleys, around chimneys (especially the up-roof side) and wherever two roofs meet. The first thing you will probably notice when inspecting flashing is that a certain amount of debris is present (leaves, twigs, etc). Carefully remove this (a soft broom works well) and then check the general condition of the flashing itself. The metal need not be shiny to do the job of diverting water off the roof, but there certainly should not be any holes present or water could pass underneath the flashing and possibly into the attic space (**Fig. 1-25**).

There are also a number of checks that you should do on a flat roof. These will have to be done while you are actually on the roof. First examine the general condition of the roofing material. The strips of roll roofing should be flat, and the edges or seams should not have any curls, bulges, or missing sections. The granular surface should also be in good condition with no bare spots. As roll roofing ages, there is a definite loss of surface granular material. Roll roofing past its prime will have a surface that is rather sparsely covered with these granules.

Indentations or bulges on the roof surface are potential problem areas because of poor drainage. The result can be deterioration of the roofing material, and in extreme cases, a failure of the roof sheathing and joists below. If you find any depressions, you will have to get below the roof and check the joists and sheathing. If this is not possible, you must remove the finish roofing material—and possibly a section of the roof decking—so that you can ascertain and correct the problem.

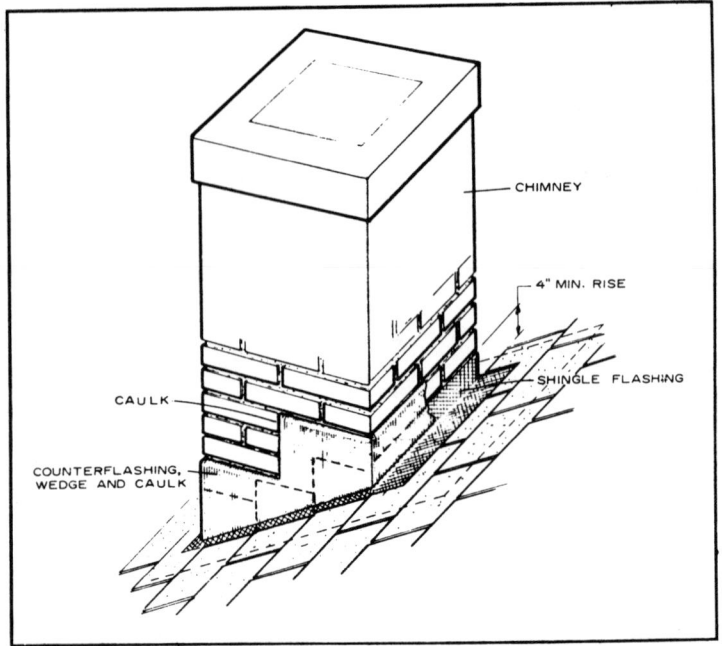

Fig. 1-25. Flashing and tar around the chimney should be in good condition.

Another flat-roof check involves having a look at anything that passes through the roof. This includes plumbing vent pipes, chimneys and skylights. The area around each projection should have flashing and a coating of roofing tar. The flashing should be in sound condition and the roofing tar should solidly cover the joints between the flashing and the roof, and the flashing and the projection. As with pitched roofs, roofing tar will dry out and crack with time. It should be recoated about once a year (Fig. 1-26).

Other flat-roof deficiencies you should keep an eye out for are raised nailheads, broken or missing section of the roll roofing, and any other signs of deterioration. You can rightly figure that a flat roof roll roofing should have a life span of about 12 to 15 years. After that time, some signs of deterioration will be present. The solution is to either repair, where possible, or to replace the entire roof.

There are two methods of applying roll roofing to a flat roof deck. These are the *concealed-nail method* and, the *exposed-nail method*.

The exposed-nail method of attaching roll roofing to a flat roof deck is probably the most widely used method. It is suitable for any flat roof that has a pitch (a rise in height) of at least 2 inches for every

Fig. 1-26. Flashing on flat roofs must have tar that is not cracked or missing.

12 inches of length. For roofs that are pitched less than this, the concealed nail method should be used.

Roll roofing is applied horizontal to the roof deck in sheets that are usually 12 to 18 feet long. As an aid in straightening the first strip (applied at the low end of the roof deck), strike a chalk line up from the roof edge at 35 inches. This will leave a 1-inch overhang. This chalk line will be your guide in positioning the first strip of roll roofing (Fig. 1-27).

Roll out the first sheet of roofing so the lower edges and end will extend approximately 1 inch over the eaves and rake of the roof deck. Drive roofing nails along a line from one-half inch to three-fourths of an inch down from the top edge of the sheet, and spaced about 18 inches apart. The top nails are necessary to hold the strip in place and more nails will be used when the second, overlapping sheet is applied. You should drive your roofing nails along the eaves and rake on a line approximately 1½ to 2 inches from the edges of the roofing. Space these nails about 2 inches apart and stagger them slightly along the eaves to avoid the possibility of splitting the edge of the roof deck (Figs. 1-28 and 1-29).

Fig. 1-27. Strike a chalk line to indicate the placement of the top edge of the first sheet of roll roofing.

Apply the second strip of roofing so that it will overlap the first strip by approximately 2 inches. Drive nails along the top edge of the sheet approximately 18 inches apart. Positioning the second sheet will be easier if you strike a chalk line 34 inches from the top of the first sheet (Fig. 1-30).

After the top edge of the second sheet has been nailed, fold the entire sheet upward onto the roof deck—toward the high end of the roof. Now you must apply a coating of roofing cement along the top 2 inches of the first strip of roofing. Because this is the area where the second sheet will overlap the first, it makes sense to add extra protection here. Next the second sheet is flopped back into position. The bottom edge of the second strip is seated into the roofing cement along the top edge of the first strip. Some roofers (myself included) like to add a coating of roofing cement along the eaves of the roof deck as well. A band of roofing cement approximately 1 foot in width will provide added protection in heavy storms and high wind (Figs. 1-31 and 1-32).

After the second sheet has been repositioned over the first, the overlapping edge is nailed into place. Make certain that the roofing is lying flat before nailing. Nails should be driven about 1 inch up from the edge and spaced about 2 inches apart (Fig. 1-33).

Whenever you are driving roofing nails into roll roofing, it is important that you do not break the surface of the roofing. Tap the nail until it is flush with the surface and no further. A hole or break in the roofing material can set the stage for a leak (Fig. 1-34).

Succeeding strips of roll roofing are applied in the same manner until the roof is entirely covered. The last strip can overlap the

Fig. 1-28. Roll out the roofing along the chalk line.

next to the last strip more than 2 inches or you can trim the last strip so that it overlaps only by 2 inches.

Whenever you apply roll roofing you will find that you will only be able to get a certain number of full-length strips from each roll.

Fig. 1-29. When the top edge of the roll roofing is aligned with the chalk line, nail the top edge.

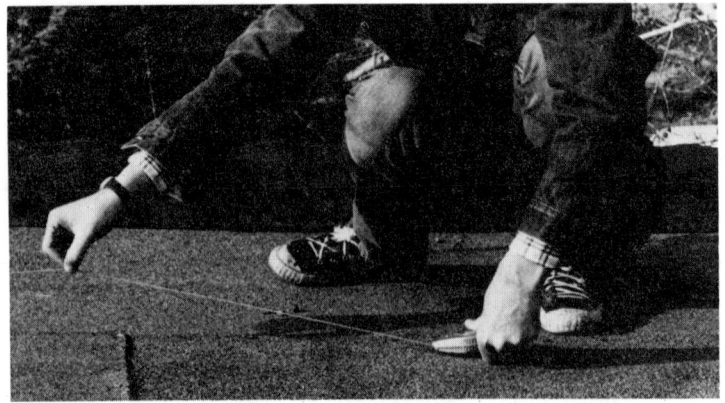

Fig. 1-30. Strike a chalk line for the top edge of the second sheet.

The excess or remaining strip will obviously be short. These short strips can be used in groups to form an entire course. The most important thing to keep in mind when using short strips is that the end lap joints must be overlapped about 6 inches. The end lap joints

Fig. 1-31. Apply a coat of roofing tar before placing the second sheet of roll roofing.

26

Fig. 1-32. Make sure you coat the edges of the roof deck with the tar.

must also be cemented along the entire joint. If you must use several end lap joints, stagger them so that an end lap in one course will never be over or adjacent to an end lap in a preceding course (Figs. 1-35 and 1-36).

Fig. 1-33. Fold the second sheet into place and nail along the bottom edge (through both the second and first sheets).

Fig. 1-34. Make sure you drive the nails flush with the roofing material.

Begin by attaching a 9-inch wide strip of roll roofing around the entire perimeter of the roof along the eaves and rake. This strip should overhang the eaves and rake by 1 inch and be secured with two rows of roofing nails. Drive the nails about 1 inch in from each edge and space them approximately 4 inches apart (Fig. 1-37).

Fig. 1-35. Coat the edges of roofing material where they will overlap.

Fig. 1-36. Overlap the edges by at least 4 inches and nail in place.

Next, lay out a full sheet of roll roofing so that it overlaps the edge strips and so that all edges are flush. Secure the top edge of the full strip by driving nails along that edge; space them about 4 inches apart. Fold the first strip upward, away from the eaves. Brush a

Fig. 1-37. A 9-inch wide starter strip is nailed around the perimeter of the roof deck.

29

Fig. 1-38. The starter strip is given a coating of roofing cement.

thick coat of roofing cement on top of the edge strip where the full sheet of roll roofing will overlap (Fig. 1-38).

The last step is to fold the full strip of roll roofing back down into place. Apply pressure to insure that the first strip is embedded in the cement (Fig. 1-39).

Succeeding courses of roll roofing are applied in a similar manner. A strip is positioned so that it overlaps the preceding course by about 2 inches. The top of the strip is nailed into place, and the strip is folded up so that a band of roofing cement can be applied along the top edge of the first strip and along the edges. Then the second strip is folded back into position and pressure is applied to firmly embed the edge of the second strip into the roofing cement.

Roll roofing is an economical method of protecting your flat roof from the elements. There is nothing really difficult about installing roll roofing using either the concealed-nail method or the exposed-nail method. There are, however, a few tricks of the trade that are used by professional roofers to help them accomplish the work quicker as well as to obtain better results.

First, it is not a good practice to apply roll roofing when the outside temperature is at or below 7 degrees Celsius. All roll roofing becomes very brittle at or below this temperature and it will

Fig. 1-39. Roll roofing is laid out and pressed into place over the tarred starter strip.

have a tendency to crack when unrolled. If you must work at lower temperatures, you can increase your chances of success by storing the roofing material in a warm place for at least 24 hours before unrolling.

When working in moderate temperatures, it is a good practice to unroll the roofing and let it lie face down (black side up so the Sun's rays can warm the material). Roll roofing that has been warmed in such a way is easier to manipulate. There is almost no chance of it cracking and it will tend to lie flatter when installed (Fig. 1-40).

For areas with high winds, the roofing industry recommends the following types of roll roofing (when installed according to the directions given above): 18-inch wide mineral surfaced, 65-pound

Fig. 1-40. Lay roll roofing out in the sun—backside up—and it will warm up. This makes working with roll roofing much easier.

31

smooth, blind nailed, and 19-inch selvage, double-coverage, roll roofing. As a general rule, the concealed-nail method of installing roll roofing will result in a longer-lived roof.

When you purchase *roofing cement*, or roofing tar as it is commonly called, buy the brand and type that is recommended by the manufacturer of the roll roofing. This way you can be certain that there will be good compatibility between the cement and the roofing material. Store the roofing cement in a warm place until it will be used. In cooler weather, you can warm roofing cement by placing the "tar bucket" in a larger container of warm water. *Never*, in any case, try to warm asphalt roofing cement with an open flame. It is highly combustible.

When you are installing roll roofing on a bare roof deck, it is important to choose the proper nails for the job. The best nails for this type of work are 11- or 12-gauge, hot-dipped galvanized nails. This type of nail will be three-eighths of an inch thick (the shank) and it will have large heads (about seven-eighths of an inch round). Nails of 1 inch in length are about right for new construction. If you are installing roll roofing over an existing roll roofing then you must choose nails that are longer so they will pass through the new roofing the old roofing, and penetrate about three-fourths of an inch into the roof deck. In most cases, roofing nails that are 1½ to 2 inches should do the job nicely (Fig. 1-41).

When a roll roofing is installed properly, you can reasonably expect 12 to 15 years of service. While roll roofing is certainly not the most attractive roof covering, it is easy to install and it will do the job of keeping the elements out.

RE-ROOFING WITH ASPHALT SHINGLES

Eventually all roofs need replacement. Asphalt roofing shingles have a life expectancy of from 15 to 30 years. Much depends on the thickness of the shingles (some types are rated for longer life than others), climate, relative air quality, installation, and general orientation of the roof.

The worst enemy of any roofing material is the sun. It causes shingles to dry out, fade, and become brittle as they deteriorate. Wind, water and temperature extremes also contribute to the breakdown of roofing materials. The signs of weathering on roofing shingles are easy to spot. These include excessive mineral granule loss, cracks in the shingles, blistering, curling, and even missing shingles. A good place to check for excessive mineral granule loss is the area around downspouts and inside gutters. There will always be some granules in these places, but there should not be an excessive amount. If the asphalt material beneath the mineral granules is visible—this material is black—then chances are very good that your roofing shingles are in the late stages of deterioration and they should be replaced. Problems of the above nature usually do not present themselves until a roof covering is about 12 years old.

Occasionally, during a heavy wind storm, it is possible for one or more shingles to lift up slightly and be broken or torn out of place. If your roof is in relatively good shape otherwise, you can simply repair the damage by replacing the missing shingle or shingles.

Before you can replace a torn shingle, you must first remove the nails that hold it in place. You will also have to remove the nails in the shingles above the damaged shingle. Begin by lifting the tabs of the shingle above and inserting the end of a pry bar (sometimes called a shingle bar) under the shingle and the nails that hold it in place. Now push down on the bar and the nail should come out. Work carefully so you don't damage this shingle. Once all of the nails have

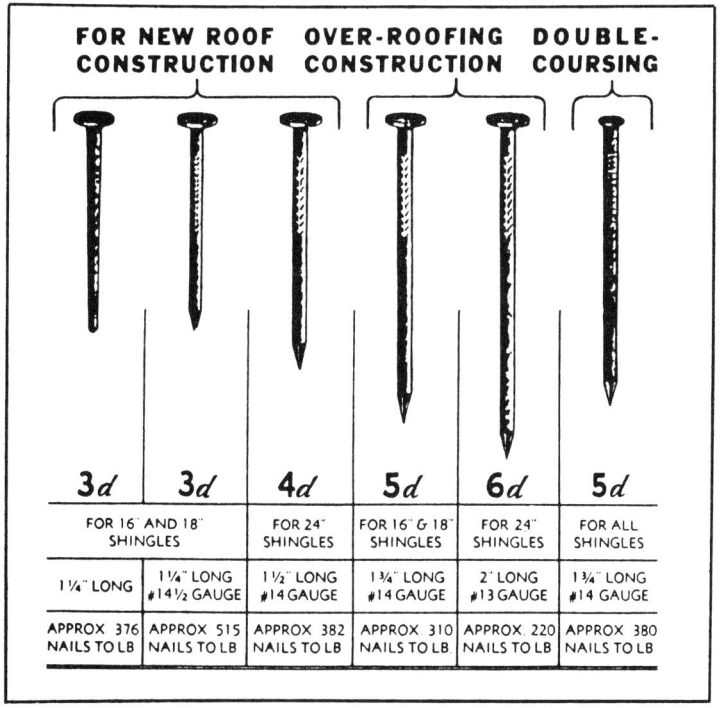

FOR NEW ROOF CONSTRUCTION		OVER-ROOFING CONSTRUCTION			DOUBLE-COURSING
3d	3d	4d	5d	6d	5d
FOR 16" AND 18" SHINGLES		FOR 24" SHINGLES	FOR 16" & 18" SHINGLES	FOR 24" SHINGLES	FOR ALL SHINGLES
1¼" LONG	1¼" LONG #14½ GAUGE	1½" LONG #14 GAUGE	1¾" LONG #14 GAUGE	2" LONG #13 GAUGE	1¾" LONG #14 GAUGE
APPROX 376 NAILS TO LB	APPROX 515 NAILS TO LB	APPROX 382 NAILS TO LB	APPROX 310 NAILS TO LB	APPROX 220 NAILS TO LB	APPROX 380 NAILS TO LB

Fig. 1-41. Roofing nail chart.

Fig. 1-42. A torn asphalt shingle.

been removed from the shingle above, repeat the process on the damaged shingle. There should be four nails in each shingle. After all nails have been removed, slide the damaged shingle out (Figs. 1-42, 1-43, 1-44 and 1-45).

A new shingle is inserted into place and the bottom edge is aligned with other shingles in the course. Nail the new shingle into place, but keep in mind that the nails must be driven in so that they will be concealed by the tabs of the shingle above. After the new shingle has been nailed, you must nail the shingle above. These nails must also be concealed. Work carefully because older shingles tend to be brittle. If you find that the old but undamaged shingles are too brittle to lift up for nailing, it might be better to face nail the culprits. If you do this, you must cover the exposed nailheads with

Fig. 1-43. Remove the nails in the shingle above the torn shingle. A special shingle bar is ideal for this.

Fig. 1-44. The nails in the torn shingle are removed with the bar.

roofing cement to prevent entrance of moisture. (Figs. 1-46, 1-47 and 1-48).

Another common problem with older roofs is that the shingles will have a curl along the bottom edge. If many shingles are in this

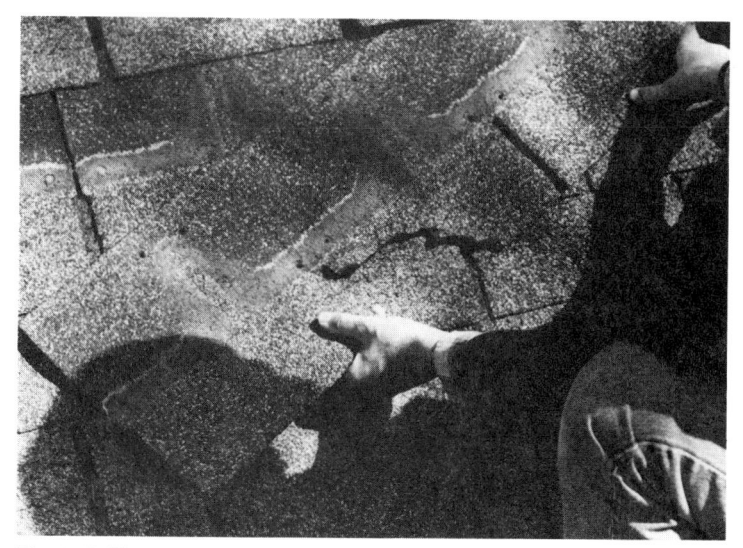

Fig. 1-45. The torn shingle is removed.

35

Fig. 1-46. A new shingle is placed into position.

condition, it would be best to remove the shingles. If only a few shingles are slightly curled, you might be able to correct the problem and get a few more years out of the roof before replacing it. Simply lift the edges of the shingle and place a dab of roofing cement underneath. Then press the shingle back into place so the edge is embedded in the cement (Figs. 1-49, 1-50 and 1-51).

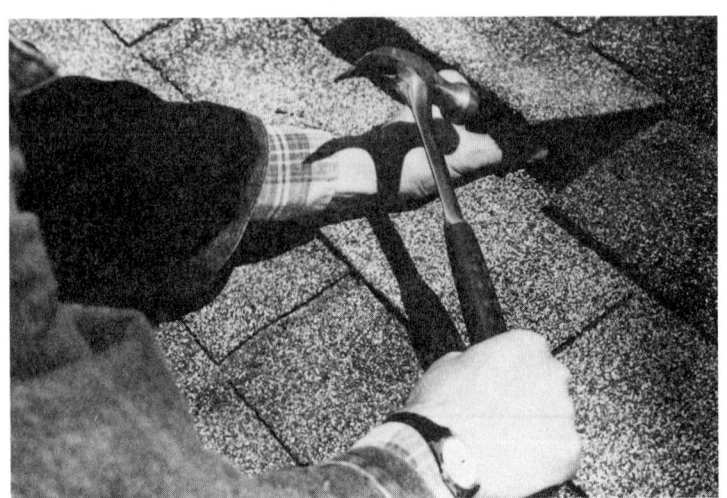

Fig. 1-47. The shingle above is nailed, but be careful not to lift the tab too high or it will break.

Fig. 1-48. A new shingle is face nailed and a daub of roofing cement is applied to the nail holes.

If you decide that your roof does need to be recovered, it is time to start computing material needs, shopping around for roofing materials, and setting aside some time to do the project. Determining the number of shingles you will need to cover your existing roof is not as difficult as it might seem at first. Standard asphalt roofing

Fig. 1-49. The edge of the shingle has been lifted by wind.

Fig. 1-50. Apply a daub of roofing cement under the edge of the shingle.

shingles are sold by the *square*. In the trade, that means 100 square feet (a section measuring 10 by 10 feet). The following instructions are based on using "standard" shingles. If you use "metric" shingles, the calculations will be slightly different. In either case, write down the dimensions of your roof and consult with your supplier when you place an order for materials. The first thing to do is to determine the square footage of your roof and simply divide this figure by 100.

Measuring your roof is very simple if you have a standard gable-type roof. Simply measure one side of the roof—length and width. Then multiply this figure by 2 to arrive at the total square footage figure for your roof. Perhaps an example will serve as an aid.

Fig. 1-51. Press the shingle down and into the roofing cement.

Let's assume that one side of your gable roof measures 40 feet long and 20 feet wide (from the eaves to the peak). This will give you 800 square feet (20 by 40). Multiply this by 2 and you have the total square footage for your entire roof: 1600 square feet. To determine the number of squares of asphalt shingles you will need to cover your roof you must divide by 100 (160 ÷ 100 = 16 squares of roofing material). Don't forget that you will also need shingles for capping the peak of the roof. This is easy to calculate. You already know that the length of the house is 40 feet. You will need approximately three cap type shingles per foot. So you will need one-third of a square, or one extra bundle of shingles (Fig. 1-52).

If your house has a roof design other than a simple gable roof, you will have a bit more calculating to do. If you have a *hip roof*, for example, you must determine the square footage of two triangles and two parallelograms. The formula for a triangle is: area = ½ base × height. The formula for a parallelogram is: area = height × ½ length of ridge plus length of eaves. Another example might be of some help to you in your calculations. Figure 1-53 illustrates a typical hip roof. Using the measurements in the diagram, results in the equation:

$$(½ \times 40 \times 18) + (18 \times ½ \times 25 + 60) \times 2$$
Area of one end   one side   sides
$$360 + 285 \times 2 = 1290$$

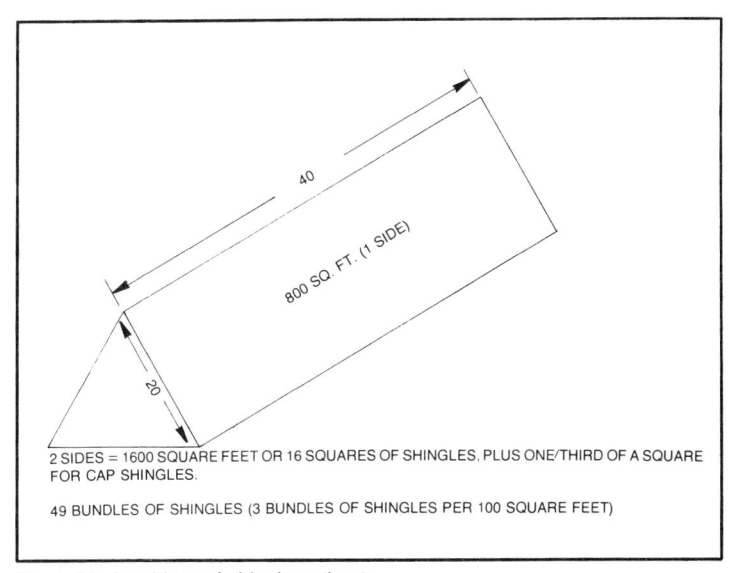

Fig. 1-52. A gable-roof shingle estimate.

```
               HIP ROOF SHINGLE ESTIMATE
```

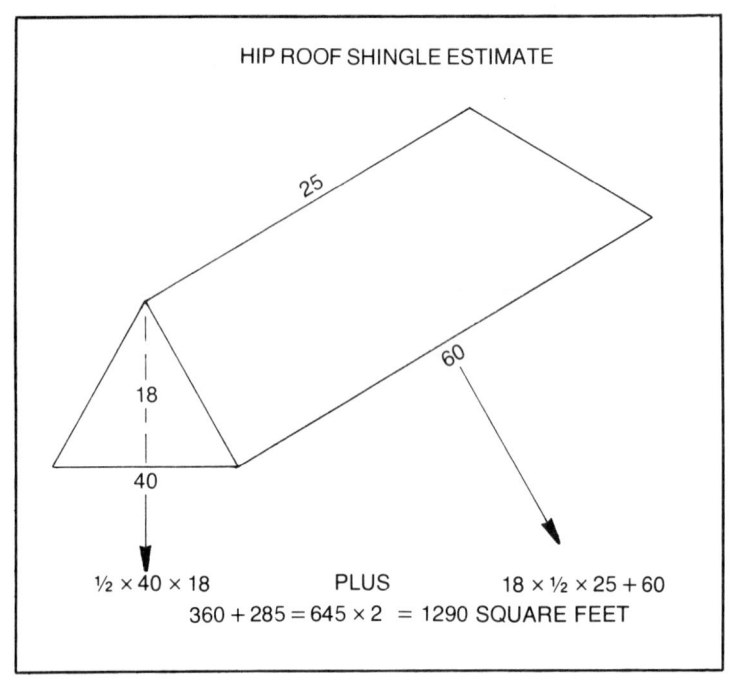

[Diagram of hip roof with dimensions: 25 (slant), 18 (end height), 40 (end width), 60 (length)]

½ × 40 × 18   PLUS   18 × ½ × 25 + 60
     360 + 285 = 645 × 2 = 1290 SQUARE FEET

Fig. 1-53. A hip-roof shingle estimate.

This particular roof has 1290 square feet. This translates into 12.9 squares of roofing shingles. You must also add the number of shingles you will need to *cap* this roof. In this case, you will need enough shingles to cap 113 feet of ridge and hip lines.

If your roof differs from the above two examples, you should not have any problem determining the square footage. A 50- or 100-foot steel tape will make short work of the measuring. It is always wise to order an extra bundle of shingles to allow for waste. Your shopping list of roofing materials should include the amount of flashing material you will need for the job. Your roof might have aluminum or asphalt flashing. If your house is very old, you might have copper. Copper flashing is rarely used on modern homes.

There is a difference of opinion over what is the best flashing material to use on a roof—aluminum flashing or a double layer of roll roofing (suitably cut). Asphalt flashing is less espensive, but it will last only as long as the rest of the roof covering. I believe best material to use for this work is aluminum flashing.

To determine the amount of flashing needed for your roofing project, simply measure the length of all valleys (Fig. 1-55) and come up with a total figure. It is wise to purchase an extra 10 percent of this material to allow for waste and overlapping of sections.

You should determine if you will need to replace any special flashing or cover materials around protrusions on the roof (Fig. 1-56). These include plumbing vent pipes, ventilators, and soil stacks. Flanges are made for these common roof projections and you can buy them ready-made. Simply measure the diameter of the pipe (they are usually 1-inch, 2-inch or 4-inch pipe).

You will also need a 5-gallon bucket of asphalt cement. While it is possible to buy this cement in 1-gallon pails, you will easily find use for 5 gallons.

It is also important to select the proper type and length of roofing nails for the re-roofing project. As with roll roofing, the best type of nails are those that are specifically designed for installing asphalt roof-covering material. Buy 12-gauge, hot-dipped, galvanized roofing nails that are long enough to pass through the new roof covering, through the old roof covering, and about three-fourths of an inch into the roof decking. See Fig. 1-41. Generally,

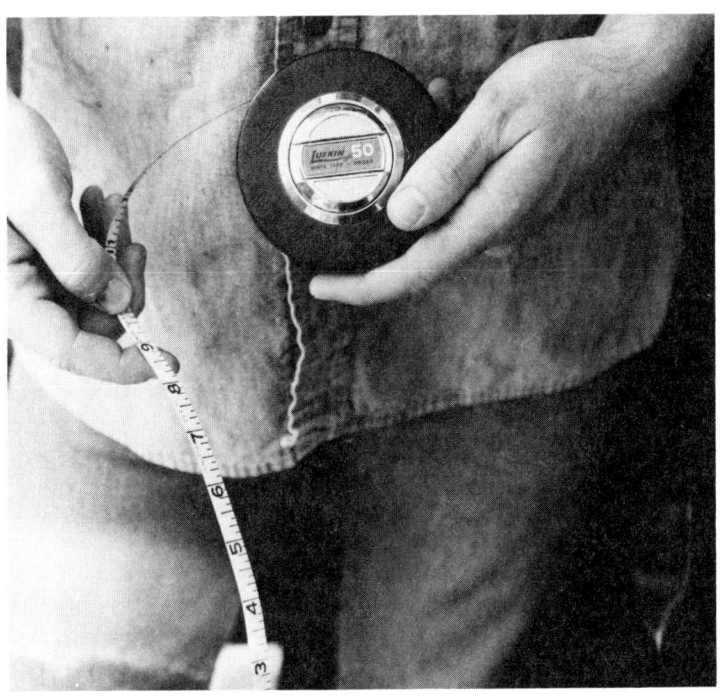

Fig. 1-54. A 50-foot steel tape is a real aid in measuring a roof.

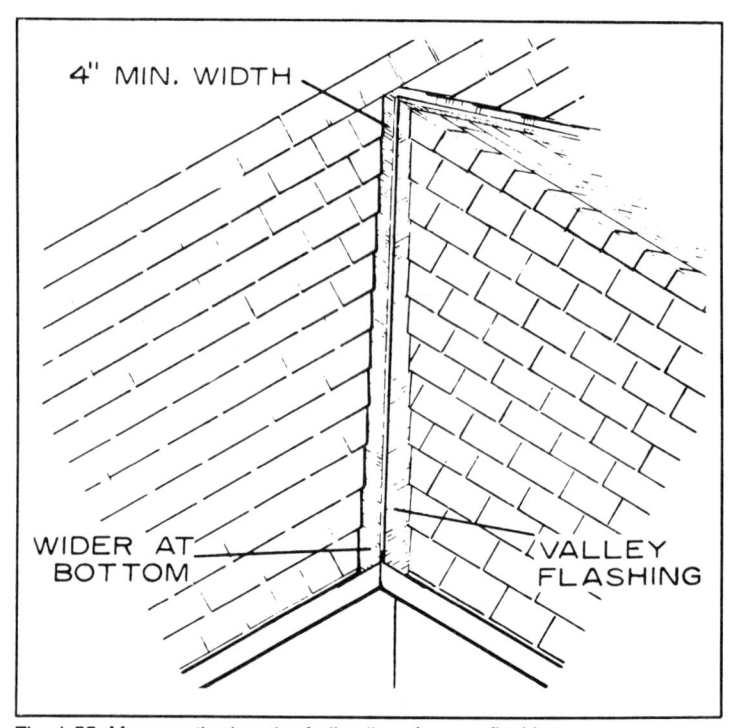

Fig. 1-55. Measure the length of all valleys for new flashing.

this will mean roofing nails 1¼ to 1½ inches in length for a second roof coating. Never apply a third layer of shingles to a roof.

Before you actually go out and purchase these materials, you should determine if you will be installing a new roof over the existing roof or removing all existing roofing materials and then recovering the roof deck with new asphalt shingles. The rule for re-roofing is that you can install up to two coverings of roofing material over a roof, but never a third covering. This simply means that if your existing roof has one layer of asphalt shingles, you can re-roof by adding another layer of shingles. If your roof already has two coverings of asphalt shingles, it will be necessary to remove both of these layers before covering the deck with new asphalt shingles.

If it is necessary to remove the old roof covering, you will—in addition to spending more time with this project—also have to cover the bare roof deck with asphalt-impregnated felt paper (commonly referred to as tar paper). Buy enough felt paper (15- or 30-pound per roll) to cover the roof deck based on your calculation of square footage for the project. One roll will cover approximately 400 square feet.

To determine how many coverings your existing roof has, pick a spot along the eaves of the house and lift up the layers of shingles you will find there. It is common roofing practice to install a double layer of shingles at the eaves. Figure 1-57 illustrates an example. If you find two layers of shingles, this will (almost certainly) mean that your roof has only one roof covering. If you find four layers at the eaves, the roof will have two layers of roofing already installed.

A little common sense helps. If you know that your house is less than 20 years old, for example, the chances of it having more than one layer of roofing are about equal. For houses older than this,

Fig. 1-56. Inspect flashing around roof projections and determine if replacement or simply a coating of new tar is required.

Fig. 1-57. Check the layers of shingles that are visible along the eaves. Divide by two to determine the number of layers of exisiting shingles.

you can reasonably expect that there are two layers of roofing or that the roof has been previously re-shingled. If you are in doubt, check other areas on the roof until you are quite certain as to the number of layers of roofing material.

If you tear off the existing roof coverings, be prepared for some very strenuous work. Everything must come off the roof until you are left with a bare wooden roof deck. A common practice among professional roofers is to remove the existing roof covering with large flat-edged shovels. Asphalt shingles and wooden shingles can be removed in this way. Keep in mind that *everything* must come off the roof deck: old shingles, nails, flashing, vent flanges, and old felt paper.

Once the roof deck has been exposed, you should inspect the boards or sheathing for soundness. Damaged or rotten roof sheeting must be replaced or repaired. Loose or missing knot holes should be covered with sheet-metal patches. Any loose boards should be renailed. Your aim during this surface preparation is to create a flat, sound, and sturdy roof deck that is ready to receive new shingles.

The first step in installing shingles on new construction or on a roof deck that has just had the old roofing material removed is to sweep off the entire roof. Next, the deck is covered with asphalt-impregnated roofing felt paper. This is installed parallel to the eaves—starting at the eaves—and stapled or nailed in place. Succeeding courses of the felt paper are overlapped at least 2 inches. The easiest way to do this is to start on one end of the roof and roll the paper (Fig. 1-58) across the deck, parallel to the eaves, make sure the course is straight, and then nail the felt with a zig-zag pattern. Repeat for the next course. Overlap hips and ridges by at least 4 inches.

Roofing felt paper will keep water out if it should rain while the roof is still uncompleted. Felt paper also serves as an effective barrier between the roof decking (which often contains resins) and

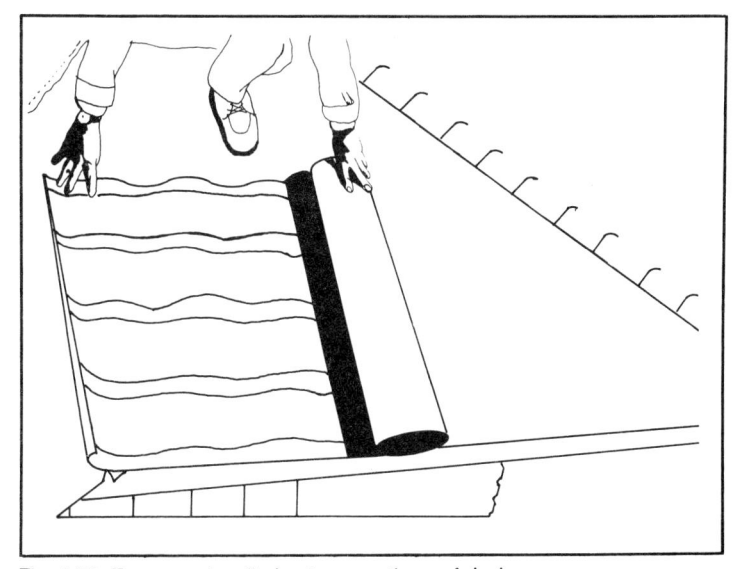

Fig. 1-58. Tar paper is rolled out across the roof deck.

the finish roofing. If the resins in the roof decking come in contact with the finish roof materials, this could cause the shingles to deteriorate quickly. That would obviously mean a short roof life. Another function of the felt paper is to help prevent the entrance of wind-driven rain from coming in contact with the roof decking.

Once the entire roof deck has been covered with felt paper, shingling can begin. The techniques for working on a roof deck that is covered with felt paper or with one layer of asphalt shingles already in place are virtually the same.

A roofing project is a big undertaking. You should consider asking a friend or two to lend a hand. Bundles of shingles must be carried onto the roof so they can be installed. As my father was fond of saying, "many hands make light work" and that certainly applies here. A bundle of asphalt roofing shingles weighs in the neighborhood of 80 pounds and there are three bundles of shingles to every square. Some of the heavier grade shingles have four or five bundles per square. If you have just an average size roof (about 1600 square feet), you will have approximately 48 bundles of shingles to carry up onto the roof. That translates into roughly 2 tons of carrying!

The best way to begin a re-roofing project is to nail down a starter course of shingles around the entire perimeter of the roof—eaves and rake. These shingles are nailed into place with the tabs up, edges butted together and they just slightly (by 1 inch) overhang the eaves and rake of the roof. See Fig. 1-59.

After the starter strip is installed, the next step is to lay down new valley flashing. There are several ways to accomplish this (such as woven valleys, concealed valleys, etc.) but I will limit this discussion to techniques for installing open valleys. These are the easiest for the do-it-yourselfer to install.

Begin by first installing a 36-inch wide strip of felt paper in the valley. The paper should be centered in the valley and secured along the edges with only enough nails to do the job. Make certain that the paper lies in the bottom of the valley so there is no tension across the face of the paper.

The next step is to lay a continuous strip of aluminum flashing in the center of the valley. Nail the flashing in place by driving nails approximately 12 inches from the center on either side of the valley. Use only as many nails as it takes to secure the flashing. Space the nails about 12 to 18 inches.

Once the flashing is secured, spread a band of roofing cement along the edges of the flashing. This will ensure that the joint

Fig. 1-59. A starter strip of shingles is installed along the eaves.

between the edges of the flashing and the existing roofing materials will be watertight. Make sure to cover all nail heads (in the flashing) with the roofing cement.

Strike chalk lines on both sides of the valley. These lines will be your guide for ending each course of shingles that would otherwise overlap the valley. When striking the chalk lines, keep in mind that open valleys should be wider at the bottom than at the top. The standard width of exposed valley flashing is 6 inches at the top and an increase of about one-eighth of an inch for every foot of length. An open valley with a length of 8 feet would be 6 inches wide at the top and 7 inches wide at the bottom where the valley meets the eaves of the house. See Figs. 1-60 and 1-61.

Other types of flashing—vent flanges, chimney flashing, and dormer/roof flashing are most commonly installed just prior to shingling.

Assuming that you have already nailed down the starter strip of shingles, the next step is to strike a chalk line parallel to the eaves. This chalk line will be a top edge guide for the first course of shingles. Measure the width of a shingle and use this measurement as a guide for striking the chalk line. Remember to leave room for a 1-inch overhang.

The first course of asphalt shingle is started at a corner of the roof where the rake meets the eaves. You can either work from above or, if the roof pitch is steep, work from a ladder. The first shingle is a full one. Succeeding courses begin with either full shingles or cut shingles. This depends on the style of shingles being installed, and the preferred overall shingle pattern. Generally, there are three major spacing variations for square butt strip shingles: *breaking thirds, breaking halves,* and *the quick method.*

The breaking-thirds method begins with a first course of whole shingles. The second course begins with a shingle that has 4 inches cut from the edge. The third course starter shingle has 8 inches removed and the fourth course has an entire tab removed. The fifth course of shingles is begun with an uncut shingle. The result will be

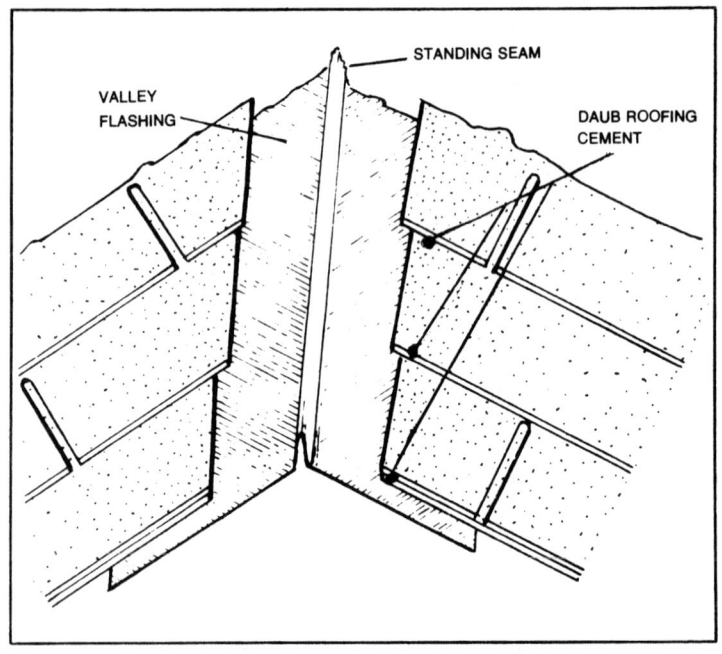

Fig. 1-60. Place a daub of roofing tar under edges of all shingles that end in a valley.

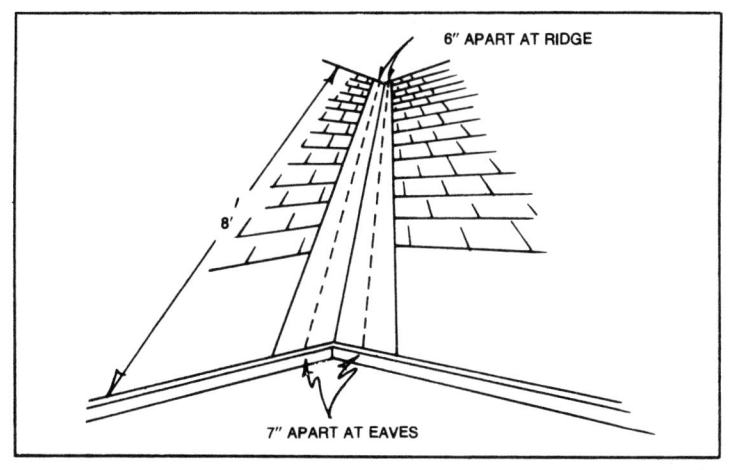

Fig. 1-61. Remember that exposed valley's are wider at the bottom than at the top (courtesy of Celotex Corp.).

that the cutouts of the rows of shingles will be offset by approximately one-third from the course above and below (Fig. 1-62).

To break courses of asphalt shingles on halves is a very simple method for the beginner. The first course is started with a full shingle. The second course is started with a shingle that has half a tab (6 inches) removed and the third course is begun with a shingle that has had an entire tab removed (12 inches). (See Fig. 1-63.)

The quick method of breaking the joints in shingle courses—and the method recommended by roofing authorities—entails starting each succeeding course after the first, up to and including the sixth course, with a strip from which an additional half of a tab (6 inches) has been removed. The seventh course begins with a full shingle and the process continues (Fig. 1-64).

Basically, all of these methods involve removing different amounts from the rake edge of the first shingle in each course. Whatever method you decide to use, keep the following points in mind:

☐ The width of any rake tab should be at least 3 inches (remember that each tab on a standard shingle is 12 inches).

☐ The rake tab widths should not repeat too closely. Never remove the same amount from every other course. Spread this out over several courses.

☐ The cutout lines of any one course should be located at least 3 inches on either side of the cutout lines for both the course above and below.

The conventional manner of applying asphalt shingles to a roof deck is to work in courses across and up the roof. This approach will minimize color shading problems because it blends together shingles from different bundles.

The proper way to nail a shingle is to start from the end nearest the last shingle applied (or when nailing the first shingle in a course, the edge closest to the rake of the roof). Nails should be driven at a right angle to the roof deck so that the edge of the nailhead will not break the surface of the shingle. In most cases, two or three blows are all that is required to drive the nail through the shingle and into the roof deck. Do not countersink any nailheads. Drive them in until they are flush with the surface of the shingle. As you work, make certain that no cutout or end joint is less than 2 inches from any nail in an underlying course (Fig. 1-65). In other words, no nails should be visible. If you make a mistake, correct it before going on.

Nailing down courses of asphalt is fairly simple even if you have never done this type of work before. As you work, you will develop a certain rhythm that goes something like this. Place the shingle in position, align the right edge with the previous shingle (assuming that you are working from right to left; that is best for right-handed roofers), align the bottom edge of the shingle so that the cutouts are offset from the previous course by at least 3 inches, reach for a nail, position the nail, and drive it through the shingle and into the roof deck. Drive three other nails into the shingle and move on. As you nail down the courses of shingles, you will naturally fall into this rhythm.

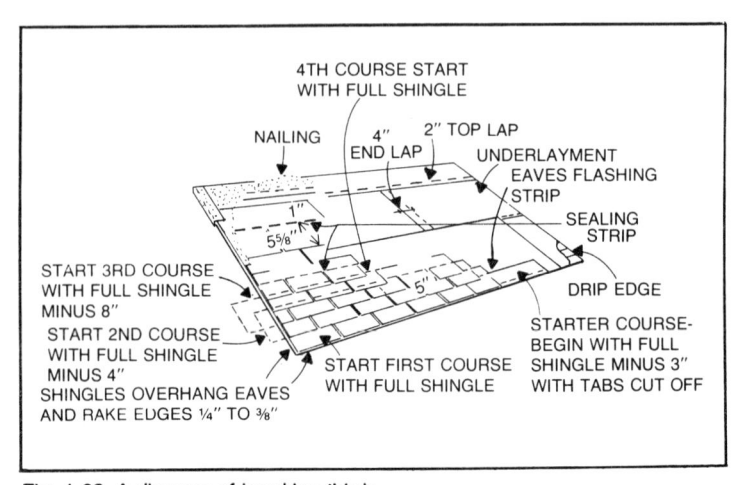

Fig. 1-62. A diagram of breaking thirds.

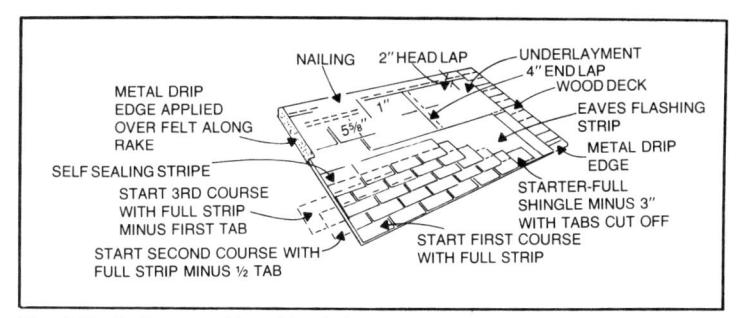

Fig. 1-63. A diagram of breaking halves.

There are several aids that will help this type of work to progress more smoothly. The first is to strike a chalk line for the alignment of the top edge of the shingles. This simple act will insure that each course of asphalt shingles remains straight.

Another aid is a nail apron for holding the nails. You will not be able to work very quickly if you have to reach to the side for some nails for every shingle. A nail pouch keeps a good supply of nails right at your fingertips. You can usually get a nail apron from the roofing supply dealer where you bought the roofing materials. If you plan on doing much carpentry, you should invest in a leather tool and nail belt. With such a belt (Fig. 1-66) you will not only have nails at your fingertips, but there are other loops and pockets for such often-needed tools such as hammer, a steel-tape ruler, a utility knife, etc.

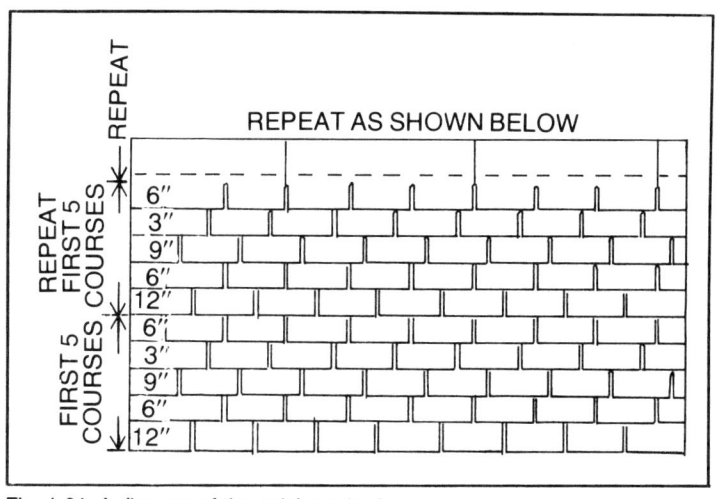

Fig. 1-64. A diagram of the quick method.

Fig. 1-65. As you nail down courses of asphalt shingles, you will begin to develop a certain rhythm for the work.

For do-it-yourselfers, a good arrangement is for one person to carry shingles and another to do the actual placement and nailing. Switch off every hour so that the carrying of shingles does not become too much of a chore (Fig. 1-67).

Roofing progresses across and up a roof. Whenever you come to a roof projection or valley, however, you must pursue a slightly different course. When you come to a soil stack, trim a shingle to fit and check the alignment with other shingles—both to the side and below. Before nailing the shingle into place, you must first apply a coating of roofing cement to the area around the stack and below the shingle. Then set the shingle into this cement and nail. The last step is to apply additional cement around the base of the stack where the shingle cutout meets. This will insure that the joint is waterproof (Fig. 1-68).

When a course of shingles ends at a valley (previously covered with flashing material), you must cut the edge of the shingle so that it will end at a right angle. The chalk lines on either side of the valley can now be used to judge where to cut each course of shingles.

When you come to a wall—such as the front of a dormer of chimney—apply shingles to the edge of this protrusion. Next, apply a coat of roofing cement at the base of the protrusion. You will have to cut shingles to fit into place so that the bottom edge is on line with the rest of the shingles in the course and the top edge is next to the protrusion. When the shingles have been suitably trimmed, apply a bit more roofing cement to the area and press the cut shingles into place. No nails are used here. The last part of this installation is to apply a coat of roofing cement along the top edge of the shingle where it joins the vertical wall (Fig. 1-69).

Eventually, as you run courses of shingles across and up the roof, you will come to the peak or ridge of the roof. If your building has a hip roof, you will come to the hip section first. In any event,

Fig. 1-66. A nail pouch is a necessity for roofing work.

53

Fig. 1-67. Before you can nail shingles on a roof deck, you must first carry them up onto the roof.

continue laying the shingles until you lay the last course. Part of the last course must extend over the hip or ridge of the roof.

After the entire roof has been covered with courses of asphalt shingles, you will be ready to cap the hips and ridges of the roof. Begin by trimming the edges of the new shingles where they pass over the ridge or hip. Do this for one side of the peak and overlap the top of the last course of shingles over the ridge. After the entire ridge has been trimmed, the next step is to strike a chalk line on one side of the roof. This line will be used as an edge guide for the cap shingles. The chalk line should be about 6 inches down from the ridge line.

The tabs used for capping the ridge and hip sections of your roof are cut from roofing shingles. A three-tab asphalt roofing shingle will yield exactly three 12-inch pieces of capping when cut at the tab slot. Cutting can be done quickly with a sharp utility knife loaded with a special hook blade (designed specifically for cutting asphalt roofing materials). See Fig. 1-70.

When you cut caps from a full three-tab asphalt shingle, you should make sure that all of the cap shingles are the same width. Use a straight edge if necessary (Fig. 1-71). You should taper cut the top edges of each cap shingle (Fig. 1-72). This will enable you to do a neater overall job with the actual capping of ridge and hips.

Fig. 1-68. Apply roofing cement in front of a chimney.

Fig. 1-69. Face nail a cut shingle into place.

Cap shingles should be bent lengthwise along their centers for an equal amount of exposure on each side of the ridge or hip. The shingles are then lined up with the chalk lines and nailed into place. Secure the shingles with a nail on each side; the nails should be about 5 inches from the exposed end and 1 inch up from the edge (Fig. 1-73).

Hip caps are started at the eaves and installed upward toward the ridge (or high point of the hip). Ridge caps are applied so the exposed edge is away from the prevailing winds. If you are unsure as to the direction of the prevailing winds, simply look at other houses in the vicinity to see which way their ridge caps face. The last cap shingle to be attached to the ridge must be face nailed. Drive one nail on each side of the ridge to hold the cap shingle in place. Apply a dab of roofing cement to each nailhead. This is to insure protection against damage for moisture.

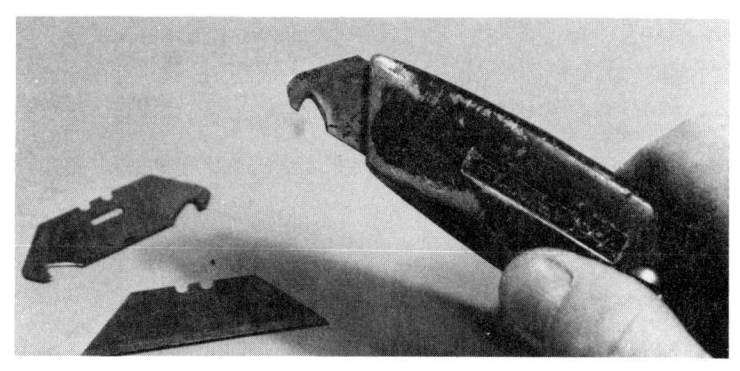

Fig. 1-70. A specially designed hook blade is made for cutting roofing materials. Always cut from the back side of the shingle.

After all hips and ridges have been properly capped, the re-roofing project is almost complete. The major work is finished, but there are a number of small tasks that should be done to insure that the project will endure. One of the first things you should do is to

Fig. 1-71. Use a straight edge when cutting cap shingles.

Fig. 1-72. Taper cut the ends of a cap shingle and they will lay better on the ridge.

clean off the entire roof. A thorough sweeping is called for here. You must remove any cut shingles or whole shingles that were left lying on the finished roof. Look for dropped nails and tools.

During this cleaning, you should keep an eye out for any damaged shingles. During the project, you might have dropped a tool or passed too many times over one particular area (where the ladder meets the roof, for example). Needless to say, any shingles that are not perfect should be replaced at this time. The shingle-bar method previously described in this chapter is a very good way for removing damaged shingles.

You should also check all shingle edges that end in valleys. A good roofing practice is to place a dab of roofing cement under the edges of all shingles that end in a valley. Simply lift up the edge of one shingle at a time and apply a small amount of the cement. This small task will increase the capability of these shingles to resist water seepage (Fig. 1-74).

As long as you are working with the roofing cement and a trowel, you should go back over all of those areas that received a coating of the cement. These include all soil stacks and vents that pass through the roof. Don't forget to apply an additional coating of cement around chimneys (Fig. 1-75), wall junctions, and any other roof projection. Because these places represent potential leak areas, they will all benefit from an extra coating of the roofing cement (Fig. 1-75).

After you have swept off the entire roof and applied a coating of asphalt roofing cement to all roof projections, you can pretty much consider the re-roofing project complete. Just because you have installed a new roof on your home don't think that you can just sit back and forget about the roof for 25 years.

There are a number of things that you can do to extend the life of your new roof. Probably the most important thing is to periodically carefully inspect the roof. This can be done in the spring and fall of each year. On these semiannual exterior checks, you should

Fig. 1-73. Nailing cap shingles on a hip.

Fig. 1-74. Apply a daub under the edges of all shingles that end in a valley.

look over the areas that have the potential for leaking. This includes all roof projections, valleys, and wherever two roofs meet. Check the condition of the flashing on these areas as well as the covering of roofing cement. Chances are that the flashing will easily outlast the roofing material, but occasionally the flashing might become damaged. Roofing cement will dry out and crack with age. You should check areas that have such a coating and renew the cement.

Clean off your roof during these semiannual checks. If your house is surrounded by trees, your roof will become a catch-all for debris. Gutters and downspouts should always be clear so rain water and melting snow can quickly run off the roof.

When you purchase roofing shingles, it is common practice to have them delivered to the job site. In some parts of the country, the roofing supplier might also provide the service of delivering the roofing shingles directly onto the roof. If this service is available in your area, you will be smart to take advantage of it. If the shingles are simply delivered to your door, have them stacked neatly, (off the ground and on a wooden pallet, for example) and as close as possible to the easiest way up to the roof. If the shingles will not be used immediately, they should be covered with a tarp or other suitable material.

If you find that you will be the one carrying the shingles up onto the roof, there are a number of professional tricks that you can use

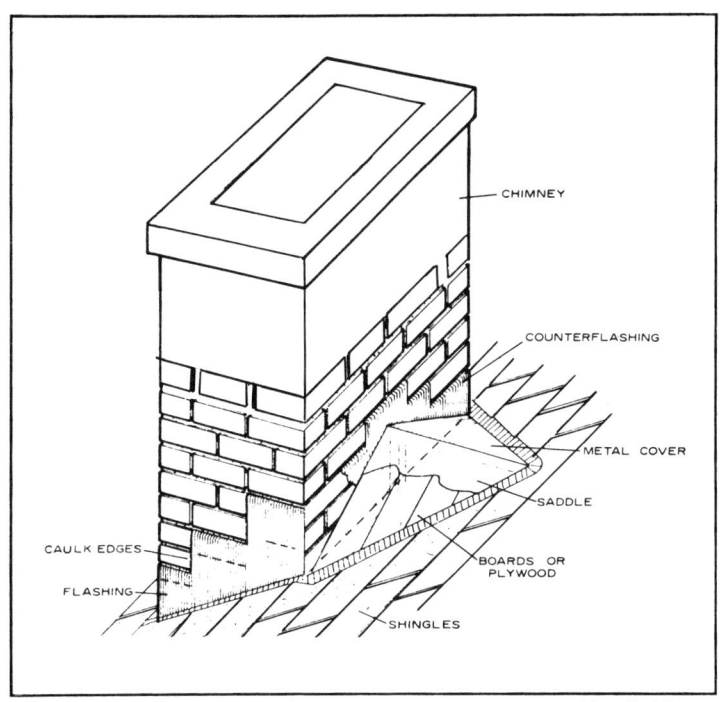

Fig. 1-75. Don't forget to apply roofing cement on the top side of chimney flashing.

to make the work go as easy as possible. First of all, keep in mind that the average weight of one bundle of standard asphalt roofing shingles is about 80 pounds.

Based on thousands of trips up a ladder with a bundle of shingles on my shoulder, I have found that the best way to carry shingles is the following. Pick up a bundle of shingles and balance the load on your left or right shoulder. Approach the ladder and climb while using one hand to hold the load steady and the other hand to hold onto the ladder rungs (Fig. 1-76). Climb up the ladder carefully. Lean slightly forward until one foot is just about even with the eaves. Step off the ladder and onto the roof deck. Walk to a predesignated spot on the roof and gently set the load down. The bundle should be placed over a rafter, for extra support (Fig. 1-76).

Most experts agree that shingles should not be stacked more than about three high in any one spot on a roof deck. If you are carrying a large number of bundles up onto the roof, spread the bundles out over the roof so the weight will be fairly distributed. Never throw or drop a bundle of shingles on the roof deck.

Fig. 1-76. Always keep one hand on the ladder when climbing with a bundle of shingles.

The weight of the falling bundle can easily break through the roof deck and cause quite a bit of damage below.

Keep the roof deck as clear as possible. Shingle-bundle wrappers, cut shingles, and anything else not of use should be removed from the roof deck. One or two areas on the ground can be designated as junk piles for this debris. It is better to litter one or two areas on the ground than to have useless material on the roof that could cause you to trip and fall.

Earlier in this chapter I mentioned that the proper footwear should be worn when you are working on a roof. You should also wear long pants, a long sleeved-shirt and a hat. This may seem a little comical, but it can get very hot on a roof. Loose-fitting clothing will help you keep cool. A hat will keep the sun's rays off your head. If you start to feel a little dizzy or nauseous, get out of the sunlight and into the shade until you feel better. You can well imagine your predicament if you were to pass out from the heat while 20 feet off the ground.

If you live in a high-wind area, you should install wind-resistant shingles on your roof. These wind resistant shingles, called *self-sealing shingles*, have a factory-applied adhesive across the middle of each shingle. After the shingles are applied, the Sun's rays heat up this adhesive and bond it to the shingle above.

For added protection in high wind areas, many professional roofers add a spot of quick-setting roofing cement under shingles that border the eaves and rake of the house. A dab about the size of a 50-cent piece is sufficient for this.

If your roof has had problems with ice dams in the past, you should consider installing ventilation in the eaves, and flashing to cure the problem. Eaves flashing is a good idea anywhere in the United States where the January temperatures during the day average 4 degrees C or less. There are two methods of installing eaves flashing.

The first method employs a strip of 90-pound, mineral-surfaced roll roofing. This material is installed so that it covers the eaves area from the edge to a point about 6 inches up from where the roof passes over the exterior wall below. The roof roofing is installed before the new roof has been laid.

The second method of eaves flashing is preferred by professionals. Aluminum flashing is used instead of roll roofing. This material is installed in the same manner as described above.

With a little care and periodic maintenance, you can reasonably expect your new roof to last for at least 15 years. If you live in a part of the country that does not experience wide extremes in temperature, your new roof may last as long as 25 years. In any case, keep an eye on the condition of your roof, keep it clean, and you can rest assured that the roof over your head will be doing the job of keeping the interior of your house dry.

Chapter 2

Gutters and Downspouts

Many of the problems on the exterior of your home are caused by moisture in one form or another. If you can control moisture, you will effectively eliminate many problems and your maintenance tasks will be less than in the past. In this chapter, I will discuss the various ways that moisture from rain and snow can lead to problems around your home, and I will offer suggestions as to how you can best deal with those problems.

Some means of catching rainwater and diverting it away from the foundation of the house is necessary. In some cases this is accomplished by placing some type of splash block (Fig. 2-1) under the downspout. Sometimes the best solution is to construct a *dry well* or a leeching field that will hold and disseminate the water so it can do no harm to the concrete foundation.

The two most common types of gutter systems are those that are hung from the edge of the roof by special straps (Fig. 2-2), and gutters that are held to the facia with evenly spaced spikes and sleeves. Gutters can be made from wood, galvanized steel, copper, aluminum, and even vinyl. Some are bare metal or galvanized metal, while the more popular types have some type of enamel finish applied at the factory. Gutters are usually shaped half round or formed in the shape of the letter K. They range in width from 4 to 6 inches.

Lengths of gutters sections range from 10 to 30 feet. The easiest length to work with, and the most readily available, are those that come in 10-foot sections. When several sections of gutter must be connected, special joint sections are available. When prop-

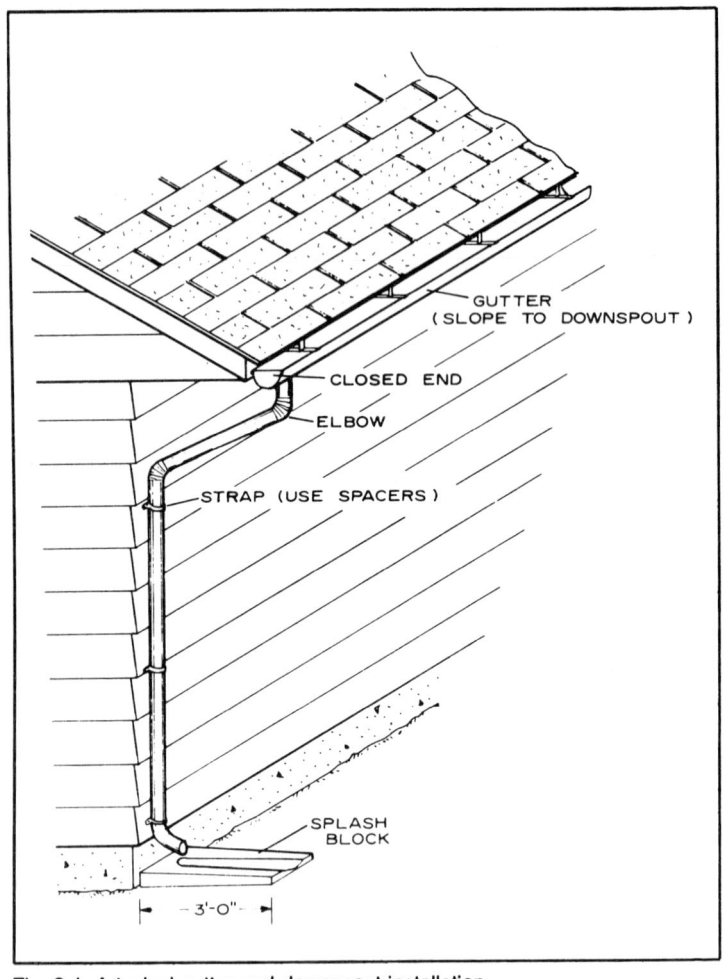

Fig. 2-1. A typical gutter and downspout installation.

erly installed, these joints (available in straight sections and inside and outside corners) will be watertight. These special slip joint connectors (Fig. 2-3) are very easy to use. The ends of the gutters are capped with special end covers. Downspout holes can either be cut into the bottom of the gutter or a special downspout section can be installed.

The downspout must be compatible with the gutter system. There are two types of downspouts: round (corrigated) and rectangular. When you are purchasing the lengths of gutter, you should also pick up the matching downspouts for the system (Fig. 2-4).

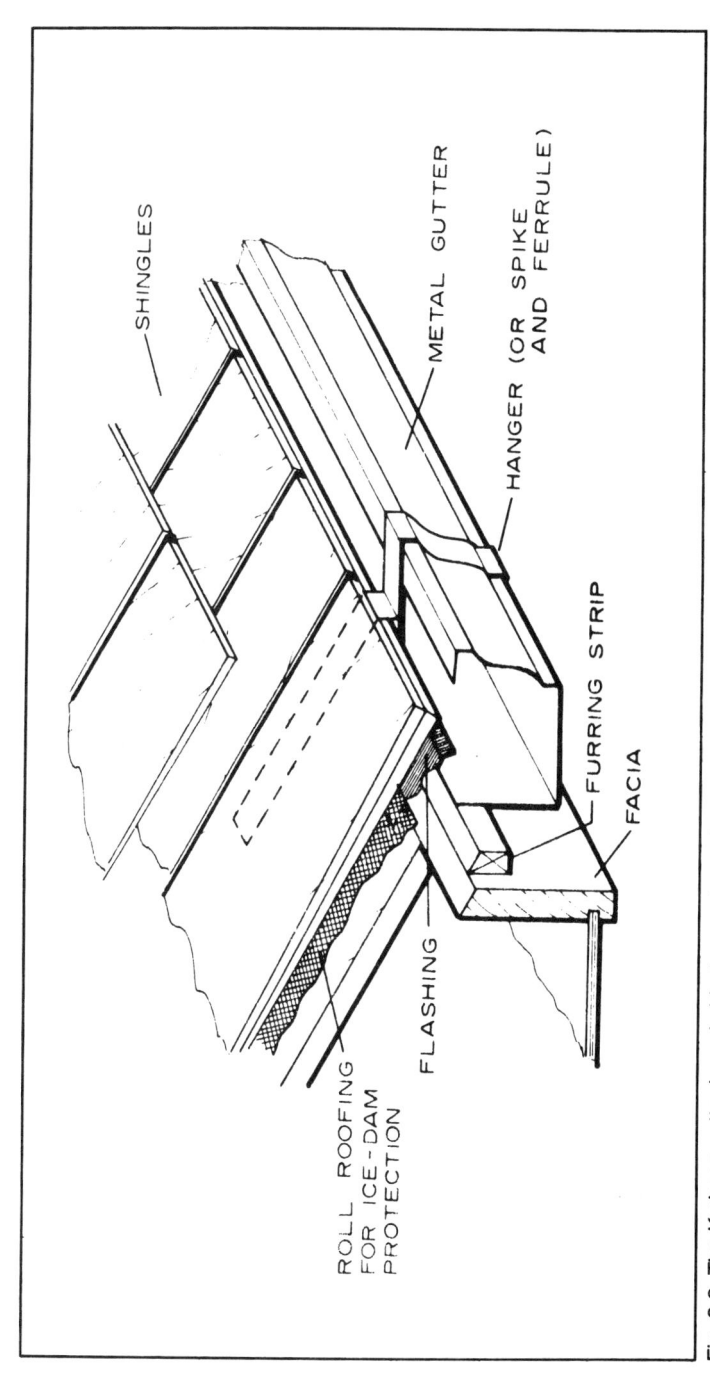

Fig. 2-2. The K-shape gutter is probably the most popular type.

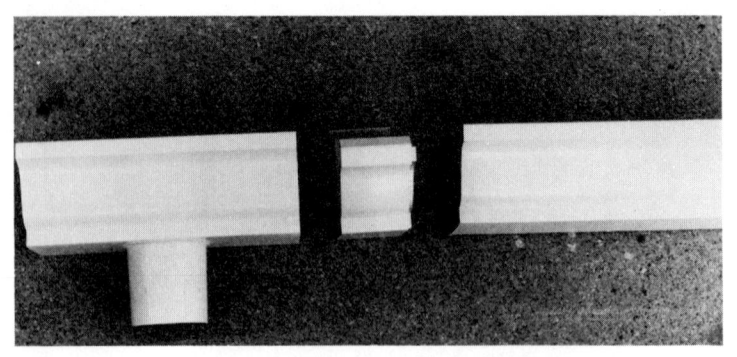

Fig. 2-3. Special downspout sections are fastened to a gutter with a straight connector.

Downspouts are connected (Fig. 2-5) to the gutter with elbows that force the rain water to take a course that brings it from the gutter back toward the siding of the house, then down, and finally out the bottom of the downspout. At the bottom of the downspout, there must always be an additional elbow that will shoot the water away from the foundation and either onto a splash block or into a specially constructed drywell.

Gutter and downspout systems must be large enough to effectively service the roof they are installed around. Generally, a 4-inch wide gutter is sufficient for a roof surface of up to about 1000 square feet. For roofs with a surface area of from 1000 to 1500 square feet, a 5-inch wide gutter is preferred. Larger roofs require a 6-inch gutter and matching downspout.

Gutters must be sloped toward the downspout so that the rain water will run quickly out and down. The standard slope for gutters calls for a drop of about 1 inch for every 20 feet of run. For a standard-length roof, usually only one downspout is required. For a roof length greater than about 45 feet, two downspouts—one at each end—are usually required.

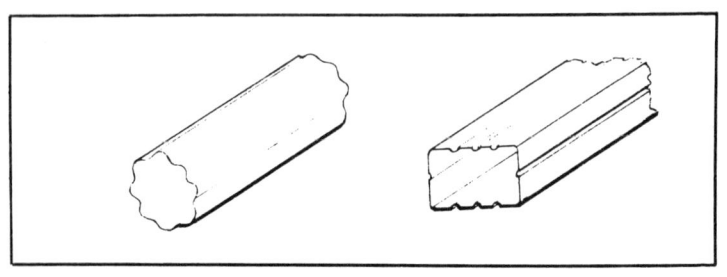

Fig. 2-4. A round downspout (left), and rectangular downspout.

MAINTENANCE

In order for the system to work efficiently, it should be cleaned of debris at least twice a year. The system should also be leak free. There are a few simple tests you can do to determine if your system is watertight.

During your spring and fall exterior inspection begin by cleaning off your roof. At the same time, checking the condition of this surface. In areas where there are a large number of decidious trees, you will often find quite an accumulation of leaf and twig debris in roof valleys and in the rain gutters. Work carefully with a broom and sweep all of this material off the roof (Fig. 2-6). After the entire roof has been swept, you can turn your attention to the gutter system along the eaves of the house.

Pick a point that is at the approximate middle of the system (on one side of the roof) and begin removing anything that you find from the gutter. Work your way toward a downspout; there you will usually find the greatest collection of debris. A paint scraper or putty knife is a very handy tool for this type of cleaning (Fig. 2-7). As you move along the gutter, check any joints in the system. They should be tight. Another thing to check is the general tightness of the gutter to the facia. The gutters will be attached with straps—nailed under the first course of shingles—or with spikes and sleeves—nailed through the top of the gutter to the facia. If you discover that the gutter is loose, you might have to renail it.

If the gutter hanger is the strap type, the best way to renail it is to first lift the edge of the shingle that covers the strap. Then remove the nails or screws that hold it in place. After the roof end of the strap is free, unscrew or unsnap the other end that holds the gutter. Next, you must reposition the strap hanger to a higher roof

Fig. 2-5. A series of two elbows are usually needed to connect the gutter with the downspout.

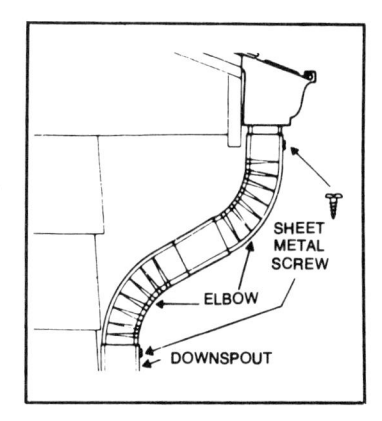

Fig. 2-6. Cleaning out the valley with a broom.

position and renail it in place (but first lift up the shingle). Use only galvanized roofing nails for this renailing (Fig. 2-8). You must also make certain that the nail head will be located at least three-fourths of an inch from the old nail hole position, and that it will be covered by the shingle. After nailing, put a daub of asphalt roofing cement over each new nail head. After the top end of the gutter strap hanger has been secured to the roof deck, you must raise the gutter into position and refasten the strap to it.

If the gutter is fastened to the facia with spikes and sleeves, you will not have to remove the loose fasteners. Fasteners are commonly available at any lumber yard or home improvement center. Don't bother removing the old spikes and sleeves. Simply leave them in place and install a new fastener about 2 inches from the original position (Fig. 2-9).

Continue cleaning the gutters—refastening if necessary—until you come to the downspout hole. Here you will most commonly find the greatest amount of debris. Usually it is in the form of decomposing leaves, and granules from roof shingles, etc. All of this material must be cleaned out. If some type of screening or leaf guard (Fig. 2-10) is not present, make a note to pick up a few at your local lumber yard or home improvement center.

Once all of the gutters around your home have been sufficiently cleaned, it is time to check them for proper drainage and leaks. The best way to do this is to run water through them with a garden hose.

Fig. 2-7. Rain gutters must be cleaned out twice a year.

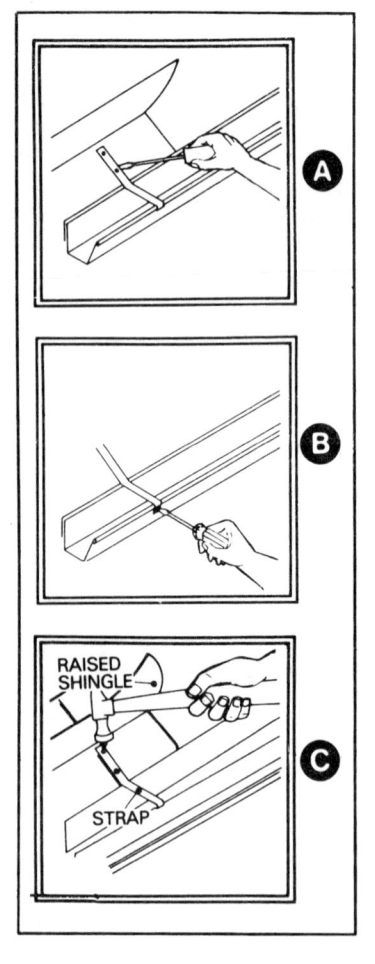

Fig. 2-8. To raise a gutter that is held in place by straps: (A) remove screws or nails that hold strap in place; (B) disconnect the strap from the gutter; (C) reposition the strap on the roof—under the shingle—and reattach the end of the strap to the gutter.

Work from above the gutters and check one section at a time (Fig. 2-11).

Keep in mind that you want water to run through the gutter system as quickly as possible. If you discover that a section of the gutter is low and water tends to puddle, you will have to remove the strap or spike and sleeve and reposition the gutter so that water runs off properly.

The areas that are most prone to leaks are any joint in the system, inside and outside corners, the area around end caps (Fig. 2-12), and the area around the downspout outlet hole and elbows. The types of leaks that can be repaired are those that are a result of a poor joint between sections of gutter, small holes, small breaks in

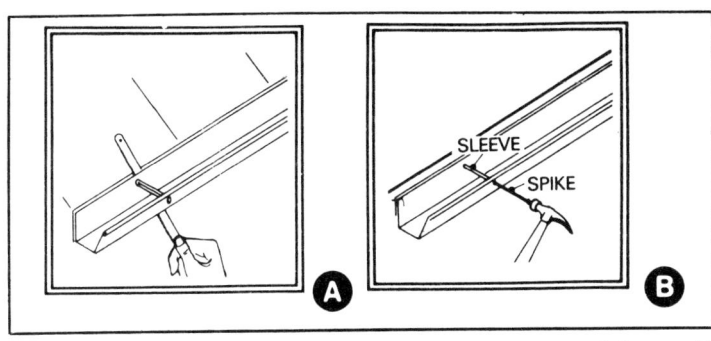

Fig. 2-9. To raise a gutter that is fastened to facia with spikes and sleeves: (A) remove the old spike and sleeve; (B) reposition the gutter and install the new spike and the sleeve.

seams of corners (both inside and outside), and poor connections around a downspout hole. The types of leaks that cannot be easily repaired include sections of gutter that have rotted out (leaving a long hole along the bottom of the gutter), and gutters that have burst as a result of ice (Fig. 2-13).

In all cases, the best type of repair is the one that does not build up the interior surface of the bottom of the gutter very much. If you build up this surface too much, rain water runoff will not readily flow past this point. For leaks in the bottom of the gutter—such as a leak around a joint—you can usually repair the area with a coating of asphalt roofing cement. Simply apply a coating of cement with a brush or putty knife. Take care not to build up the area too much (Fig. 2-14).

If this does not fix the leak, you will have to resort to more drastic measures. Pay a visit to a store that sells automobile body repair materials and purchase a fiberglass fender-repair kit (Fig. 2-15). These kits contain fiberglass resin, hardener, fiberglass cloth

Fig. 2-10. A leaf guard must be installed over the downspout hole in the gutter.

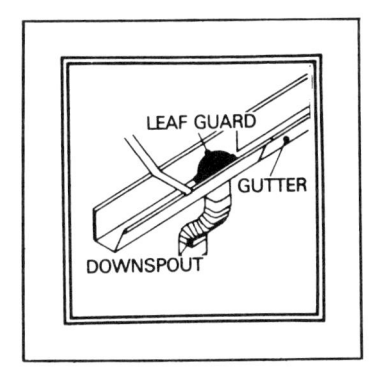

Fig. 2-11. Test your rain gutters from above with a garden hose.

and usually a container for mixing the resin. Follow the directions on the kit for mixing the resin and hardener. Apply a coat of the mixed resin, then a layer of fiberglass cloth, then another layer of resin. When this patch dries, the leak should be permanently fixed.

Fig. 2-12. End caps on rain gutters are potential leak areas so give this joint a coat of tar.

Fig. 2-13. Rain gutters that look like this should be replaced rather than repaired.

For leaks in the sidewalls of gutters you can usually make a satisfactory repair with roofing cement. Because the leak is not on the bottom of the gutter, you need not be as concerned about applying too much asphalt cement. Brush on enough to fill the seam

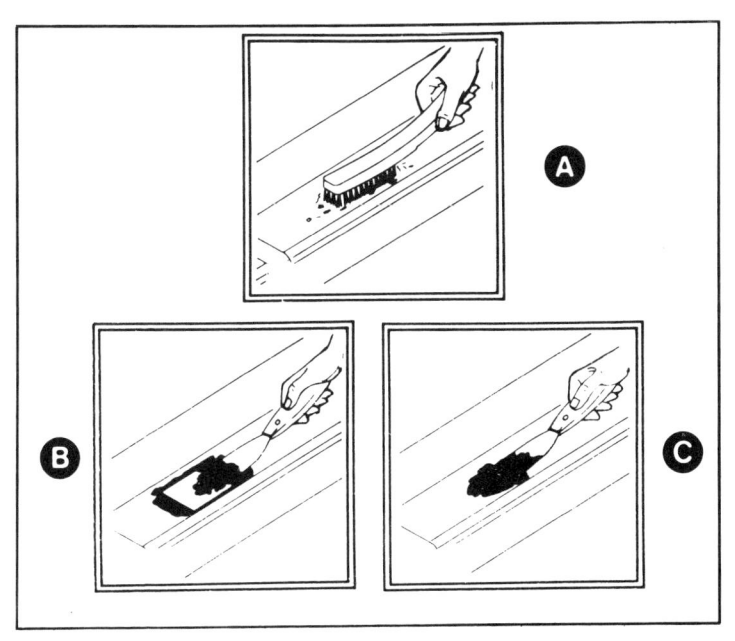

Fig. 2-14. To patch a small hole or crack in the bottom of a rain gutter: (A) clean the area with a wire brush; (B) coat the area with roofing tar; (C) apply a tin patch and cover with more tar. Don't build up the area much or water will not flow past.

75

Fig. 2-15. For strong patches on rain gutters, use a fiberglass repair kit. They are available at auto parts stores.

(Fig. 2-16) and effectively stop the leak. If the seam is spread apart very wide (more than one-fourth of an inch), use the fiberglass repair method.

INSTALLATION

While there is nothing particularly difficult about installing a gutter and downspout system around your home, there are a number of things that can and should be done to ensure that the system works. The installation of a gutter and downspout system will go much quicker and have a greater chance of success if two people take on the task. There are a number of tasks that are very difficult for a lone worker to accomplish, but they are a simple matter for two people. Holding a 10-foot section of gutter along the facia while nailing in place is one example. One of the first things you should do when you are planning a gutter and downspout system installation is to recruit some help.

The next thing you must do is determine how many feet of gutter and downspout you will need for the project as well as number of elbows, connectors (straight, inside corners, and outside corners). You will also need spikes and sleeves (or hanger straps) as

Fig. 2-16. Small leaks in the sidewall of a rain gutter can easily be patched with a daub of roofing cement.

well as special metal straps for holding the downspout to an exterior wall.

Begin by drawing a diagram of the roof deck of your home. For a standard gable roof, you will have gutters only on the eaves of the

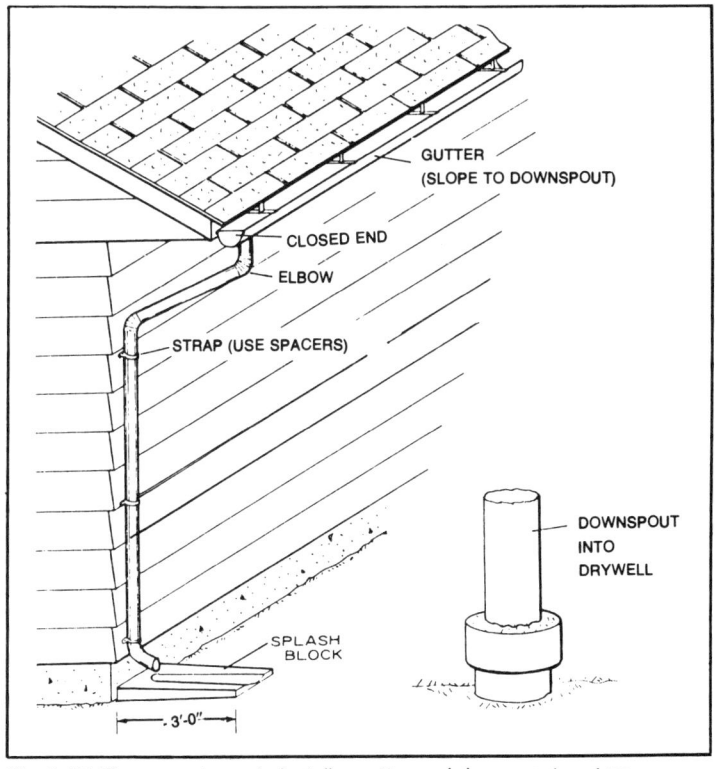

Fig. 2-17. The correct way to install a gutter and downspout system.

77

Fig. 2-18. Asphalt roofing cement is handy for sealing joints and making minor repairs in the gutter system.

house. For a hip roof, you must install gutters around all sections of the roof deck.

On your diagram, you should indicate the length of eaves as well as distance from eaves to the ground. One key to measurement, that is often overlooked, is the distance from the facia board to the exterior wall of the house. Remember that you will want to install the downspout to the sidewall of the house rather than straight down from the gutter outlet hole. To do this, you will have to use two elbows and a length of downspout as in Fig. 2-17.

Once you have determined the number of 10-foot lengths of gutter and downspout pipe, you must also calculate the number of connectors, elbows, and downspout straps. Add to this spikes and sleeves and a can of roofing cement (Fig. 2-18) and you should have all of the materials needed.

While determining the number of spikes and sleeves for attaching the gutter to the facia boards, keep in mind that these should be spaced about 2½ feet apart. It makes sense to purchase a few extra spikes and sleeves (Fig. 2-19).

After you have purchased and carted home all of the gutter and downspout materials needed for the job, lay them out on the ground approximately where they will be installed. This will aid you in assembling the gutter sections. The best way to go about this is to attach straight connectors (Fig. 2-20) at the end of each 10-foot section. Do not connect the gutter sections to one another until they are actually placed in position on the facia. At this time, you can also install end caps on both ends of the gutter run and a downspout drain hole section. Use your predetermined measurements to arrive at the exact gutter length, including connectors.

The next step is to climb up a ladder and drive a nail at one end of the gutter run. Keep in mind that the gutter system will have a high and low end. This assumes that the run is no more than about 40 feet in length. If the run is more than 40 feet you should install two downspouts (one at each end of the run). This will mean that the gutter will be higher in the middle than at both ends. Nevertheless, the first nail you drive into the facia is the high end of the run. Remember that the gutter system should drop about 2 inches for

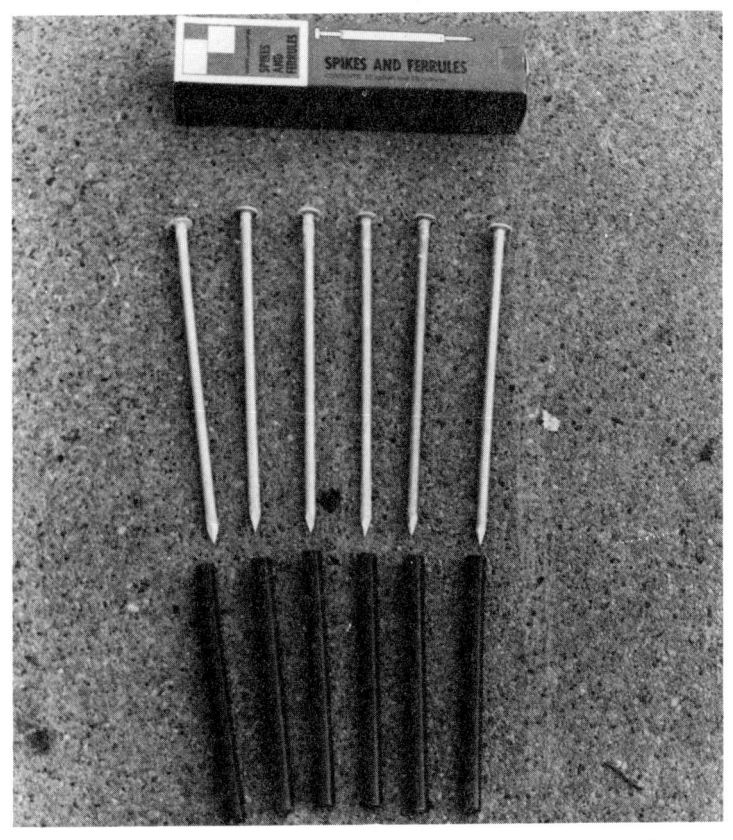

Fig. 2-19. Spikes and ferrules are easy to use when you are attaching rain gutter to the facia.

every 20 feet of run. Drive a low end nail at the proper height (Fig. 2-21).

Now you must strike a chalk line between the two nails. This line will be your top edge guide for installing the gutter system.

Installing gutters is most easily accompanied with two workers—one at each end of the gutter section. If you cannot find someone to give you a hand with the work, there is an alternative method that, while requiring more time, will enable you to do the work alone. To aid the solo installer, attach a loop of wire or strong cord to the high end of the gutter run. You can then use this nail to hold one end of the gutter while you nail the other end in place along the chalk line. You can use the same nail that was used to strike the chalk line for this. While this method is a little on the jury-rigged side, it will enable one person to install a gutter system.

Raise the gutter into position and align the top edge of the gutter with the chalk line. Work from the low end of the run toward the high end. The gutter should not extend more than is necessary beyond the eaves or rakes of the house (Fig. 2-22). If cutting is required, do this on the ground. The end of the gutter should be slightly extended from the edge of the rakes (about one-half of an inch). Figure 2-22.

The top edge of the gutter is aligned with the chalk line and nailed in place. If you are using gutter spikes and sleeves (the

Fig. 2-20. Install end caps while the gutter is on the ground.

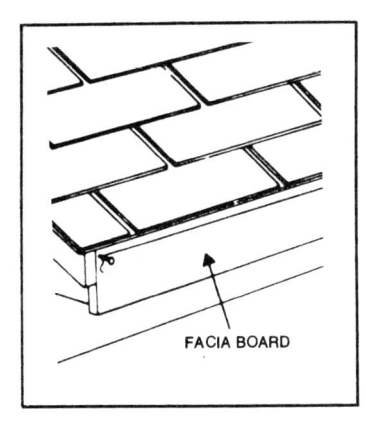

Fig. 2-21. Drive a nail into the facia, at the high end of the gutter run, and then strike a chalk line from this to the low end of the system. Use this line as a guide for aligning the top edge of the rain gutter.

easiest to install), the nails should be spaced approximately 2½ feet apart. Ideally, the nail should be driven into the end of the roof rafters whenever possible. It is usually best to have one person hold the gutter while another person works from the end of the eaves, nailing as he goes along.

As you install sections of gutter around the roof, you must exercise extreme caution when you come to any area where electrical wiring is present. Because every home has incoming power lines, you will surely be faced with the task of installing gutters around these potentially dangerous wires (unless your electrical service line is buried underground). For safety sake, never touch electrical wires.

If you use gutter straps, they must be nailed under the flat course of shingles. For gutter straps, a second pair of hands are very handy for positioning the length of gutter before nailing the straps in place.

Fig. 2-22. Extend the gutter about one-half inch beyond end of roof.

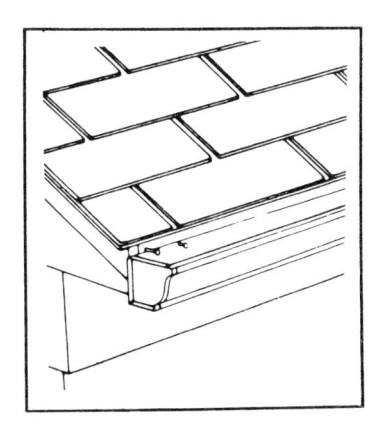

Fig. 2-23. Make straight cuts—on the ground—with a hacksaw.

After the first section of gutter has been securely fastened to the facia (along the chalk line), lift the second section into place and make the connection with the special straight connector. Usually, the gutter will slip into position easily. Occasionally you might have to open the end of the connector slightly for a secure fit. After the connection has been made, you must bend the top of the connector into the gutter to make the joint tighter. Continue fastening lengths of gutter along the chalk line until the run is complete. The last section of gutter must have both a downspout hole section and an end cap. The last section should also not extend more than about one-half of an inch beyond the end of the rake. See Figs. 2-23, 2-24, and 2-25.

After all lengths of gutter have been securely fastened to the facia, you must go back over the work and apply a coating of asphalt roofing cement to all joints in the run. A few daubs, spread evenly

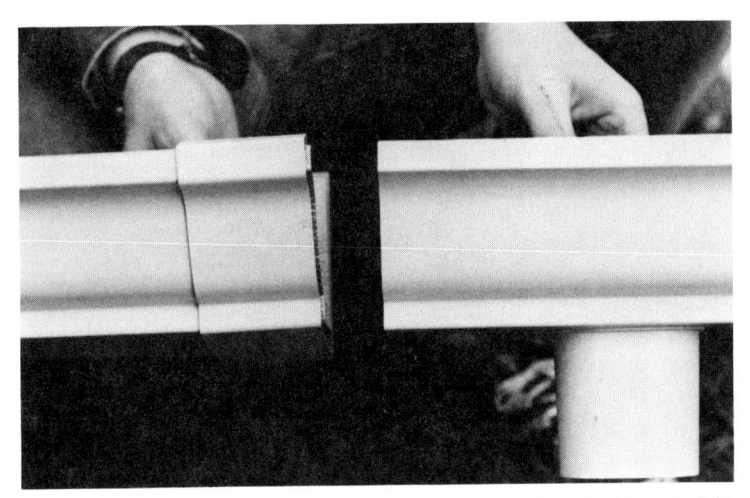

Fig. 2-24. The gutter and downspout hole section are joined with a straight connector.

with a trowel, should do the job of sealing nicely. You should also apply a coating of tar around the end caps as well (Fig. 2-26).

The next step in this project is to attach a downspout or two downspouts if the run is more than 40 feet long. Downspouts direct the flow of water from the roof, down and away from the house. They are connected to the gutter at an outlet hole (most

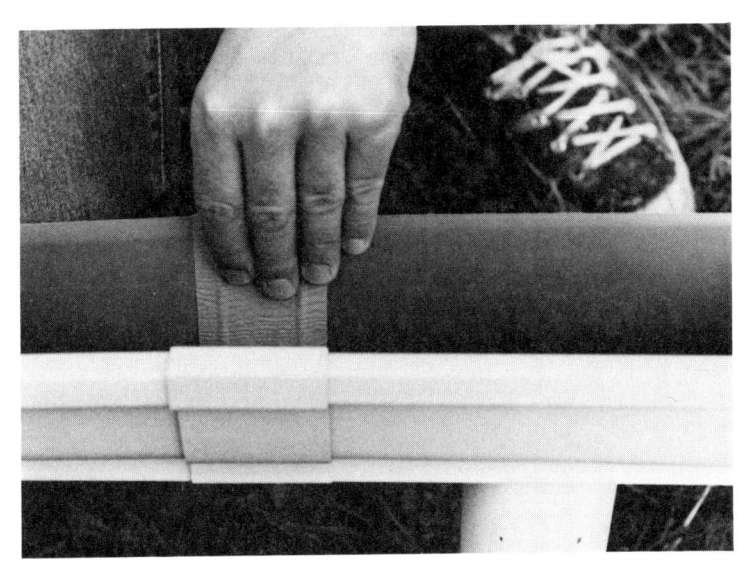

Fig. 2-25. Press the straight connector edges for a secure joint.

83

Fig. 2-26. Seal the joint with daubs of roofing cement.

commonly with two elbows). The purpose of the elbows is to direct the flow of water from the gutter, back under the eaves and, into the downspout pipe. In some cases, it might be necessary to attach a small section of straight downspout pipe between the two elbows to make up the distance from the gutter outlet hole to the sidewall of the house (Fig. 2-27).

The downspout should always be attached to the sidewall of the house. It is always amusing to notice a downspout that is attached for a straight run from the outlet hole to the ground. Aside from looking quite ridiculous, a downspout installed in such a manner is vulnerable to being knocked or blown down during a storm. The proper way to install a downspout is to attach it to the sidewall of the house (Fig. 2-28).

Downspout straps are sold as flat pieces of metal that must be bent to the contours of the downspout and then nailed to the sidewall of the house. Most professionals use hot-dipped galvanized roofing nails for this type of nailing. You should never use ordinary steel nails; they will surely rust and stain the house siding. For single-story homes, it is common to use two downspout straps (Fig. 2-29). One is positioned about 1 foot from the top and another is positioned about 1 foot from the bottom. For longer runs, downspout straps should be spaced about 6 or 7 feet apart.

The bottom of the downspout should have an elbow attached to the end to direct the flow of water away from the foundation of the house. Underneath this bottom elbow there should either be a splash block—to further direct the flow of water away from the foundation walls—or a special dry well.

SPLASH BLOCKS, RAIN BARRELS, AND DRY WELLS

If the ground area around the bottom of a downspout slopes away from your home, and there is good overall drainage in the soil, you can install a splash block under the downspout outlet elbow. As the name suggests, a splash block is a simple device that take the force of moving water and directs it away from the foundation of the house. Without a splash block, water from the gutter and downspout

Fig. 2-27. Two elbows are used to connect the gutter with downspout pipe on the exterior sidewall.

Fig. 2-28. Downspout pipe should not run straight from the gutter; this would make it vunerable to damage.

system would quickly wash out a hole around the foundation. In heavy rainfall areas, the absence of a splash block might cause a section of lawn to be washed away, leaving a gulley.

A splash block can be nothing more than a flat concrete block placed in such a way as to eliminate the destructive forces of runoff. A better choice is a specially made concrete or plastic splash block that will not only take the force of the rain water, but direct it away from the foundation of the house as well. To be effective, splash blocks must be placed under each downspout outlet elbow (Fig. 2-30).

During your semiannual exterior check, have a look at the area around your splash blocks. In some cases, you might have to do a little adjusting so that rain water flows away from the building's foundation.

If the ground around your home is flat, or not able to easily absorb rain water, chances are that a splash block will not do you any

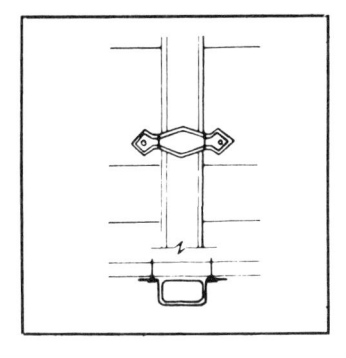

Fig. 2-29. Downspout pipe is held to the sidewall with special straps.

good. In such cases as these, a better solution might be to construct a dry well. It seems like a waste, however, to simply channel rain water into a cavern where it cannot be used. Some enterprising homeowners, especially those who are inclined toward gardening, are reverting to an age old practice of installing a rain barrel above ground to hold rain water. This water can then be used for watering small gardens, shrubbery, etc.

If you think that a rain barrel might be useful around your home garden, there are a few things that you should do to ensure that the project succeeds. A 50-gallon steel drum will hold enough water for several weeks of watering a small garden. The only problem with a steel rain barrel is that they tend to rust. Vinyl liners are available and might be worth the small investment to keep your rain water clean.

Another alternative is to find a wooden barrel. In any case, your rain barrel should have some type of cover to keep insects, rodents, small animals, and children out of the water. A hinged lid can be easily made for this. The downspout should run into the barrel only about 3 to 4 inches. If you really want to make a useable rain barrel, consider installing a spigot a few inches up from the bottom of the

Fig. 2-30. Install the splash block under the downspout.

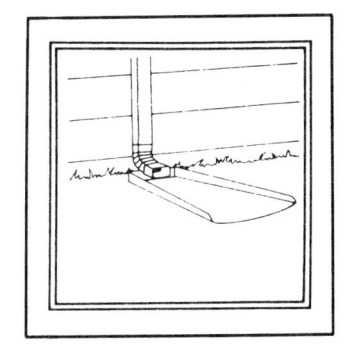

barrel. With such a setup, you can attach a hose for easy use of the water in the garden. A plumbing supply house is probably a good source for materials. If your area experiences freezing weather during the winter, empty the rain barrel and store it upside down during the colder months.

If you decide that a rain barrel is not really suitable for your home, you should give some thought to constructing a special dry well to take care of rain water runoff. A suitable dry well can be constructed using a 55-gallon drum obtained from a local farm supply store. You might also check your local telephone directory for a source of large drums. The container need not necessarily be new, but it should be in sound condition. In addition to the drum, you will also need some 4-inch pipe (asphalt composition, vinyl, or clay tile). This pipe will carry water from the end of the downspout to the dry well. Be sure to get enough to cover the distance.

Most experts suggest that a dry well be located at least 5 feet from the foundation wall. I feel that 5 feet is a minimum distance and, as far as I am concerned, the further away from the house the better.

You will have to dig a hole large enough and deep enough to hold the drum. The top of the drum should have at least 1 foot of soil on top of the cover. You will also have to dig a trench from the downspout outlet hole to the drum. If your soil is easily worked with a shovel, this task should not take very long. If your soil is rocky, you will spend a fair amount of time with pickax, pry bar and other tools. In extreme cases, you might have to rent heavy-duty digging equipment to dig the hole. If this is the case, consider calling in a professional to dig the hole.

After the trench and hole have been dug, the next step is to line the bottom of the hole with about 2 inches of stones and gravel to help drainage. Then you can turn your attention to the drum that will be your dry well (Fig. 2-31). Begin by punching about 50 holes around the side of the drum. Cut out both the top and bottom of the drum. The last hole you must make in the drum is an inlet hole for the pipe.

The perforated drum is set into the hole and connected to the downspout. Then the drum is filled with stones and gravel. A cover is then placed on top of the drum; this, in turn, is covered with either plastic sheeting or tar paper. The last step is to refill the hole with some of the dirt from the original excavation. If you were careful when first breaking ground, you will have a few pieces of sod that can be used on top of the dry well.

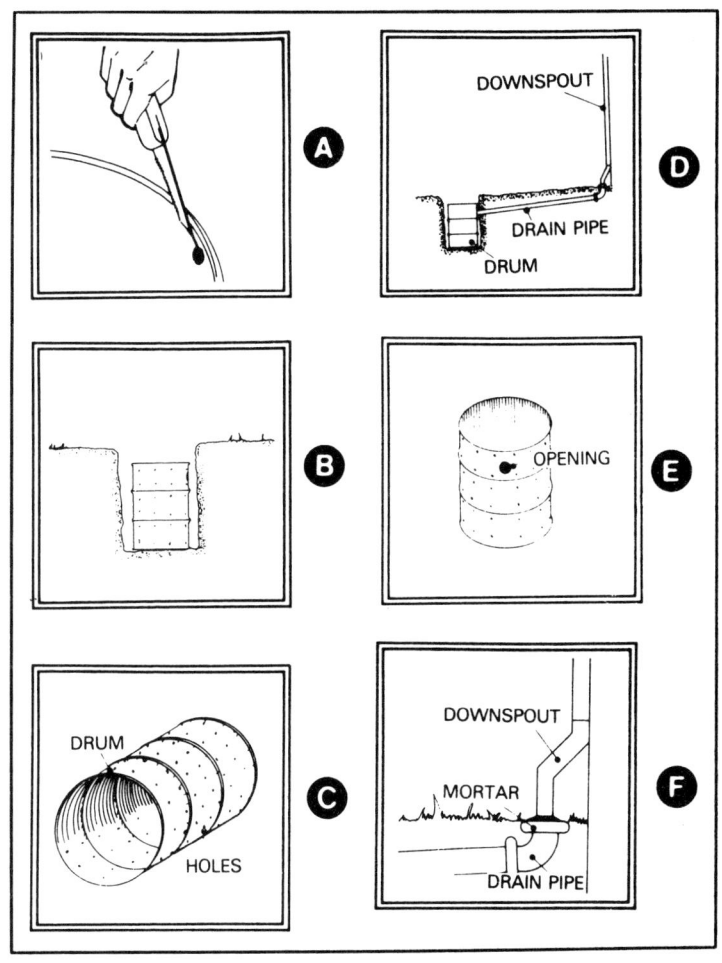

Fig. 2-31. Dry well procedures: (A) cut out the top and bottom of a large drum; (B) punch holes around the drum to aid drainage; (C) make a hole in the drum for incoming pipe; (D) place the drum in the hole; (E) dig a trench for the water line from the downspout; (F) connect the system, and re-cover with soil.

In order for your drywell to be effective, you must make certain that nothing can possibly get into the system to clog it. The most effective and simpliest way to do this is to install special strainers or screens in the gutter at each downspout location. Such strainers will effectively keep your system free flowing. But keep in mind that you will have to clean out your rain gutters at least twice a year to keep the system operating well. Your dry well should operate without malfunctions.

# Chapter 3

Painting

If there is one thing that almost all American homes have in common it is that they have some surface covered with paint. Most houses have, at the very least, a painted trim. Many have siding that has a coating of paint. Even the more modern, so-called Western Designs, with redwood and cedar siding, are protected by a clear coating or stain. There are other surfaces such as railings and fencing that are painted. Concrete surfaces are also commonly painted. These might include foundation walls, stucco siding, and flat masonry surfaces such as floors in carports and garages.

SELECTING PAINT

A quick glance in any store that sells paint is enough to confuse even an experienced painter. Some of the things you can find on the shelves of a typical paint store include primers, latex paint, oil-base paints, stains, sealers, fillers, varnish, polyurethanes, lacquers, thinners, and even special paints and primers for unusual applications (Fig. 3-1).

The most popular paints in use today—for both professional and do-it-yourself painters—are latex-base paints. Latex paints can be successfully used for most types of painting projects. The only possible exceptions are those surfaces that require a special coating such as metal or concrete. Keep in mind that developments in the painting industry happen often; it is entirely possible that a latex paint is being developed for use on these special surfaces. If you are not convinced that latex paints are suitable for most painting surfaces, consider the following points in favor of latex paints.

91

☐ Cleanup of painting equipment used for latex paints is simplicity in itself. Use warm water and a mild soap (Fig. 3-2). There is no need to purchase special thinners or solvents, and there are no dangerous fumes to breathe.

☐ Latex paints are ideal for exterior surfaces. They can be applied at almost anytime of the year, but the best temperature range is from 50 to 80 degres F. You can even apply latex paints after a rainy period, providing the surface is dry to the touch. You should never paint a wet surface because latex paint will not have a good adhesion base and it will be thinned by surface water.

☐ Latex paints dry very quickly; it takes less than two hours, in most cases. This means that it is entirely possible to give two coats of latex paint in one day. Another advantage of this quick drying is that little airborne dirt or few insects will become part of the finish coating before it dries.

☐ Latex coatings, while appearing dry, actually have the capability of stretching or contracting along with the surface on which they are applied. This capability helps to eliminate many of the paint-failure problems commonly associated with other (oil base) paints. Cracking is one example.

☐ Latex paints have a better color retention than oil-base paints. This will generally mean that a latex-coated surface will retain its original color for a long period of time. The color will stay brighter, longer than if the same surface were painted with an oil-base paint.

☐ Latex paints can be touched up anytime. If a section of siding is repaired, it can be painted with some leftover latex paint and the patch will be practically invisible. This is something that is not generally possible with oil base paints.

All of these qualities add up to a very versatile paint coating for both the professional painter and homeowner faced with a painting project. To give you an idea of the developments in the latex paint industry, you can now purchase latex systems for an entire house. These include a primer, siding color, trim paint, and porch and deck enamel—all in a latex base. One real advantage of such a paint system is that it is possible to have an almost perfect match of colors over the entire exterior of your home.

Latex paints are widely used for repainting as well as painting over previously unpainted surfaces. Modern latex paints lend themselves well to repainting. They can be applied over existing paint even if the previous coating is an oil-base paint.

Fig. 3-1. A vast selection of paints is available to the do-it-yourselfer.

When painting bare wood or new surfaces, most paint manufacturers (and professional painters as well) recommend that a special primer be used. Until fairly recently, the only primer suitable for this type of work was an oil-base primer. Now latex primers are available that have all of the good characteristics of latex paints. They will do the job of priming bare wood just as well as oil-base primers. For best results, it is always a good idea to use a latex primer that is manufactured by the same company that produces the latex paint. Don't use one brand of primer and another brand of trim or body paint.

While latex primers have been developed for most types of surfaces around the exterior of the home, there are a few cases where an oil-base primer is preferred. These are concrete surfaces, porches, decks, and metals (such as railings, gutters and downspouts, etc.). The reason that oil-base primers are preferred for these surfaces is that the surfaces themselves generally receive more traffic than, for example, wooden siding. Most paint manufacturers also recommend that, if you use an oil-base primer for such surface, you should also use an oil-base top coating as well. It is generally accepted that oil-base primers and top coatings dry to a harder finish thin latex and they are better able to withstand foot traffic.

Painting exterior metal surfaces also requires a special oil-base primer and top coating. This includes both new metal (never been painted), previously painted metal surfaces and, galvanized metals. Special metal primers contain approximately 80 percent metallic zinc dust and 20 percent zinc oxide in an oil vehicle. These primers (and top coatings) are used widely in industry because they inhibit rust and they last for a long time. The homeowner faced with painting metal should also use these special metal primers and top coatings for long-lasting results.

Most wooden surfaces, either new wood or previously painted, can be coated with a latex primer during the surface preparation stages of the painting project. You will find more information about surface preparation later in this chapter.

Some exterior surfaces are not painted, but they are stained or covered with a clear finish. Exterior stains are used on the home to achieve certain color shades or tones. If cedar shingles, or the more rustic handsplit shakes, are attached to an exterior sidewall, their original reddish color will change, over a period of time, from red to grey and then finally to a very appealing golden brown color. This color change will happen naturally, but it will take many years. If

Fig. 3-2. Latex paints can be removed from painting tools with soap and water.

you want to hasten the process of natural color change, you can apply an exterior stain—most commonly a penetrating resin type—that will not only stain the cedar, but seal and protect the surface as well.

Another type of stain—a semitransparent stain—seals and protects the surface while at the same time it allows the naturalness of the wood show through. With such a stain, you allow the wood to age and develop its own natural color while protecting the wood at the same time.

There are also solid-color stains for exterior application. These actually mask the natural color of the wood, but they also make the overall color or tone uniform. Solid-color stains also hide blemishes and irregularities on the wood over which they are applied. For example, if the exterior siding on a home is plywood, it is not uncommon for this material to have special patches or plugs (Fig. 3-3). These are installed at the plywood mill and they simply make the surface of the sheet of plywood uniform. Unfortunately, these plugs are unsightly. To cure the problem it is a common practice among professional builders and painters to cover the siding with a solid color stain.

You are probably wondering why anyone would want to stain wooden siding when time will bring about a pleasing natural wood tone. Why not simply cover wooden siding with a clear finish that would protect the wood and do nothing to change the natural color of the wood. The answer is that many people do coat exterior siding with a clear finish such as varnish or any of the urethanes. But there is presently no clear finish that is designed to last very long on the exterior of any house.

The problem originates with the Sun. The Sun's ultraviolet rays quickly work on the deterioration of clear coatings; in most cases they must be redone, or at least touched up, about once a year. A much better alternative to a clear coating for exterior surfaces is a transparent stain or semi-transparent stain. While these stains are not totally clear, they do let the grain of the wood show through and at the same time they provide adequate protection for the wood underneath.

Even though a clear finish will not have a very long life when applied to an exterior surface, nevertheless many people do apply them. Some people feel that the extra amount of attention is a small price to pay. They simply touch up or repair the clear finish annually.

Varnishes are easily the largest group of clear finishes on the market today as well as the easiest to apply. Other groups of clear

Fig. 3-3. Solid color stains are commonly used to cover plugs and other surface irregularities on exterior siding.

finishes include shellac and lacquer. At one time, in the not too distant past, all varnishes had to be thinned before use with linseed oil or other solvents. Now, after many advancements in the industry, varnish is simple to use right as it comes from the can. There are even a few water-base varnishes available, similar to latex-base paints, that dry to a clear, hard, durable finish much the same as conventional varnishes do. The obvious advantage of a water-thinned clear finish is easy clean up.

Also included in the varnish category are the relatively new synthetic resin formulations. These are principally epoxies and urethanes. Epoxy base clear finishes (also available in colors) are most commonly a two-part formulation (mixed just prior to use). Epoxies go on easy, they are very durable, and they have an excellent resistance to abrasion, water, alcohol, stains, and many types of chemicals. Epoxy-based clear coatings are widely used for industrial purposes and they are generally available.

Urethanes are relatively new and they are becoming more popular each year. Urethanes—commonly called polyurethanes—are expensive, but they provide about the toughest clear coating available. Urethanes are also available in a variety of colors.

PAINTING EQUIPMENT

As with any type of project, exterior painting can be made easier with the right kind of tools. It is a fallacy to think that you can achieve professional-looking results if you use poor-quality paint or inferior painting tools. It is not uncommon for many people, when they are faced with a painting task, to buy or pick up the first brush that comes to hand and use it for the work. More often than not, the results of the painting will leave much to be desired. You must use quality painting tools (as well as quality paints) if you want to achieve professional-looking results.

Paintbrushes

Any store that sells paint will also have a selection of paintbrushes ranging in price from less than a dollar to over $20. A common misconception among casual painters is that you can paint with any paintbrush. This is just not so. A $10 paint brush will paint clean circles around a 50-cent cheapie. More often than not, the least expensive paintbrush is purchased with the intention of using it for one task and then thowing it away. This is unfortunate because a quality paintbrush, while costing a few extra dollars to buy, should last a lifetime. With just a bit of care, it will actually get better with age. A paintbrush will get broken in, so to speak, and enable you to paint cleaner lines as well as hold more paint so you can paint larger areas with less effort.

In order for you to be able to determine the quality of any paintbrush, there are a few things that you should know. All paintbrushes consist of three parts: handle, ferrule and, bristle. Each of these parts has a specific function and each must accomplish this well or the result will be a paintbrush that is actually a hinderance to painting rather than an aid.

The paintbrush handle—which can be made from either wood or plastic—should fit your hand well (Fig. 3-4). This is no small point. A brush that fits your hand well can be used for hours on end without fatiguing your hand. But a brush that does not fit the hand well will cause you to paint poorly.

Fig. 3-4. A paintbrush handle must fit the hand well.

The ferrule on any paintbrush has only one function and that is to hold the bristles firmly in place. Generally, better-made paintbrushes will have a ferrule that is riveted or nailed onto the handle. A brush of poorer quality will have a ferrule that is simply pressed onto the handle. A pinned ferrule (Fig. 3-5) is less prone to coming loose than a crimped ferrule. A loose ferrule will cause you to paint poorly and the end result will be an unsatisfactory painting job.

The real business end of any paintbrush is the bristles. Twenty years ago, all bristles were made from natural materials such as camel's hair and hog bristles. With the invention of nylon, this material came into use for bristles as well. Today, it is possible to find quality paintbrushes with either nylon or natural bristles. Nylon bristles have a number of advantages over natural bristles. They are not affected by chemicals, they are easy to clean, and they will not absorb paint the way natural bristles do.

There seems to be an ongoing debate among professional painters as to which type of bristle is best for a particular paint and I doubt if this will ever be resolved. As a general rule, however, natural bristle brushes tend to be better for applying clear finishes and oil base paints. Nylon bristles are ideal for latex (and water-thinned) paints.

There are a number of very important considerations that should be taken into account concerning paintbrush bristles. These apply to both natural and nylon bristles. First of all, the bristle length should be approximately 50 percent longer than the width of the brush. For example, a 2-inch brush should have bristles that are 3 inches long. There are exceptions to this rule. A 1-inch brush, for example, will usually have bristles that are 2 inches long and a 4-inch (or wider) brush will usually have bristles that are about 4 inches long.

A quality paintbrush will have bristles of different lengths. These are packed into the ferrule (or trimmed after in place) so that the bristles on the outside of the brush are actually shorter than the bristles in the center of the brush. Poor-quality paintbrushes will have bristles that are all the same length. One easy way to determine if the bristles on any given brush are tapered is to look at the brush from the side. The ends should form a slight pyramid (Fig. 3-6).

The tips of the bristles are also important as a determination of quality. A good brush will have bristle tips that are smooth in addition to being tapered. The bristles on a poor-quality paintbrush will have ragged tips. One very good way to test the quality of the tips on any paintbrush is to brush the palm of your hand—as if you were painting it—with the dry brush. A quality brush will feel soft; a poor brush will feel very rough (Fig. 3-7).

Another consideration for paintbrush bristles is the amount of flex in the bristles. A good brush will be flexible at the tips and less

Fig. 3-5. A good paintbrush will have rivets holding the ferrule to the handle.

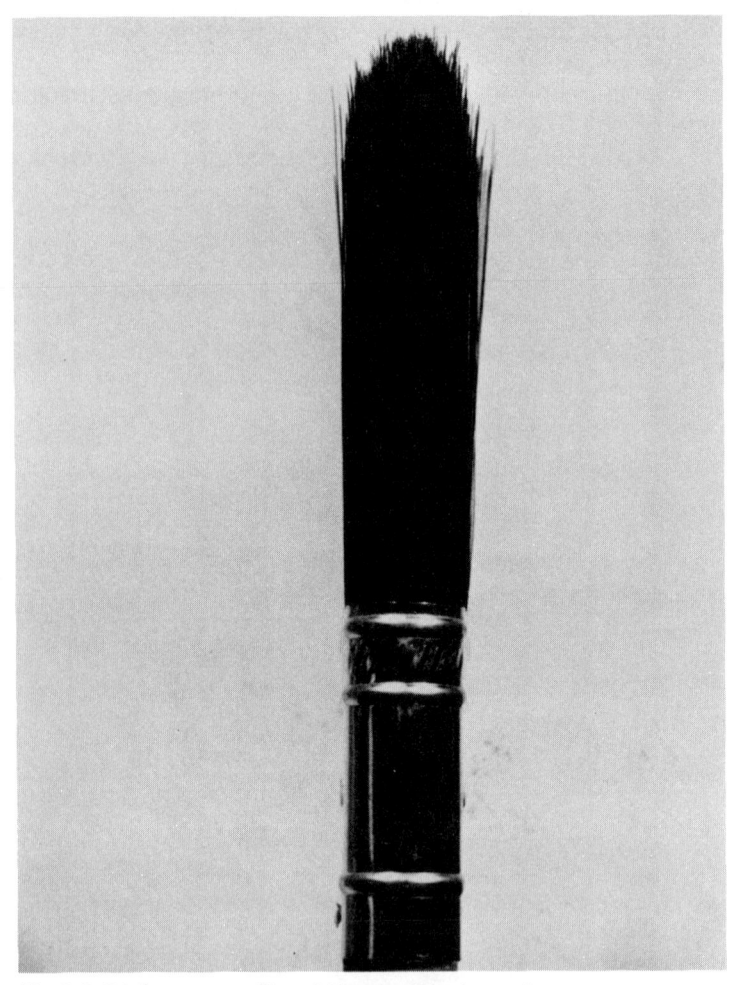

Fig. 3-6. Bristles on a quality paintbrush will be tapered.

so where the bristles join the ferrule. While it is entirely true that the flex of any given paintbrushes' bristles is directly related to the length of the bristles, it is also true that a quality paintbrush will flex more at the tips than at the ferrule end regardless of length of the bristles.

When you go shopping for a paintbrush, pick a store that specializes in paint and supplies. Here you will find a good selection of brushes in several price categories. You will also be able to very easily see the difference between quality brushes and those that are not much good for anything.

One good way to make a purchase decision about a paintbrush is to first take the brush out of its wrapper. If the brush doesn't have a protective wrapper, pass it by because this is one sure indication of a poor-quality paintbrush. Next, hold the brush in your painting hand. The handle should fit comfortably and the brush should feel well balanced. Keep in mind that the bristles will weigh more when coated with paint.

Hold the brush about 1 foot from your eye, sideways, and look at the bristles. There should be a definite taper to the bristles. Those bristles on the outside should be shorter than those in the middle of the brush. Next, pretend to lightly paint the palm of your other hand. The bristles should practically glide across your palm,

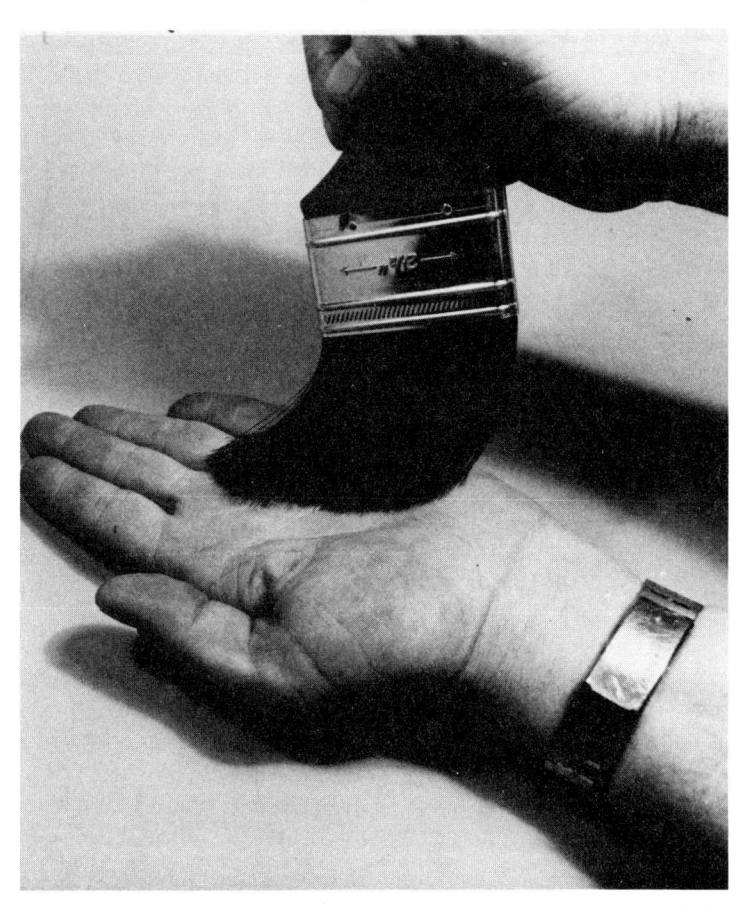

Fig. 3-7. The bristles on a quality brush should feel smooth when you brush the palm of your hand.

and they should not feel the slightest bit rough. If the brush passes all of these tests, it is probably a worthwhile investment. Make sure to try several paintbrushes—in different price ranges—so you will have a good idea about what quality in a paintbrush really means.

A quality paintbrush is a sound investment, just as is any other quality tool. With such a brush, you will be able to paint well and quickly. A poor-quality paintbrush is as useless as a dull saw blade.

Once you have purchased a quality paintbrush, you will want to keep it in good shape for years to come. It is no secret that the best time to clean a paintbrush is as soon as possible after it has been used for a painting task. Cleaning at this time will insure that the paintbrush bristles remain in good condition and, of no small importance, the brush will be ready for use the next time you need it. After all, quality paintbrushes are an investment that will last for many years, but only if you give them the care that they require.

Freshly used paintbrushes are cleaned in the same manner. Different paints require different types of cleaners to restore the brush, but the method of cleaning is about the same.

For latex paints, use warm water and a mild soap (I use dish soap with good results). Begin by rinsing the brush in a steady stream of warm water. After most of the paint has been rinsed off, squirt a few drops of mild liquid soap into the bristles and work this cleaner into the bristles with your fingers. Pay special attention to the butt ends of the brush where the bristles pass into the ferrule. Then rinse the brush again.

It is important that you direct the stream of water into the bristles to force the paint (and soap) out of the brush. When you are satisfied that you have removed all of the paint, shake the excess water from the brush, comb the brush with a steel comb, then let the brush hang (handle up) until dry. The brush should next be wrapped in its original wrapper or in clean newspaper and stored in a dry place until you need it again (Figs. 3-8, 3-9 and 3-10).

To remove oil-base paint from a brush, you should use the paint thinner recommended by the manufacturer of the paint. Use turpentine or mineral spirits to remove varnish, and use alcohol to remove shellac. The best way to remove freshly used oil-base paint, varnish, enamel, or shellac is to soak the brush in a container (with the appropriate cleaner) for about 10 minutes. Then, press the brush down into the cleaner and agitate until the brush is clean. You might find it helpful to spin the brush handle between your palms while pressing down.

After the brush is cleaned to your satisfaction, wipe it dry with a clean, dry rag. Some painters prefer to give brushes cleaned in this fashion a quick wash in warm water and mild soap after first cleaning in the proper cleaner. After the brush has been cleaned thoroughly, it should be combed with a steel comb and dried in a warm place before wrapping for storage (Fig. 3-11).

If you follow these simple cleaning procedures your paintbrushes should last for years. Occasionally, however, something will happen which will prevent you from cleaning your brush after use. When this happens, you usually end up with a paintbrush

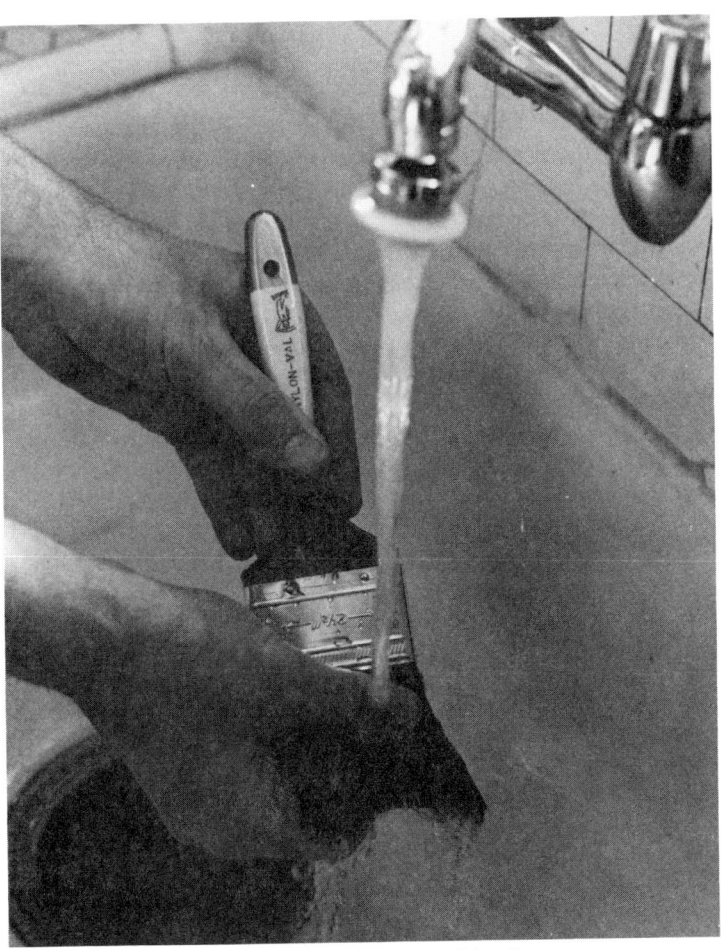

Fig. 3-8. Wash out a paintbrush as soon as possible after use.

Fig. 3-9. Comb bristles with a steel comb to keep them straight.

that has a solid mass where the bristles used to be. To clean a brush that is loaded with dried paint or a brush with paint buildup at the butt end of the bristles, you will need a special cleaner. Your local paint store or home improvement center should sell at least one kind of paintbrush cleaner.

All brush cleaners work very much like standard paint remover, but they have additional additives. Begin by soaking the brush, for about 10 minutes in the cleaner, until the outer layer of paint has been softened. Next, scrape this first layer off and resoak the brush in the cleaner. Repeat this process until all of the old paint has been removed from the brush. The final cleaning is usually done with warm water and a mild soap. Follow this with a combing, drying, and wrapping for storage. It will take a little work, but you should be able to restore an otherwise useless paintbrush to near new condition (Fig. 3-12).

Rollers

You might never have thought about using a paint roller on the exterior of your home, but a roller can help you paint large flat surfaces on the outside just as quickly as for interior painting. Some of the more obvious surfaces on the exterior of your home that lend themselves to being painted with a roller include sidewalls (particularly those covered with asbestos siding), porches and decks, exterior ceilings, and concrete surfaces.

Just as there are differences in quality among paintbrushes, there are also distinctions between a good roller and one that will not do the job of spreading paint well. A roller, often called a *sleeve* or *cover*, is composed of two basic parts. These are the tube, and a covering (most commonly a fiberous material) called the *nap*.

Roller tubes are best when made from a hard plastic material. This type of roller will not absorb any moisture and it will insure that the roller will last for a long time. Beware of rollers that have a cardboard tube. They will not last very long, but their price is usually appealing.

The roller nap is made from a synthetic fiber, and like the plastic tube, is unaffected by moisture, paint thinners, or solvents. There are many types of synthetic materials being used for roller covers. two of the best are Union Carbide's Dynel and Du Pont's Orlon. When buying a roller cover, try to find one that is specifically

Fig. 3-10. After a brush is dry, wrap it in newspaper before storing.

Fig. 3-11. Soak the brush in paint thinner to remove oil-base paint.

labeled Dynel or Orlon. If you cannot find such a roller, you can usually use price as a guide. Inexpensive rollers ($1 each, for example) use lesser quality synthetic materials for the cover. A roller costing a few dollars each usually will have both a durable nylon core and the better synthetic fibers for the nap.

The nap length on any given roller cover will give you a good indication of the type of surface for which it is best suited. While short nap rollers (one-fourth of an inch) are good for interior surfaces such as walls and ceilings, they are practically useless for exterior work. For exterior surfaces that are not heavily textured, you can probably use a roller with a nap of about one-half of an inch deep. For heavy-textured exterior surfaces, however, you should use a long-napped roller cover, that is about three-fourths of an inch to 1 inch deep (Fig. 3-13).

One other thing to consider is the density of the fibers on the roller cover. A roller with a thick covering of nap will not hold as much paint as a cover with a thinner density. There is, to be sure, a certain trade off between density of nap fibers and paint holding capability. Generally, the better roller covers will have a good dispersion of fibers that will hold a fair amount of paint and give good coverage over a surface.

One check that you should do, when considering a roller cover, is to simply spread the nap fibers apart with your fingers. If you can see the tube, chances are the nap is too sparse (Fig. 3-14). Other than this simple test and type of fibers, about the only other indication of quality that is fairly reliable is the price of the roller cover. Generally, you cannot purchase a quality roller cover for under $3 dollars each. Much less than this price and the quality is questionable (unless the roller is on sale).

In addition to helping you to paint well, another reason for investing in a quality roller cover is that it will last for many years with just a minimum of care. Care in this case means cleaning the roller cover as soon as possible after use.

Fig. 3-12. For dried paint, soak the brush in a special brush cleaner.

Fig. 3-13. A long nap roller (right) will hold more paint than short nap roller.

As soon as possible after painting is completed, the oil-base, paint-soaked roller cover should be put into a cleaning solution. Kerosene is a good all-purpose solvent for cleaning oil-paint-soaked rollers. It is relatively inexpensive to buy. Let the roller soak (Fig. 3-15) in the cleaning solution for at least five minutes; agitate every so often to help the solvent to remove the paint. Then remove the roller from the solution and blot it dry with clean rags or paper towels. Repeat this process until the roller is clean. About two or three times should do it. Remember to use clean solvent each time, however.

Once you are satisfied with the cleaning, you should wash the roller in warm, soapy water to remove the solvent. If the roller will only be used for oil-base paints, this step can be eliminated. After the roller has been washed, stand it on end until dry. Then store it in a plastic bag until it is needed again.

Part of the beauty of working with latex paints is that they can easily be cleaned off painting equipment (providing that you do not let the paint dry). For this reason, it is always best to clean painting equipment as quickly as possible after painting is complete. If you have to put off cleaning a roller that has been used for latex paints, you can prevent the paint from hardening by simply placing the roller (still wet) into a plastic bag and sealing the bag. You could put the wet roller into a bucket of water to soak until you are ready to clean it. You can also do this for painting tools that have been used for oil-base paints. Just make certain that the tool or roller is submerged in the cleaning solvent.

After the roller has soaked in water for about five minutes, take it out and place it under running water. This will remove quite a bit of the latex paint. Then apply a little dish soap and work this into the nap with your fingers. Rinse well and the roller should be clean. For rollers that have been used for long periods of time (for several hours), you will have to rinse the roller several times before it is really clean (Fig. 3-16). Dry the roller standing on end. When it is totally dry, store the clean roller in a plastic bag that has been sealed.

An alternative to this roller cleaning method involves using an electric drill, a large paper bag, and an old roller handle. The idea is to use centrifugal force to quickly spin clean a roller. Begin by cutting the old roller handle and straightening it so that you end up with a straight rod with a roller sleeve insert at one end. Chuck the free end of this rod into an electric drill and slip the paint-soaked roller sleeve onto the other end (Fig. 3-17). Next, immerse the roller into a cleaning solution (water for latex paints and kerosene for oil-base paints). Let the roller cover soak for a few minutes to loosen much of the paint.

Put the roller into the paper bag and turn on the drill. The roller will spin and the thinned paint will fly off into the paper bag due to

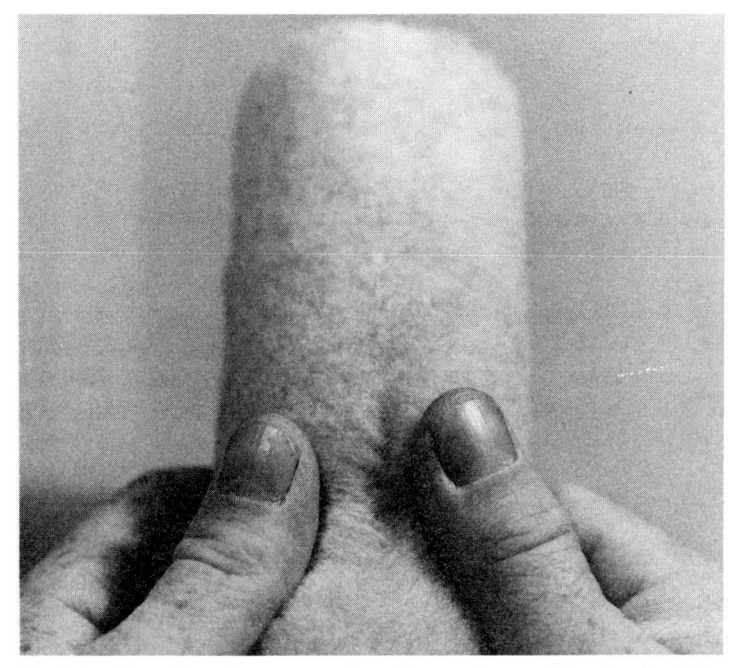

Fig. 3-14. Spread the fibers on a roller with your fingers. The pile should be dense.

Fig. 3-15. Soak a roller in thinner to remove oil-base paint.

centrifugal force. The process is repeated two or three times until the roller is clean. One added benefit of this method is that the roller, in addition to being clean, is almost dry as well. Simply discard the paper bag when the cleaning is complete.

A quality roller cover will last for many years with just a little care. In time, however, even the best roller covers will need a little trimming. As you press on a roller while painting, the edges will have a tendency to flare out slightly. On long nap rollers, this tends to happen frequently and it will show up as ragged streaks on the painted surface. To correct this problem, the edges of the roller can be trimmed with a pair of snips (Fig. 3-18).

There are three other important parts to a paint rolling system: the handle, an extension rod, and a tray. Several types of roller handles can be found on the market, but the only ones worth considering are those that have four steel rods onto which the roller sleeve slides and is held in place. The handle grip should be made from tough plastic and the end should have a threaded hole. This is where you attach the extension handle. The frame of the roller handle should be made of rigid steel that will not bend or even flex very much during use. Probably the best words to describe a quality roller handle are "heavy duty." Such a roller handle will cost $6 or more. That might seem like a lot when you can buy other types for less than $2. But a quality roller handle (Fig. 3-19) should last quite a long time.

About the only care a roller handle ever needs is a rinsing after use. Do this while you are cleaning the roller cover. Occasionally, however, paints will buildup and cake on the end caps and the cross bar. This dry paint is easy to remove with a sharp knife (Fig. 3-20).

Whenever you are painting with a roller, you should have an extension handle attached to the roller. You will get less paint on yourself simply by being further away from the roller. More importantly, however, an extension handle moves you further away from the work. This enables you to see more of the work and to obtain generally better coverage. Still another reason for an extension

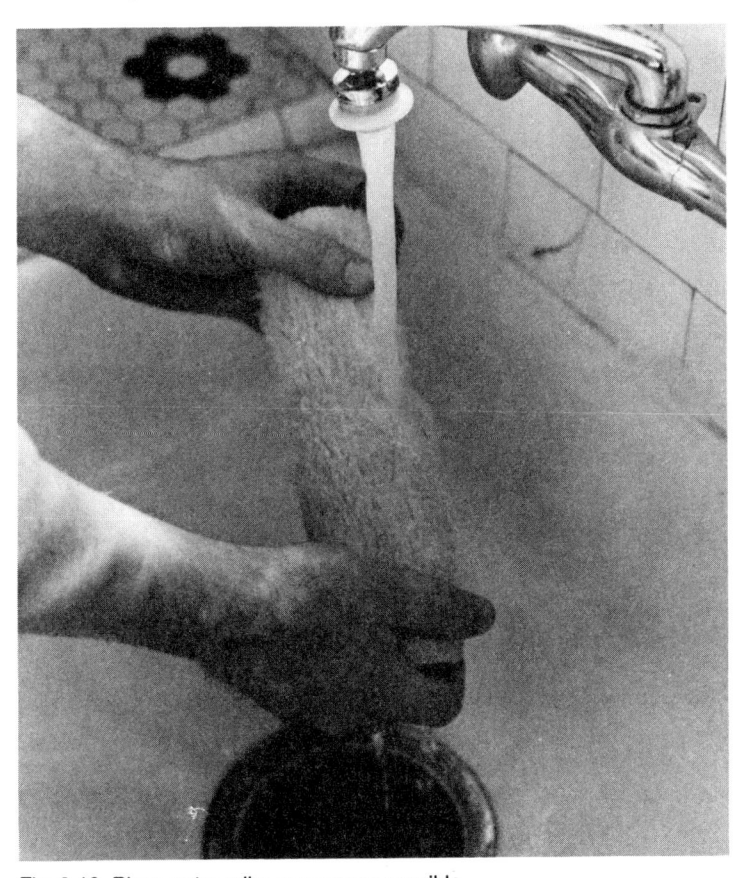

Fig. 3-16. Rinse out a roller as soon as possible.

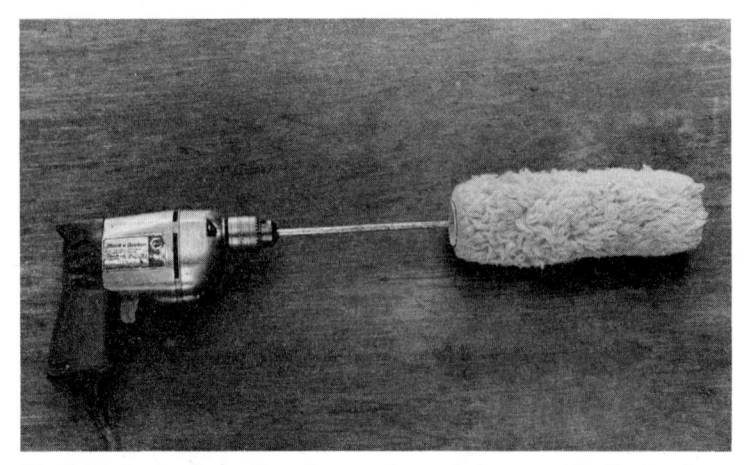

Fig. 3-17. A spin cleaner for rollers can be made from an old roller handle.

(Fig. 3-21) on your roller is that you will be able to paint for longer periods of time with less fatigue. You can fill a roller, apply the paint and, then refill the roller again without having to bend down, stand up and bend down again. Instead the paint tray is left in a central location and you simply reach for the paint with the aid of the extension handle.

Almost any threaded rod can be used for an extension handle. Examples are the common broom handle and a specially designed professional painter's handle extension. The latter might be a good investment if you do a lot of painting with a roller. These are usually

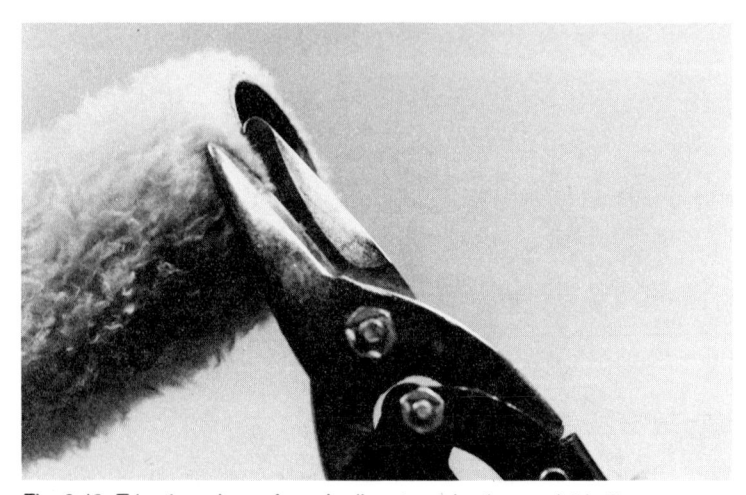

Fig. 3-18. Trim the edges of used rollers to make them paint better.

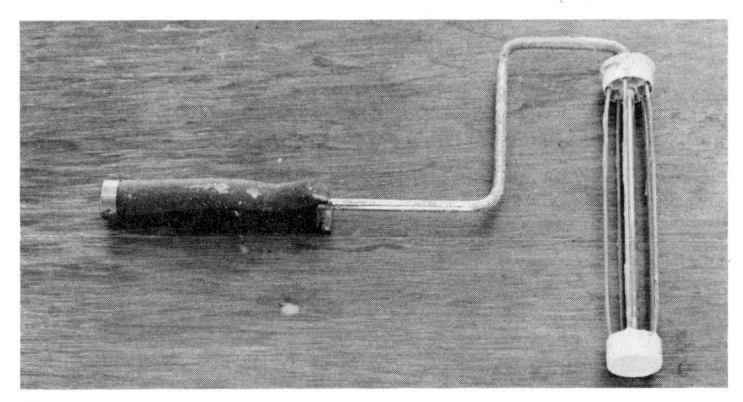

Fig. 3-19. A roller handle should be sturdy.

made from a lightweight aluminum alloy and they can be telescoped. The real advantage to these is that you can adjust the extension handle for different types of painting. Painting the walls in a hallway or an alcove, for example, requires a shorter extension than painting a ceiling.

Another part of a paint-rolling system is a paint tray. There are many types of trays available, but best choices are those that can

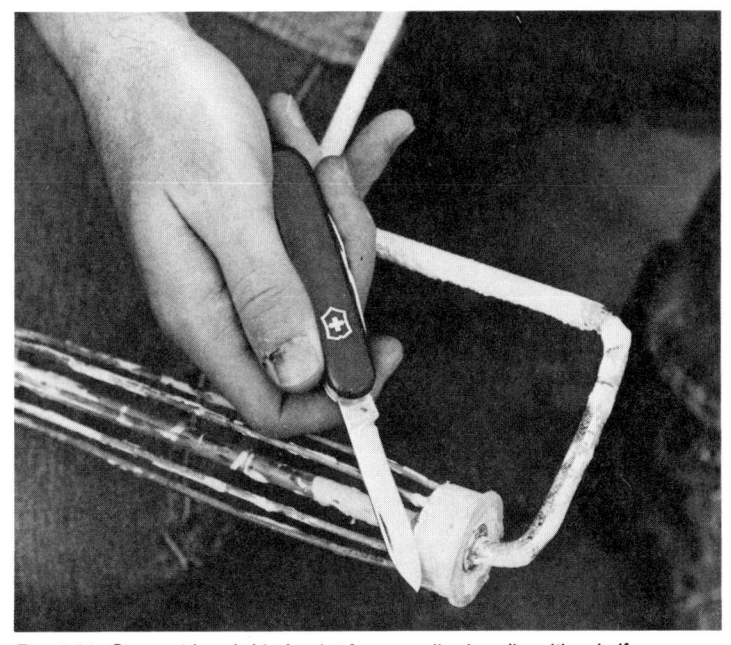

Fig. 3-20. Clean old and dried paint from a roller handle with a knife.

Fig. 3-21. An extension handle on a roller.

rightly be considered heavy duty. To be worthwhile, a paint tray must have a one-half gallon capacity, be made of heavy gauge steel or aluminum, and have some type of grid system that will enable you to roll off excess paint while you are filling the roller. The price for a good paint tray will probably be about $5, but you can expect this type of tray to last for a very long time. Rinse out the tray as soon as possible after each use.

Other Tools

In addition to the basic painting tools already mentioned there are a number of other tools that are often needed for painting projects. Many are used for both interior and exterior painting, while others are strictly for exterior work. You should have an extension ladder that is adequate for the height of your home. Such a ladder can be used for cleaning out gutters and downspouts, checking the condition of your roofing, caulking second story windows and, of course, painting.

Extension ladders are commonly sold in three grades ranging from lightweight to heavy duty. The best bet for the homeowner is the middle grade. These sell for a reasonable price. They are light enough for one person to move around while at the same time durable enough to last for many years. The length of your extension ladder is quite important. A 24-footer will be about right for the average-size 1½-story house. A 32-foot extension ladder should be long enough to reach the peak of an average size 2-story house. These estimates assume that your house is located on level ground. If it is not, you will have to go with a longer ladder.

One workable alternative to purchasing an extension ladder is to rent one. In most parts of the country, a heavy-duty extension ladder can be rented for just a few dollars a day.

Fig. 3-22. A folding ladder has many uses around the home.

Fig. 3-23. A good paint scraper is sometimes called the painters "right hand."

While a folding ladder is generally used for interior work, there are many uses on the outside of your home as well. Probably the best length choice of a folding ladder is about 6 feet (working height). With such a ladder, you can reach first-story windows, porch ceilings, and other low overhangs (Fig. 3-22).

All ladders should be kept in first-class working order; this is usually a simple task. Store the ladder out of the weather and make certain that all moving parts are operating properly before it is used.

Another handy item for the do-it-yourselfer painter is a canvas drop cloth. You might never have considered using a drop cloth when painting outdoors, but it is a good idea nevertheless. With a standard 9-by-12-foot tarp, you will be able to cover cement walkways, bushes, railings, and many other areas that you would want to protect from an accidental paint spill. In addition, there are a number of other projects around the home that will benefit from the use of a tarp.

There are several hand tools that are very useful when you are preparing an exterior surface for painting. Because most surface preparation involves removing old, loose, or peeling paint, the best tool for this type of work is a paint scraper. The most popular paint scraper among professional painters has a stiff blade and it is from 3 to 4 inches wide. The stiffness of the blade is crucial for efficient paint removal. The front edge of the scraper should have a square and flat edge. This type of edge will be an aid in removing loose or peeling paint—much more so than a sharpened edge. Keep this in mind when you are using a scraper (Fig. 3-23) and touch up the edge from time to time to keep it square and flat. A file is very handy for this (Fig. 3-24).

Some other handy tools for surface preparation include a wire brush, sandpaper and holder (or a sanding block), and a nail set and hammer for countersinking exposed nail heads (Fig. 3-25).

SURFACE PREPARATION

The most important part of any painting project is surface preparation. Your method of approach and the amount of time you

Fig. 3-24. Dress up the edge of a paint scraper with a file.

Fig. 3-25. Some of the more common surface preparation tools and materials.

spend prior to painting will have a direct effect on the finished paint job. The fundamental idea behind all surface preparation is simple. You are trying to make the surface, which will be receiving a new coat of paint, as receptive as possible to the new coating. Your aim is to remove any old, loose, or otherwise unsound paint, patch any areas in need of repair, and prime any bare wood surfaces.

To obtain long-lasting results, there are several important steps that must be taken in any exterior painting project. These include a thorough examination of all exterior surfaces, and the surface preparation (which means cleaning, scraping, and sanding). Next, bare wood areas must be primed. In many cases, this will simply involve spot priming. Then comes the painting of the house. Also involved is periodic examination and cleaning of the painted surfaces, and making repairs and paint touch ups as required to keep the painted surfaces in good condition.

Before you decide to paint the exterior of your home, you should carefully look over all surfaces to see what the job will entail. Keep in mind that if extensive repairs or surface preparation are necessary, it might be in your best interest to call in a professional to do the repainting. You could also consider having a new type of siding installed.

Every homeowner should get into the habit of periodically checking the exterior of his home (Fig. 3-26). There are definite indicators that will tell you the condition of your existing paint coating. It is important to keep in mind that modern paints have a lifespan of from seven to 10 years. Much depends on how the paint was applied, the type of area you line in (urban or rural), as well as the type of weather in your area.

Fig. 3-26. Check all exterior surfaces at least twice a year.

During the life of a paint coating, there is a natural wearing away of the paint through the actions of the elements of wind, sun, and moisture. When a house is initially painted, the coating is applied at a thickness of about 7 mils. As the paint ages, approximately one-half mil per year of the coating wears away. When the thickness of the coating is down to about 4 mils, it is time to repaint and build the surface coating back up to a thickness of at least 7 mils once again.

Keep in mind that this gradual wearing away is a natural process. As the paint wears away, dust, dirt, and other airborne material that has adhered to the surface will also be carried off by rain and wind actions. The result is a painted surface that keeps looking fairly good over its entire life.

The stage is set for exterior paint problems when paint is applied too thickly. Temperature changes, humidity, and the difference between inside and outside environments all cause siding to contract and expand through different seasons of the year (even over the course of one day). If the paint coating on the exterior of the house is much thicker than about 7 mils, the coating will crack. This problem is usually most apparent on the sunny side of the house where the heat from the sun causes rapid expansion of the siding. Another area is under the eaves where rain cannot wash away as much of the coating as on other, lower parts of the house. This cracking is called *alligatoring* and it is easy to spot (Fig. 3-27).

Still another problem caused by applying a coating too thickly is called *cross-grain checking*. These cracks are most commonly

Fig. 3-27. An example of alligatoring.

long horizontal lines and they are quite common on older homes that have had several coats of paint applied in the past (Fig. 3-28).

There are a number of other paint problems that you should keep an eye out for when you are checking the general condition of your home. These include chalking, blistering, peeling, scaling, mildew, and decay. You might have heard of the term *chalking* in relation to a paint coating. Chalking is the gradual wearing away of the surface coating (remember about one-half mil per year is to be expected). Excess chalking, however, is caused when a paint coating is applied too thickly or if a new coating is applied over an old coating that has not sufficiently been worn away.

It is a simple task to determine if the paint coating on your home is chalking excessively. Brush your fingertips or a piece of double-knit fabric over an 8 to 10 inch area. If your fingertips or the cloth come away with a lot of dry powder—enough to fill your fingertips or the weave in the double-knit fabric—then you have an excess chalking problem (Fig. 3-29).

If this simple test reveals an excess chalking condition, you must obviously correct the problem before repainting. The best way to do this is to wash the exterior of your home with a strong stream of water from a garden hose (Fig. 3-30).

While washing will cure a variety of paint problems, it is a sound practice to use a scrub brush on heavily soiled areas as well as those with a buildup of grime and soot. If necessary, use a liquid detergent or a powdered detergent (Fig. 3-31) to help lift the dirt off

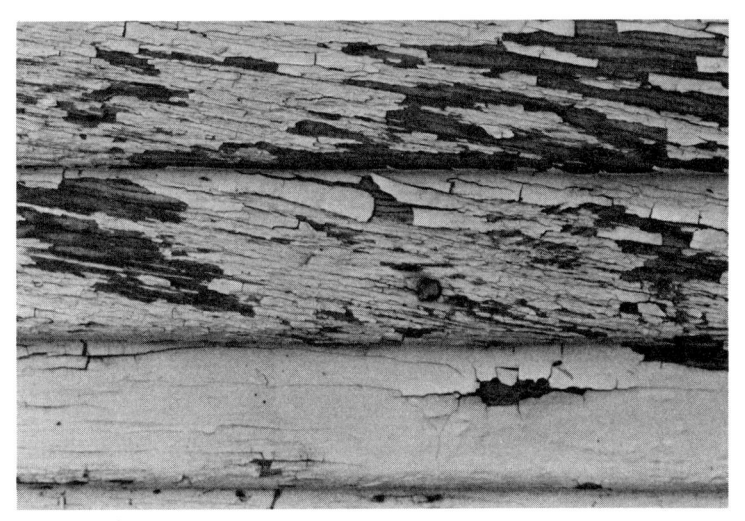

Fig. 3-28. Cross-grain checking paint failure.

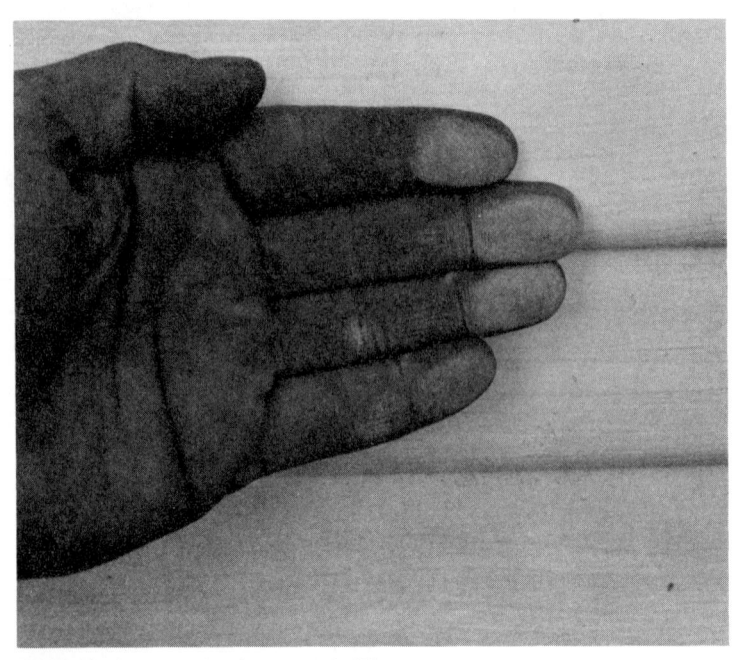

Fig. 3-29. An example of excess chalking.

the surface. After a thorough washing and after the area dries, retest for chalking. In most cases, the problem will have been corrected by the washing and scrubbing. After you are certain the surface is dry (perhaps after 24 hours), you can begin painting the house.

Blistering is caused by moisture in wooden siding. This excess moisture can come from several places, but the most common source is moisture that is trying to escape from the interior of the house. This moisture problem is particularly prevalent during the home-heating season when windows and doors are closed and the humidity of certain areas is relatively high. The kitchen and the bathroom are examples. In an effort to escape, this moisture passes through the interior wallcovering, insulation, and siding, and then it pushes the paint coating outward causing blistering paint (Fig. 3-32).

If you discover an excess of blistering (Fig. 3-33) on the paint coating of your home, you must do something to correct the problem or it will present itself each year. One solution is to install some type of venting system in the kitchen or bathroom to remove the excess moisture in the air. Exhaust fans designed specifically for this purpose are generally available in home improvement centers.

Fig. 3-30. Excessive chalking can often be removed by washing the siding.

Fig. 3-31. A scrub brush and detergent can be used for extreme cases of excessive chalking. Rinse well after scrubbing.

Other solutions to an excess moisture problem is to install dehumidifying systems in the rooms that have a lot of moisture in the air or to install special ventilators in exterior walls of your home, especially around problem areas. Vents will enable moisture to easily escape rather than have to take a route through your siding. For the best results, vents should be installed under eaves and overhangs at intervals all around the house. The easiest vents to install are those that require drilling a 1-inch hole into which the round vent is inserted. Check these small vents periodically to make sure they are open. Flying insects like to make nests in these places. When you are painting around these vents, be careful not to paint them or they will clog and be ineffective.

If you discover areas that are suffering from blistering paint, you must—in addition to finding a solution to the problem—scrape off all blisters during surface preparation. This is a simple matter and it can be quickly accomplished with a paint scraper. In most cases, a little scraping will remove all paint and you will be faced with bare wood. If the siding underneath is damp, you must let this dry out for a day or two before priming.

Once the area is dry, sand and spot prime as necessary (Figs. 3-34 through 3-36). Keep an eye on problem areas even after they are painted to see if the problem recurs. If it does, you will have to take more steps to correct the problem. In some cases this will mean calling in a professional carpenter to rectify the problem.

Peeling paint is a common problem on homes that have been painted several times. Peeling usually is a result of improper surface preparation before painting. Remember that new paint will not adhere well to a glossy surface unless it is sanded first and it will not stick well to a surface that has a coating of dirt, grime, or soot. To correct a peeling paint problem, begin by scraping off all loose paint, and then sand to make the surface smooth. If the scraping or peeling results in bare wood, you should sand this area. Apply a primer before repainting.

Occasionally peeling paint will be a result of excessive resin in the wood siding. This can be a problem if the siding has many knots, and it will be easy to spot (Fig. 3-37). To correct the problem, scrape and sand the knot until it is smooth. Apply an oil-base primer to the area. When the primer dries, paint as with any other area and the problem should be corrected.

Fig. 3-32. An example of blistering paint.

Fig. 3-33. A vent fan will help to remove water vapor from the interior of your home and help prevent paint failure.

Scaling of a paint covering is another moisture problem that is most often caused by water entering the wooden siding through cracks or breaks in the siding. Scaling can also occur if a blistering paint problem is not corrected. In addition to scraping, sanding and priming, you must also determine the cause of the scaling problem. Areas to check include those around windows and doors, around gutters and downspouts, and around chimneys. If any holes or cracks are discovered, they should be caulked to prevent the problem from recurring.

Mildew is a very common paint-coating problem in the more humid areas of the country. On the surface—usually on the north

Fig. 3-34. Scrape the blistering paint.

side of the house, under eaves or in areas with poor air circulation—mildew looks very much like a build-up of dirt and soot. If the area will not come clean with soap, water, and a scrub brush, chances are good that it is mildew (Fig. 3-38).

Fig. 3-35. Sand the area after scraping.

Fig. 3-36. Spot prime.

To test the area for mildew, put a few drops of ordinary household bleach on the suspected area (Fig. 3-39). If gas bubbles appear and the area bleaches out, you are faced with a mildew problem. If the area simply turns white as a result of the bleach, the problem is simply dirt and grime that will come off with soap and water and a scrub brush.

Mildew is a living organism that feeds on wood, paper, and paint. Mildew can survive on almost any surface such as glass, metal, plastic, etc. and it can be found on superficial layers of dirt, grease, or any other organic matter. Due to its uncanny adaptability and myriad of species, mildew is extremely difficult to control and practically impossible to erradicate. Another interesting fact is that mildew is cyclical in nature. Every few years, due to various climatic and environmental factors, the incidence of mildew can either be very high or low.

Once you have determined that a mildew problem exists, you must strive to eliminate as much of it as possible. All paint manufacturers seem to agree that the best method of removing mildew from a painted surface is to wash the area thoroughly with a solution of trisodium phosphate, household bleach (one cup each) and three quarts of water. Trisodium phosphate is available at any store that

Fig. 3-37. A bleeding knot on siding: scrape, sand and spot prime.

specializes in paint and painting supplies. The affected area should be scrubbed with this solution and a stiff brush. Then rinsed with a strong stream of water from a garden hose. Next, the area should be given a coat of bleach solution (50 percent each of water and household bleach). This mixture should not be rinsed off; it should be allowed to dry. After the area is totally dry, it can be painted with a quality paint that contains a special fungicide. All quality paints have this additive specially formulated for your general geographical area.

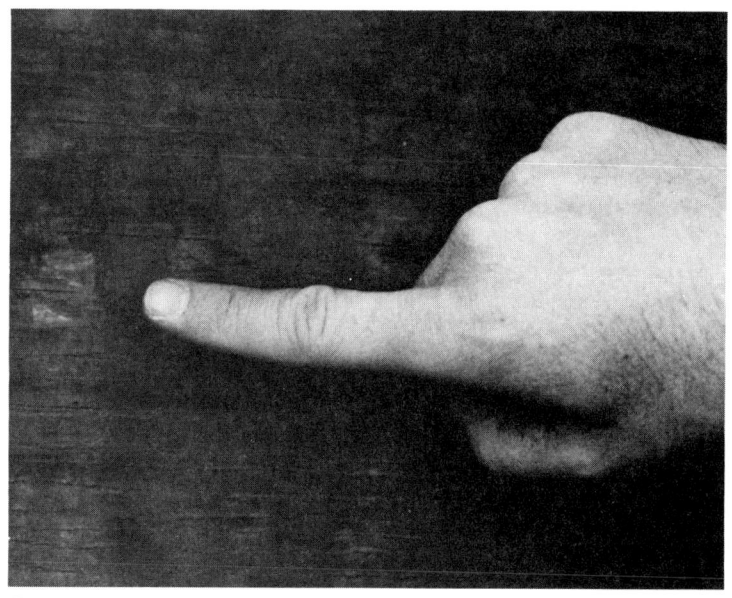

Fig. 3-38. An example of mildew.

Fig. 3-39. The bleach test for mildew.

It is important to keep in mind that even though a paint contains a mildew resistant additive, it will not be mildew proof. If you clean the area affected as outlined above, you will keep mildew growth to a minimum and it might even appear dormant for a long period of time. Because mildew feeds on paint, an untreated area will grow if it is simply painted over.

One of the conditions that promotes and encourages mildew growth is poor air circulation. If you discover mildew on your siding, chances are very good that the air circulation around that area is poor or the siding is sheltered from the prevailing winds by shrubbery. Part of your defense should be to prune any foliage in the area so that it is no closer than 2 feet from the siding of your home. This will permit fresh air to circulate around the area and it will provide a poor environment for the growth of mildew (Fig. 3-40).

Fig. 3-40. Bushes too close to siding reduce ventilation and increase chances of mildew. Prune back at least 2 feet.

Decay is still another moisture-related problem around the home and it is not always apparent on the surface. Occasionally, while you are scraping and sanding areas of peeling paint or blistering paint, you will notice that the siding underneath seems spongy. This is a sure sign that decay is taking place. The problem must be corrected before you even consider repainting. Decay is a very real sign that you have some type of leak that is causing rain water to run down an interior wall (inside the wall cavity) rather than outside. Some of the more common causes of this type of leak are faulty gutters and downspouts, roof valley flashing with holes, the area around a chimney, any inside corner, anywhere the siding is less than 6 to 8 inches above grade, around roof projections such as dormers; and wherever shrubbery or other plants grow within 2 feet of an exterior sidewall.

If you discover an area of decay on your exterior siding, you must determine the cause of the problem. Keep in mind that in addition to replacing the decayed portion of siding, you will also have to repair the cause of the decay. A leaking gutter is one example (Fig. 3-41).

It is very important that the cause of the decay be discovered and corrected because decay will spread if left unchecked. If you have the tools and the know-how to do the repairs, by all means do the work yourself. But you must be honest with yourself about your capabilites. Don't be afraid to call in a professional carpenter.

Fig. 3-41. Decay caused by water leaks.

While you are performing surface preparation tasks that need to be done prior to painting, you will probably notice rusted nail heads. This can be quite a problem if ordinary nails—rather than galvanized nails—were used to attach the siding to the house. When nails are painted with a water-base paint, without first priming, the result is usually rust spots on the siding. The only solution to this unsightly problem is to sand the area until all traces of the rust have been removed. This requires lots of elbow grease. You will probably have to sand the nail head itself to remove the rust. After the area has been sanded smooth, prime the spot with a good oil-base primer.

Another solution to rusted nail heads, and one that can also be used for popped nails, is to countersink the nail head, and then fill the depression with a good-grade exterior filler. Some of the better choices for this task include exterior plastic wood and exterior spackle. After the filler has dried hard, sand it smooth so the patch will blend with the surrounding area, and then spot prime. This should solve the problem. See Figs. 3-42, 3-43, 3-44, and 3-45.

Fig. 3-42. Countersink popped nail heads with hammer and a nail set.

Fig. 3-43. Fill the depression with good exterior filler material.

During the surface preparation stages, there are several other tasks, in addition to those outlined above, that should be accomplished in an effort to make the overall painting project easier and to keep your home in sound condition. For example, remove all shutters, screen doors, mail boxes, lighting fixtures and house numbers. All of these house accessories should be painted unless they are anodized aluminum or they have a baked-on enamel finish.

They will usually be painted a different color than the body of the house—trim color for example—and you will find the work to go much easier if it is done in a garage or workshop. By removing these items, you can paint them when time allows, when you cannot work outside such as during the evening, or while it is raining. You will also find it much easier to paint doors while they are laying across two saw horses rather than while they are hanging by hinges.

By painting these items out of the way of general traffic, you can also be fairly certain that someone will not mar the freshly painted work. Make repairs, scrape, sand and, prime where necessary. When these house parts have been put into first-class shape, place them in a safe place until you are ready to re-install them—after the entire house has been completed.

Other surface preparation tasks include repairing broken windows and screens, and caulking around windows and doors. The time to replace a broken window is when the break occurs. During the surface preparation you might discover a window with a crack or break (Fig. 3-46). See Chapter 4.

Surface preparation is undoubtedly the most important stage of any painting project. Before a fresh coat of paint can be applied, the

Fig. 3-44. Sand the patch to blend with the surrounding area.

137

Fig. 3-45. Spot prime.

surface must be in sound condition and ready to accept the new coating. This means that all loose, existing paint must be removed, all areas in need of repair must be tended to, all bare wood surfaces must, at the very least, be spot primed, and all existing caulking must be checked and replaced as necessary. After all of these tasks have been completed, then the actual painting project can begin.

EXTERIOR PAINTING

Painting the exterior of a home is a large project composed of several smaller tasks. Each task which must be accomplished in its turn. Before you begin the project, you should be both physically and mentally prepared. While painting is not particularly difficult, it will require long hours of standing on a ladder with brush in hand. A well-thought-out work plan that attacks the project in segments is probably the best approach for success.

Painting tends to get a little messy when you are working on a project as large as the exterior of your home. You can be certain that you will get some paint on yourself as well as some other places that you never intended to paint. Prepare yourself for this by wearing suitable clothing. A good combination is a light pair of pants, a long-sleeved work shirt, and a painting hat. You can get a painting hat for free from most stores that sell a line of quality paint (Fig. 3-47).

Along with protective clothing, you should wear some type of sturdy footwear such as a pair of strong shoes or a pair of boots (Fig. 3-48). Keep in mind that you will probably be spending many hours standing on a ladder while painting. A pair of lace-up boots will give you the extra support you will need to be able to go the distance.

I also suggest that you wear a pair of cotton gloves while painting. While rubber gloves might at first seem like a better choice, I have found that they get too hot. I use several pairs of brown cotton gloves (the kind with red linings) while painting outside. When one pair becomes wet with paint or perspiration, I simply change them for a dry pair. With gloves on, your hands tend

Fig. 3-46. Repair broken windows during surface preparation.

139

Fig. 3-47. Painting clothing should be comfortable to work in and include a hat.

to take less abuse and you don't have to wipe or clean your hands every time you stop painting (Fig. 3-49).

For exterior painting I always wear a pair of sunglasses (Fig. 3-50). The glasses not only help to take the glare off the surface I am painting but, they also protect my eyes from paint chips (while scraping) and paint drops during painting. A chip or drop of paint in the eye could have disasterous results when you are 20 feet off the ground. It is not only a good idea to wear some type of eye protection, it is a necessity.

After all exterior surfaces have been washed, scraped, sanded, primed, and repaired as required, you can get ready to paint. The first step is to mix (box) all paints you will need. Boxing is necessary whenever more than one container of paint (of the same color) will be used for the painting. Sometimes there is a slight difference between cans of paint due to different batch numbers, for example. If these paints are used straight from the can, you might see a difference—a slight variation in color or tone—where one can was finished and another started. By mixing all of the paint of the same color together, you are assured of one uniform color and tone. Boxing paints is more important with body paint, where as many as 10 gallons will be needed, than with trim color where usually 1 gallon will do the job.

To box paint, you will need a container that is large enough to hold several gallons of paint. A 5-gallon plastic pail is a good choice. Make sure that it is clean before boxing. Open several gallons of the paint and pour them into the large container. Mix by stirring and then put the paint back into the original containers. You will never have a color variation if your first box all paints (Fig. 3-51).

One painters' trick worth mentioning here involves the use of a 10-penny nail, a hammer, and the rim of a paint can. If you have ever done much painting, you know that every time you dip a brush into a paint can and wipe the excess paint off the brush on the rim of the

Fig. 3-48. Boots will enable you to spend long hours on a ladder more comfortably than lighter footwear.

Fig. 3-49. Wear cloth gloves while painting.

can, you build up more paint to this area. In a short time, this paint will build up and harden in the rim. This makes it almost impossible to seal the can. One very simple solution to this problem is to punch holes all the way around the rim of the can (Fig. 3-52). Then, when you wipe the excess paint off your brush, the holes permit the paint to drip back into the can where it will not harden. In addition, you will be able to easily seal the container with the lid.

Most professional painters agree on the best basic approach to painting any size, shape, or style house. After all surfaces have been brought up to first-class condition, begin painting the trim of the house from the highest point and work downward. Start with the eaves and the overhang at the peak of the house. As you complete one section—as far as you can safely reach in both directions—you must climb down and move the ladder. Then climb back up and repeat the trim painting until it is complete.

Most of the trim painting will be done with a brush and while you are standing on a ladder. Do not work with a full can of paint. Use a paint bucket, a plastic pail, or partially full paint can that is never more than about one-third full. The reason for not carrying too much paint up a ladder is that you cannot possibly use very much in one location. Why make more work for yourself. In addition, all paints contain dryers that evaporate and cause the paint to harden. If you work with a full container of paint, it will become thicker and harder to spread easily. Still another reason for not carrying a large quantity of paint is that if an accident should happen—dropping the paint for example—you will not have wasted much paint and what you have spilled will be easier to clean up than a full gallon of paint.

The paint bucket you are working from will be much easier to use if it is equipped with a special hook for holding it to the ladder while you paint. Bucket hooks are available from any paint store or you can make one from strong wire. Welding wire works fine for this. It is also a good idea to attach a piece of wire or string in the

Fig. 3-50. Sunglasses can save you from eye injury while scraping.

Fig. 3-51. Boxing paints.

shape of a loop to the handle of your paintbrush. The loop will enable you to hang your paintbrush on the bucket hook while climbing up or down the ladder (Fig. 3-53).

When working under eaves or other overhangs, do not apply too much paint as it will have a tendency to run or drip down the side of the house. You also do not want to build up too much of a paint coating or paint problems such as cracking will develop later on. Brush the paint out for uniform coverage. Paint the underside of the overhang first, and then paint the vertical parts such as facia boards.

While doing this type of overhead work, it is important, from a safety standpoint, that you always keep one hand on the ladder. The other hand does the painting (from right to left if you are right handed). This is the safest way to paint from a ladder and the only approach you should use (Fig. 3-54).

As you paint the trim of the house, paint all of the eaves, overhangs and facia first, and then paint around windows and doors and trim around these openings. Painting window trim is fairly simple once you get the hang of it. Before you begin, make certain that the existing paint is scraped, sanded, and primed (if required), and that the window putty around the glass is in good shape (Fig. 3-55).

Painting window trim is the most time consuming part of all trim painting. With double-hung windows, begin by lowering the upper half and raising the lower half to expose the edges of these parts and to expose the upper and lower parts of the sash as well. The idea is to expose all of the areas that are concealed when the window is closed, but visible when the window is open. Paint these areas and include the edges (top or upper, bottom or lower) of the window. After these areas have been painted, raise the upper and

Fig. 3-52. Punch nail holes around the rim of a paint can to allow excess paint to drip back into the can.

Fig. 3-53. Make a hook for your paint bucket so you can hang it while you work.

lower the bottom sections until they are almost closed. Do *not* close them all the way or the wet paint will act as an adhesive.

The same approach is used for other types of windows such as casement windows. Open the window and paint those parts of the frame and window that are hidden when the window is closed. Then close the window *almost* all the way and paint the rest of the window.

The next part of the window to paint are the muntins. These are the strips of wood that hold the panes of glass in the frame. You will find it helpful to begin painting all vertical muntins first and then all of the horizontal pieces. This procedure is helpful when you have windows with many muntins. Usually, because I am right handed, I begin painting on the right side of the window first and work toward the left (Fig. 5-56).

As you paint any window, work carefully so that you do not get too much paint on the glass. Painting experts claim that an overpaint of about one-eighth of an inch is permissible when you are painting a window muntin. The slight excess around the glass is almost invisible (from the inside) and it also tends to seal the glass a bit better into the frame (Fig. 3-57).

After all window parts have been painted, paint the sash, the molding, the sill, and the apron under the window. You should work from the deepest parts of the window outward until the entire window and molding have been given a coat of paint.

Trim painting, including windows, is easily the most time consuming part of any home exterior painting project. This is simply because of the amount of detail work involved. On an average size

Fig. 3-54. Painting the eaves of a house should be done first. Work from the highest point down.

Fig. 3-55. Remove all old paint and peeling paint from windows before painting.

house, it will probably take one day for the surface preparation—assuming that expensive repairs are not required—one or two days for the trim painting, and about one to one and one-half days for painting the body of the house. Much depends, of course, on the height of the house and the method used to apply the paint.

After all of the trim has been painted to your satisfaction, you can begin painting the body of the house. If the siding on the house is relatively flat, such as asbestos shingles or plywood sheeting, you can probably paint the body of the house with a roller. If the siding is shiplap, hand-split cedar shingles, or other irregular siding, you will have to paint the house with a wide brush.

Even if your home siding is flat, don't think that all of the painting can be done with a roller; there will always be some brush work. There are always some areas that cannot be painted with a roller such as inside corners, where trim meets the body of the house, the area around window and door frames, and those areas that do not lend themselves to practical use of a roller such as very high parts of a house.

All brush work should be done carefully and with the intention of making the roller work go smoothly. In short, paint all of those areas that cannot be painted with a roller first. Then switch from brush to roller.

Generally, the best rolled painting project will be done with a long nap roller that is three-fourths of an inch to 1 inch thick. A roller

Fig. 3-56. Paint windows from the deepest parts first.

Fig. 3-57. Overpaint window muntins by no more than one-eighth of an inch.

of this type will enable you to apply paint to those areas that are not totally flat such as where one asbestos shingle overlaps another. If you were to paint with a short nap roller, you would not cover the surface thoroughly. In addition, a long nap roller will enable you to hold more paint on the roller.

When you paint the exterior siding of your home with a roller, begin at the highest point you can reach and work downward. By painting in this manner, you will be able to see any running or splashed paint as it falls onto the unpainted portion of the house and you can correct as necessary. You should do all of your painting with a roller that has an extension handle attached. This will give you a much greater range with the roller as well as move you back from the work so that you will have a clear picture of what you are doing.

Paint stores sell extension handles for rollers that have the capability of telescoping up to about 12 feet. Such an extension would enable you to paint a single-story house from the ground and it might, therefore, be a worthwhile investment for the do-it-yourself house painter.

As you work from the high parts of the house down to the bottom, you will discover how much area can be covered with each roller full of paint. Do not roll the paint out too thickly or thinly; remember that a thickness of about 7 mils is ideal. If you are right handed, work from the right to the left all the way around the house.

After you have completed each side of the house with a roller, take a few minutes to look over the work before going on to another side. If you discover any areas that are not covered properly or are missed entirely, touchup as required. After you are satisfied that a side is properly painted, move on to the next side and continue painting until the entire house is complete.

If your siding is of the type that does not lend itself to being painted with a roller, you will have to do the work with a brush. A quality 4-inch to 6-inch brush will help you to do the work most efficiently. The approach is pretty much the same as with a roller. Begin at the highest part of the siding and cover as much area as you can from your position on the ladder. Do not overextend yourself. A good general rule for painting from a ladder is that your hips should always be centered on the ladder. Work with your paint bucket securely hooked to a rung on the ladder as you paint downward.

While different types of siding must be painted differently, brush work is all basically the same. Always paint with the direction of the grain. For vertical siding such as shingles, paint from the top downward. For horizontal siding, paint in a horizontal direction (right to left if you are right handed). Work carefully and concentrate on brushing the paint onto the surface rather than slopping it on. This will ensure the best coverage and appearance. Complete one side of the house before moving on to another.

Keep in mind that all brush work takes time for best results; don't try to rush the work. After a short time, you will develop your own rhythm of brush work, and you will begin to notice that the work is progressing smoothly and efficiently. Although brush work is much slower than painting with a roller, brushed-on paint usually results in better coverage than with a roller.

No matter what painting tools you are using to paint your home, there are a few professional tips that can make the work progress more quickly without sacrificing quality. When you are painting the exterior of your home, always follow the sun. You should paint those areas that have already been in the sun and are now shaded for the day. For example, begin painting on the east side of your home in the morning, then the south side, then the north side, and finally the west side of your house. Unless it is unavoidable, you should never paint an exterior surface that is in direct sunlight. This would cause the paint to dry too quickly and result in paint failures within a short time.

Latex paints are easiest to work with and apply when the outside temperature is between 50 degrees F and 80 degrees F. At temperatures below 50 degrees F, latex paint does not harden as quickly as it should. The result can be paint failure. At temperatures above 80 degrees F, the paint will dry too quickly and this will also result in paint failures.

Latex paint can be applied to a damp surface—such as when there is early morning dew on siding—but never on a wet surface. Oil-base paints, on the other hand, must only be applied to a totally dry surface for best results.

Carry a rag in your back pocket while painting. You will use the rag hundreds of times while painting to wipe up accidental spills, for dusting an area before painting, for swatting insects and even for wiping excess paint off your brush.

If your house is two or more stories, consider asking for help with the painting project. At the very least, get some help with moving the ladder as you paint. Moving a 40-foot extension lader, extended even partially, is no easy task for one person.

PAINTING METAL

The average home will have a number of metal surfaces that will require some type of periodic attention to prevent them from deteriorating. Some of the more common metal surfaces include hand railings, metal garage doors, rain gutters and downspouts, chain link fencing, stove pipe, mail boxes, and house numbers. In some cases, the metal surface will not require painting except to make it blend or contrast with surrounding. Metals in this group (non-rusting metals) include galvanized metals, anodized metal, chrome, stainless steel and baked on finishes. In other cases, metal surfaces must be painted to prevent rust. Unpainted metal is not only unslightly to look at but, it will breakdown and fail if it is not protected.

As with any painting project, surface preparation must be accomplished first. The amount of work needed for surface preparation will be determined by the type of metal you will be painting as well as the present state of the metal. The first step is to remove all traces of rust. The best way to remove rust from a metal surface is with some type of abrasive. Small areas can be sanded with an abrasive (sandpaper, emery cloth, wire brush, etc.) (Fig. 3-58). Larger areas require the use of some type of electric sanding tool such as a disk sander.

After the surface has been completely cleaned of rust and the metal is visible, the priming (Fig. 3-59) can be done. The only way that the reforming of rust can be prevented is to seal air and moisture from the metal. This is the job of a metal primer. Some metals require a special primer for this. Others can be sealed, in effect, with one or two coats of conventional paint of the type used for topcoating.

Steel and iron require a special red lead primer. If you have ever seen a metal bridge being painted, you probably have noticed reddish orange spots over certain areas of the bridge. This is red lead primer. It is available at most paint stores and it should be applied to areas that are prone to rust problems.

There is a new steel and iron primer that has a latex base. While I have never tried this primer, I understand that it is suitable

Fig. 3-58. Clean metal railings with a wire brush.

Fig. 3-59. Prime cleaned metal railings with a zinc primer.

for priming steel and iron with the added advantage of being nontoxic. Red-lead primers definitely are toxic.

Galvanized metals do not require paint; the special coating on these surfaces will prevent rust. You might want to paint galvanized metal around your home to make it blend or contrast with the surrounding structure. The most common uses of galvanized metal around the home are for gutters, downspouts, and stove pipes.

If you decide that you want to paint galvanized metal, there are a few things that must be done to the surface before priming or painting can be expected to be successful. First of all, no primer or paint coating will adhere to new, shiny galvanized metal. This is because the surface will have been coated with a special coating to protect the galvanized metal during storage and shipping. This coating must be removed before priming new galvanized metals, but it will usually have weathered away (after about six months) on older galvanized metal.

Protective coatings on new galvanized metal can be removed by cleaning the metal with paint thinner. Simply saturate a rag with paint thinner and wipe the surface of the galvanized metal. After the surface dries, a primer can be applied (Figs. 3-60 and 3-61).

In order for a primer or topcoating to adhere to a galvanized surface—which has either been cleaned with paint thinner or allowed to weather for at least six months—you must choose a coating that is compatible with the zinc used during the galvanization process. Paints containing a pigment of approximately 80 percent metallic zinc dust and 20 percent zinc oxide in an oil vehicle have been used successfully for both primer and topcoating. At this point, there might also be a new latex formulation available. The best place to find out is at your local paint store.

Aluminum is a common metal around the home and part of the beauty of it is that it will not rust. It will corrode, however, and it might not blend in well with the trim color of your home unless it is anodized in a color that blends. Surface corrosion on aluminum can be easily removed with steel wood (Fig. 3-62) or a wire brush. Before painting aluminum, check the label of the paint you are using.

Fig. 3-60. Wipe galvanized pipe with paint thinner to remove oils.

Fig. 3-61. Prime galvanized metal with special primer.

Many paints can be applied directly over aluminum without first priming the metal.

Copper and brass do not rust, but time and the elements will cause the surfaces of these metals to take on a colored cast. If painting is necessary, the surface color can be removed with steel wool or emergy cloth. Check the paint container label; many paints can be applied directly over copper and brass without a special primer.

If you are painting metal that will be subject to heat, such as a metal smokestack, use a special heat-resistant paint. There are a number of these on the market that were originally designed for automobile exhaust manifolds. Most commonly sold in spray cans, these heat-resistant paints are easy to apply. First check the label to see if a primer is required. In all cases, any rust must be removed before painting begins (Fig. 3-63).

Painting any type of metal is not particularly difficult. Clean the surface, apply a special primer if required, and then apply a coat or two of finish paint. Because developments in the paint industry happen often, it would be best—if you must paint a metal surface—to check with your paint dealer to learn if any new metal paints have recently been marketed.

PAINTING CONCRETE

There are a number of concrete surfaces around the average home that will benefit from a coating of paint. The more common of these are foundation walls and garage floors. Surface preparation is important when you are painting concrete surfaces. The success of the finish coating is directly related to the condition of the surface before painting. To ensure that the topcoating will penetrate properly, there are a few things that must be done to a concrete surface before painting begins.

First of all, you should never paint a concrete surface that is less than six months old. New concrete contains additives, such as lime and salts, that help the concrete to set up and cure properly. As the cement hardens, usually within a period of about six months, these additives rise to the surface of the concrete and are worn

Fig. 3-62. Remove corrosion from aluminum with steel wool.

Fig. 3-63. Use special heat-resistant spray paint for chimney pipe.

away. If the surface is painted before the concrete has fully cured, the additives, as they rise to the surface, will cause the paint to peel or otherwise deteriorate.

When concrete additives rise to the surface, they appear as a white powder. This is commonly referred to as *efflorescence*. Before paint can be expected to adhere, this white powder must be removed from the surface. Usually a scrubbing with a stiff broom or a wire brush will remove efflorescence, but it is also a good idea to wash the surface with a strong cleanser to make sure all traces are removed (Fig. 3-64).

The first step is to thoroughly clean the surface. Begin by sweeping or brushing. Next, you should look over the surface for areas that will require special attention. Look for whitish areas (efflorescence), grease and oil stains, and areas in need of repair. All of these signs represent potential problems for the top coating and they must be corrected before painting. In most cases, this will mean a thorough washing with a strong detergent and a rinse with clean water.

Another area that might cause problems for the painter is any area that has been steel troweled and appears glossy. Concrete steps are usually finished this way. Paint will not adhere to a glossy surface unless the area is "roughened" slightly to make it slightly porous. A stiff wire brush will quickly take the gloss off most concrete surfaces. For extreme cases, you might have to use a solution of muriatic acid and water or equal parts of water and white vinegar. Scrub the glossy area with either the acid or vinegar solution (Fig. 3-65), let it penetrate for a few minutes, and then rinse with clear water. If you use muriatic acid, work carefully following label directions and heeding cautions.

Large cracks and loose or missing sections of concrete (Fig. 3-66) must also be repaired before painting. Begin by removing any loose concrete with a chisel and a hammer. Next, dampen the crack and let water soak in. This will prevent the patch from drying too quickly. The crack can then be filled with a premixed concrete patch or any of the many products designed for repairs to concrete. Most paint stores and home improvement centers offer several patching materials for this type of work. If you use a ready-mixed concrete mixture (sand mix), remember that the patch will be new concrete and it must be allowed to cure properly for at least several weeks before painting. If you are in a hurry, investigate some of the epoxy-base patching materials that can be painted in about 24 hours.

After the concrete surface has been cleaned, washed, repaired, and allowed to dry for at least 48 hours, you can begin painting.

Fig. 3-64. Wash concrete surfaces before painting.

Fig. 3-65. Scrub the surface of concrete to roughen it slightly. This will make paint adhere better.

Undoubtedly the fastest and easiest way to paint any large, flat surface is with a roller. You do not have to use a paint tray for floors. Simply pour about 1 pint of paint directly on the floor and roll it evenly over the surface. For vertical surfaces, however, a paint tray is required.

Most areas can be painted quite easily with a roller and extension handle. With a little practice, you will be able to roll paint along vertical surfaces, steps, and other 90-degree angled areas. Certain areas such as around basement windows, for example, will require that you use a brush for accurate painting. Small areas, such as a foyer, are easier to paint with a brush.

As you spread the paint, it is important that you apply it evenly, and that you avoid puddles. Remember that two light coats of paint are far superior to one heavy coat. If low spots are present on a floor, give them a little extra attention so that paint will not accumulate.

Paint manufacturers have developed several types of paints for use on concrete surfaces. These include latex paints, oil-base and epoxy-base paints. Probably the most durable are the epoxy-base paints. They are also the most expensive.

There are several schools of thought concerning the priming of concrete before painting. In the final analysis, the type of topcoating will determine if priming is necessary. Quality paint manufacturers spend considerable sums for research and product development. The result of this testing is what you will find in a good concrete paint. Some paints work best with a primer; others do not require a primer at all. The best place to find out if a primer is necessary is on the label of the paint can. If a primer is recommended, you should use one.

Many paints designed for painting concrete are glossy when dry. These surfaces have a tendency to become slippery when wet.

Fig. 3-66. Repair cracks in concrete before painting.

Fig. 3-67. Remove peeling paint from concrete with a paint scraper before painting.

This is especially true in a garage where water will sometimes be present. To avoid the possibility of a slippery floor, many paint manufacturers sell an anti-skid additive that can be added to their product. Sears Roebuck, for example, offers Safe-Step that is mixed with paint before application. Other traction additives as well as anti-skid paints are available.

As an alternative, you can use an old painter's trick. Paint the floor. While the paint is still wet, broadcast fine sand—pool filter sand works well—over the surface of the floor. The wet paint acts as an adhesive to the tiny sand crystals, and as it dries, the particles are held in place. If you use this method, it is important that you use only fine, clean sand and you must spread it thinly and uniformly over the surface. One of the features of using fine sand is that it can be applied a little heavier in certain high traffic areas such as steps. If you are applying two coats of paint, spread the sand between the coats.

It is common practice to give two coats of paint to an uncoated concrete surface and one coat to a previously painted surface in sound condition. Surface preparation is a bit simpler on previously painted surfaces because problem areas are easier to spot.

Problem areas are scraped and cleaned with a strong detergent, paint thinner or other cleaner suitable for the task at hand (Figs. 3-67 and 3-68). If the old paint is in sound condition, but glossy, the gloss must be removed. This can be done with sandpaper, steel wool or any of the solutions designed to remove gloss (such as Surface Deglosser, made by the DAP Company). Repainting will usually be successful with one new coat of paint.

If problems exist on a previously painted surface, these must be corrected before repainting. Some of the common paint problems are listed in Table 3-1 along with suggestions for corrections.

After you have painted a concrete floor, you should let it dry thoroughly before use. To aid drying, especially in an enclosed area, use an electric fan to blow air over the floor. While most floor paints

Fig. 3-68. Gloss must be removed before repainting concrete that has previously been painted with an enamel paint.

Table 3-1. Paint Failures and Solutions.

FAILURE	CAUSE	SOLUTION
White crystal formation (efflorescence)	Moisture from below forcing salts to the surface.	Scrape loose paint, scrub area with detergent, rinse twice, let dry, apply new paint
Poor paint adhesion	Improper surface preparation. Surface too smooth.	Remove loose paint, scrub area with brush and detergent, rinse let dry, repaint. Remove loose paint, roughen surface, repaint.
Slippery surface	Enamel or epoxy paints become slippery when wet.	Repaint with paint containing sand or broadcast fine sand over freshly painted surface.
Peeling paint	Moisture forcing alkali to the surface.	Remove loose paint with scraper wire brush, wash, let dry, repaint with latex or epoxy enamel—not oil base.
Slow drying, sagging lack of gloss	Paint applied at too low a temperature. Surface too porous; high humidity	Paint only when surface temperature is above 60 degrees F. Increase air circulation with fan.

Fig. 3-69. Paint will adhere better if the surface is cleaned first.

are dry to the touch within 24 hours, they will not be totally setup until after about 48 hours. After that time the floor can be used as normal. Garage floors might take a longer period to dry. It would be best not to park a car on the floor for at least five days.

Modern paints for covering concrete are easy to apply and they will give years of protection to your foundation walls and floors. In addition to protection, the concrete surfaces will blend in well with the house color.

MAINTAINING PAINTED SURFACES

After you have successfully painted the exterior of your home, you will want to keep the coating looking good for as long as possible. Generally, a good exterior paint will have a life of at least six years. Much depends on the type of paint used, climatic conditions for your area, the color of the paint, and even the amount of pollution in the air. It is entirely possible to extend the life of this coating to 10 or more years by following some sort of routine maintenance program. This should include cleaning, checking, and touching up where necessary.

An annual or semiannual (best) exterior check is something that every do-it-yourself homeowner should do. Spring and fall are the two best times of the year for this. In the spring, you can determine how your home's exterior survived through the winter, and you can note repairs and maintenance that is required. Additionally, you have a string of warm months in which to do the work. A fall check is also advisable to make certain that the exterior is in good condition for the colder months to come.

During the spring check, it is a good idea to wash the exterior of your home. A strong stream of water from the garden hose (Fig. 3-69) works well for this. Some areas such as moldings around

Fig. 3-70. Soap, water, and a scrub brush should be used to clean heavily soiled areas before painting.

Fig. 3-71. Prune all bushes at least 2 feet back from siding.

doors might require some work with a detergent and scrub brush (Fig. 3-70).

Keep in mind that some surfaces will wear or weather faster than others. The eaves of a house do not weather as quickly as the siding. Pay particular attention to fast-weathering areas and touch up where necessary. This will extend the overall life of the paint coating.

Occasionally, paint will wear off exterior siding because shrubbery, tree branches, or bushes have grown too close. More than touching up the paint covering is required here. The only real solution to this type of problem is to prune all growth so that it is at least 2 feet from the siding (Fig. 3-71). Not only will this prevent wear, but it will also enable fresh air to circulate around the house. This reduces the chances of mildew conditions presenting themselves.

During the periodic maintenance of the exterior of your home, you should also check caulking around all openings, clean out rain gutters and downspouts, and remove any debris that has accumulated on the roof. Because the paint on the exterior of your home is probably the most noticeable feature of the house (aside from the design, of course), you should do your best to keep the exterior looking as good as possible. By following a periodic maintenance program, you will not only increase your investment value, but you will also live in a home that you can be justly proud of.

Chapter 4

Plugging Leaks and Drafts

Ever since man started living in shelters, he has been trying to do something about drafts, heat loss, and leaks. This has been accomplished in various ways; chinking with sphagnum moss between the logs in a log cabin is one method that you might have heard of. In the 1980s, homeowners use different methods to plug cracks and leaks in building materials.

Wherever two building materials meet—such as a window frame and siding of a building—there is always the potential for movement of the materials. During the course of a year, you are very likely to find spaces, cracks, and gaps around the exterior of your home. During the heating season when the interior of the typical home is very dry one interesting estimate puts the humidity of the average American home at approximately 5 percent. That is also the relative humidity of the Arizona desert during the summer months.

With this kind of dryness, there is always bound to be a certain amount of shrinkage of building materials. If you have wooden strip flooring in your home, even if it is covered with carpeting, you have probably noticed that the floors tend to squeek during the heating season, but not at all during the warmer months when windows and doors are opened more frequently. If shrinkage of building materials is taking place, that means that spaces, cracks and gaps are opening and permitting heat to escape. This also allows cold air to seep into the home.

It is no secret that the cost of energy to heat and cool our homes seems to go up almost monthly. This alone should be a good enough reason to think about plugging up any gaps on the exterior of your home as well as increasing the R value of your insulation.

CAULKING

When you think that even small leaks around window and door frames can tack on a few extra hundred dollars to your heating and cooling costs every year, you start to see the value of caulking. In addition to heat loss, another reason for keeping the caulking around the exterior of your home in good condition is to prevent the entrance of water from rain and snow melt.

A good point to keep in mind, when thinking about caulking in general, is that there has never been a building that did not move. Settling is a characteristic of any home. Expansion and contraction of all building materials, as a result of temperature and humidity changes, is a natural phenomenon. For this reason, it is important that the caulking around the exterior of your home be slightly flexible. It should expand or contract along with the building materials. At the same time, the caulk should effectively seal gaps or spaces.

There are several types of caulking (Fig. 4-1) generally available for the do-it-yourselfer. Some have a life span as long as 20 years. Others start to dry out—and thus become less effective—almost from the moment they are applied.

Oil-base caulking compounds are the least expensive type of caulking available; many brands sell for less than $1 per 11-ounce cartridge. They work best for seams and cracks that have only minimal expansion or contraction. Examples are wooden door frames or small cracks in wooden siding. Although the price of oil-base caulking compounds is attractive, their service record is not. These compounds tend to shrink—as much as 20 percent—and they usually do not last more than one year. As you can see, this is false economy. They generally have to be renewed each year to be effective. Although it is possible to extend their service life by painting each fall, better choice of caulking would be a higher priced, longer lived, base-type caulking compound.

Latex-base caulking has a base very similar to that of latex paints. These caulking compounds are easier to use than oil-base caulking and they have a much greater range of application. Their price, however, is more than double that of oil-base caulking. For exterior applications, acrylic latex caulk is the favored choice among professionals. This type can be applied to a damp surface and it can be painted as soon as it "skins" (usually in about 30 minutes).

In addition, latex caulking is very flexible and durable and it will generally last from seven to 10 years. Two other points worth mentioning about latex caulking are that they adhere well to most types of building materials, and they are available in a wide range of colors that will not bleed or stain exterior siding.

Silicone-based caulking compounds make excellent structural adhesive sealants, but they usually require extensive surface preparation before they can be used. For example, many types of wood commonly used in construction require priming before silicone caulking can be applied. This is done to prevent the natural chemicals in the woods from coming to the surface and causing the adhesive in silicone caulking to fail.

Silicone caulking is very resistant to degradation by sunlight. In addition, these materials have the capability of withstanding extremes in temperatures and they adhere well to all non-porous materials (glass, metal, glazed ceramics) and some porous materials.

Silicone caulking has a long life (from 15 to 20 years), but it is rather limited in elongation and tear-resistance strength. Silicone

Fig. 4-1. Caulking is a small investment that pays off in big savings.

caulks are extremely sensitive to moisture and they have the distinct tendency to prematurely set up in the tube or cartridge. For best results, once a tube of silicone caulking has been opened, it should be used entirely. These caulks cannot be painted over even though claims are made by various manufacturers to the contrary. They cannot usually be used over themselves (unlike most other caulks) unless some type of priming is first applied. Nevertheless, under certain conditions, silicone caulking is an excellent choice.

Butyl caulking is a solvent-based material that is ideal for sealing joints that have a moderate amount of movement (rain gutters, metal window frames, roof flashing, etc.). Butyl formulations—some of which contain polymeric caulks and other proprietary rubbers—range from high quality to highly filled composites that have traditionally been referred to as oil-base caulking compounds.

Generally, all of these materials will exhibit good adhesion over a wide range of building materials. The better formulations, characterized by higher price and lighter by actual weight, will contain a sufficient level of fillers to optimize certain preferred properties.

Butyl caulks have an excellent resistance to water in all forms, but they might not hold up well to the effects of sunlight unless a special stabilizer has been added to the compound. This is usually indicated by price as well as a description of the product on the packaging. Butyl caulks require a heavy pigmentation and the proper filler incorporation in order to maximize their resistance to the effects of the elements. Higher-priced butyl caulks have good flexibility over a wide range of temperatures. They can also be painted over, in most cases, without first having to prime the area. Adhesion of butyl caulks is achieved by special additives (tackifiers or promoters) and, as a consequence, water resistance is slightly sacrificed for adhesion.

Most butyl caulking compounds are rather limited in their capability to withstand excessive movement of the area in which they are applied. Because the elasticity of any rubber-based material is directly affected by sunlight, butyl caulking tends to become quite rigid and occasionally brittle after a six-year period. Nevertheless, butyl caulking compounds make good exterior sealants when used within their range of capabilities.

Elastomeric sealants are a relatively new addition to the caulking line and they are being used with greater frequency commercially as well as by the do-it-yourselfer. This is true even though they are probably the most expensive of all caulking compounds. Undoubtedly, the biggest attraction of elastomeric sealant caulking is their wide range of application. They adhere to almost any building material and they actually seem to stick better with time.

After curing, elastomeric sealant caulking will stretch and conform as the caulked joint settles (relieving its own stress and thus preventing tension rupture). The caulk does not dry out, it can be reapplied over itself, it will reset and adhere with normal ambient summer temperatures, and it has good insulation properties. All of these features add up to an excellent caulking material with a life span of at least 20 years. About the only black marks against elastomeric sealant caulkings are that they are very expensive. Usually they sell for about $6 for an 11-ounce tube. They can be difficult for the casual user to use. But this problem can be eliminated with a little practice.

WEATHER STRIPPING

Weather stripping is another way to seal cracks and spaces around the exterior of your home. While usually more useful for filling large spaces—such as around door frames—weather stripping can also be used in conjunction with conventional caulking. The technique most often used here is to first fill up the large gap or space by packing with weather stripping. Then applying a bead of good caulking on top. This is a very economical way to seal large spaces.

There are four types of weather stripping: felt, rubber, putty, and foam. Each has various characteristics as outlined below.

Felt weather stripping is probably one of the oldest of all weatherstripping materials. It is most commonly sold in one-half inch to 1-inch wide strips that can run in length up to about 50 feet. Felt weather stripping has durability and low price in its favor and it can generally stand up well to abuse. It is commonly used around door frames (placed very close to the door when closed) and it effectively seals against incoming and outgoing air leaks (Fig. 4-2).

Rubber weather stripping (there are many versions) is widely used as a door and window sealing material. One use that you might be familiar with is a rubber sweeper attached to the bottom inside of an exterior door. When the door is closed, the rubber weather strip seals the threshold (Fig. 4-3). Usually, a special nailing tab or strip is attached along the top edge of rubber weather stripping for easy attachment to various surfaces. Wear and sunlight contribute to the

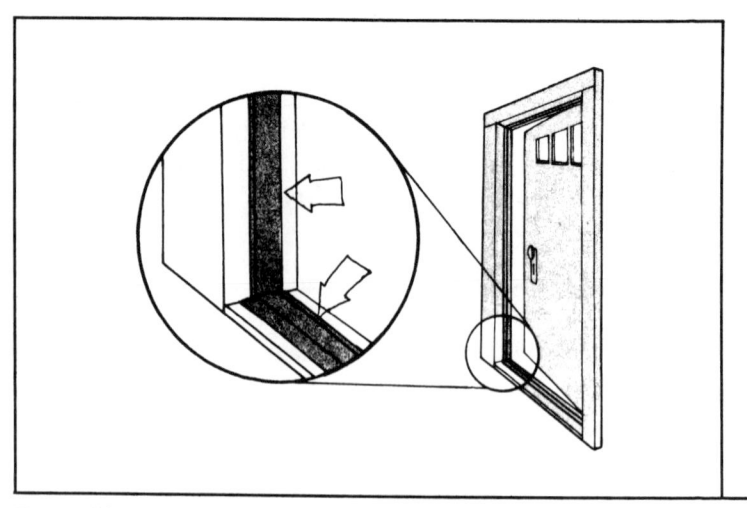

Fig. 4-2. Weather stripping should be used around all doors to cut down on leaks.

demise of rubber weather stripping and it must usually be replaced every three to five years.

Putty (Fig. 4-4) has been used for centuries to seal cracks and small openings in exterior siding. Unfortunately, putty does not have a long life. This is largely due to the fact that most putty compounds have a linseed-oil base. As the oil dries out, the putty shrinks and becomes ineffective at sealing. The life of a putty weather strip usually can be extended by periodic painting.

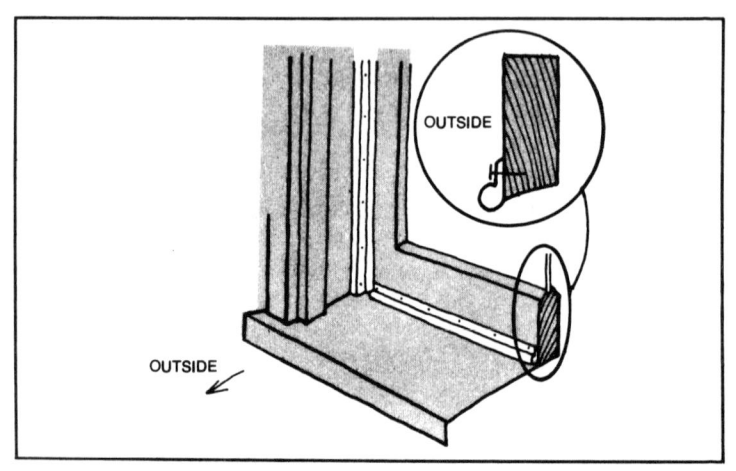

Fig. 4-3. Loose fitting windows are more efficient when weather stripping is applied around the outside.

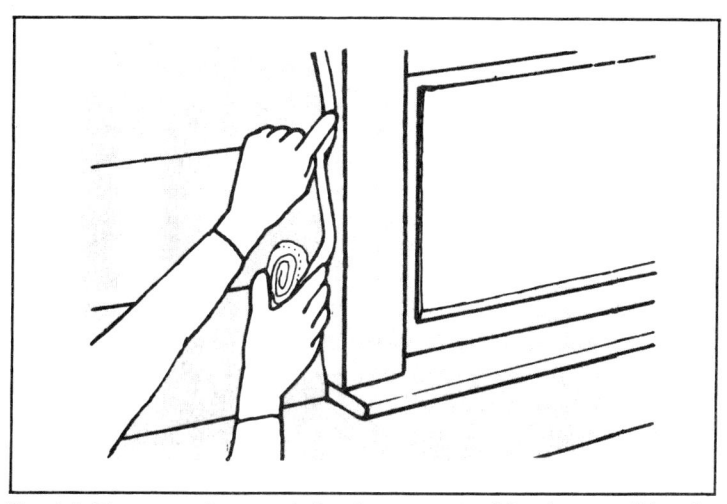

Fig. 4-4. The area where a window frame meets siding is a candidate for weather stripping, putty, and caulking.

Foam weather stripping (Fig. 4-5) is available in a variety of widths and thicknesses. Like felt, it is used largely around window and door openings to form a tight seal. Foam weather stripping is very popular because it forms an almost airtight seal when properly installed. Because it can be compressed and still form a seal, it can be placed around door edges and along window bottoms and tops. There are adhesive-backed foam tapes that can be installed quickly as well as those that must be tacked or stapled in place. Foam weather stripping is readily available, effective and easy to install.

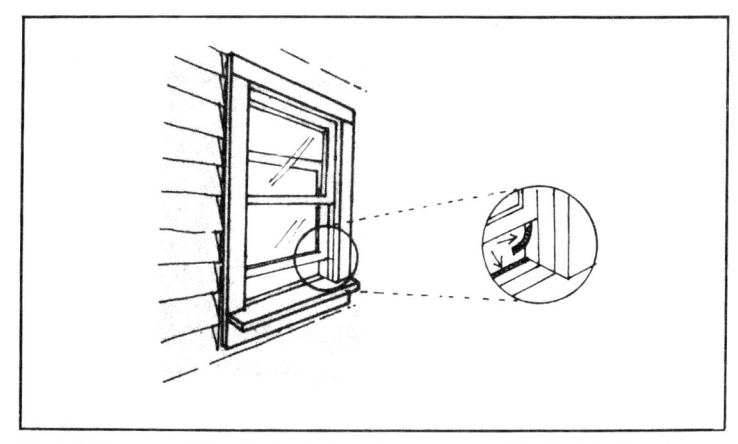

Fig. 4-5. Foam weather stripping is easy to apply around the inside of windows.

Fig. 4-6. Pack insulation around outside water faucets to cut down on air leaks.

It also tends to be the highest priced of all weather stripping materials.

Fiberglass insulation can be packed into large spaces on exterior surfaces to seal them tight. Some of the spaces insulation is commonly packed into includes the areas around outside faucets (Fig. 4-6) and electrical outlets. Whenever you have a large area to seal, consider packing fiberglass insulation into the space as described later in this chapter.

WHERE TO APPLY CAULKING AND WEATHER STRIPPING

Doors often benefit from an application of caulking and some weather stripping. Caulking should be applied around the edge of the exterior trim or frame. For added protection, the same procedure can be followed for the interior trim around the door. Before applying new caulking, it is a good idea to remove the existing caulking if it appears cracked or shrunk. This can be accomplished with the tip of a screwdriver or other suitable tool. Run a bead of caulking wide enough to fill this joint area (Figs. 4-7, 4-8 and 4-9).

Fig. 4-7. Remove old and useless caulking from window frames with a suitable tool.

After the door frame has been caulked, you can turn your attention to applying weather stripping around the inside of the door frame. When the door is closed, the weather stripping should form an effective seal around the interior edges of the door. This is most commonly accomplished by tacking or stapling weather

Fig. 4-8. Apply a new bead of caulking around window frames.

177

Fig. 4-9. Make sure the new bead of caulking seals the joint well.

stripping—felt or foam works best here—so that it will just touch the edge of the door when it is closed (Fig. 4-10).

You should also check the threshold (sill) for a tight seal. Consider adding a sweeper to the bottom inside of the door or consider installing a new threshold in the doorway. Some of the more modern thresholds have a special rubber strip that pushes up against the bottom of the door when it is closed to form a very good air seal (Figs. 4-11 and 4-12).

Windows undoubtedly present the largest potential for heat loss, drafts and water entrance around your home. By sealing all

Fig. 4-10. Felt weather stripping is installed around the inside of a door frame (flush when the door is closed).

areas around windows, you can be sure that you will greatly reduce heat loss. Begin, as with doors, by removing all old and deteriorated caulking around the exterior of the window frame or trim. Then run a bead of caulking around the frame. All joints around the window casing should receive a bead of caulking. This includes the sides, the top (where you will also find flashing), and around the bottom or apron of the window (Figs. 4-13, 4-14 and 4-15). After this has been completed, you can turn your attention to the interior of the window.

Inside the room, check the joint between the window casing or trim and the interior wall. If a space or gap is apparent, you should apply a bead of caulking to the area. Whenever you are working on interior trim, apply only enough caulking to effectively fill the seam (Figs. 4-16 and 4-17). Consider using a clear caulking so that it won't be too visible. In some cases, you might also have to give the interior caulking a light touchup with paint to conceal it. Keep in mind that you spend much more time looking at windows from the inside than from the outside. If you apply the caulking too thickly, it will be unsightly—although effective.

To test your window for a good seal, open the window and slip in a piece of paper or a dollar bill so that it will be touched by the window when closed (Fig. 4-18). Then close the window and try to remove the paper. If it is difficult to remove the paper, you have a good seal when the window is closed. If the paper comes out easily,

Fig. 4-11. A door sweep, attached to the bottom of the door, will seal this joint against air leaks.

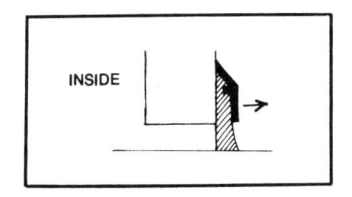

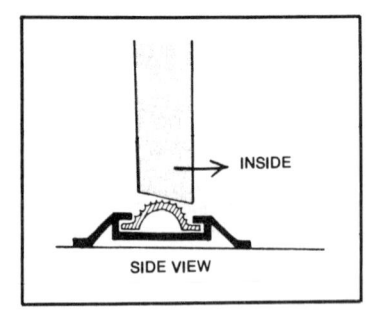

Fig. 4-12. Some of the newer thresholds have a rubber or vinyl center that seals this joint when the door is closed.

you will want to apply a strip of weather stripping along this area (Fig. 4-19).

Windows probably require more time than any other part of the exterior caulking task. For this reason it is always a good idea to work in stages. For example, caulk all exterior joints around windows, then work on caulking the interior casings, if needed, then apply weather stripping where you feel it will be most effective. While working on the exterior, always keep an eye out for window glazing that is in need of repair. Putty often dries out and becomes ineffective. In extreme cases, the window glass or pane will actually be loose in the frame. Fix this type of problem as soon as possible.

You might discover a window that has a crack in the glass or broken, cracked, dried out, or even missing putty. This must be

Fig. 4-13. Remove old caulking with a pocket knife.

Fig. 4-14. Brush out the joint to remove dust and anything else that might prevent a good seal.

repaired as quickly as possible. Begin repairing a broken window by first removing the broken glass. If the putty is just in poor shape, you can skip this part and simply repair the putty. While removing the broken glass, wear a pair of heavy leather gloves to protect your

Fig. 4-15. Apply a new bead of caulking.

Fig. 4-16. Seal the inside of window frames with a bead of caulking.

hands (Figs. 4-20 and 4-21). You must remove all old window putty. A paint scraper is very handy for this type of work. After the window frame is free of all glass and old putty, measure the inside of the frame and buy a new pane of window glass cut to the proper measurements.

Fig. 4-17. Paint inside caulking.

Fig. 4-18. Place a dollar bill in an open window, close the window, and try to remove the bill. If it comes out easily, you need to seal the joint.

When you purchase the window glass, you should also buy some glazier's points and window putty. Glazier's points are small triangular pieces of metal that are pressed into the window frame to hold the glass tightly in place before the putty is applied. Window

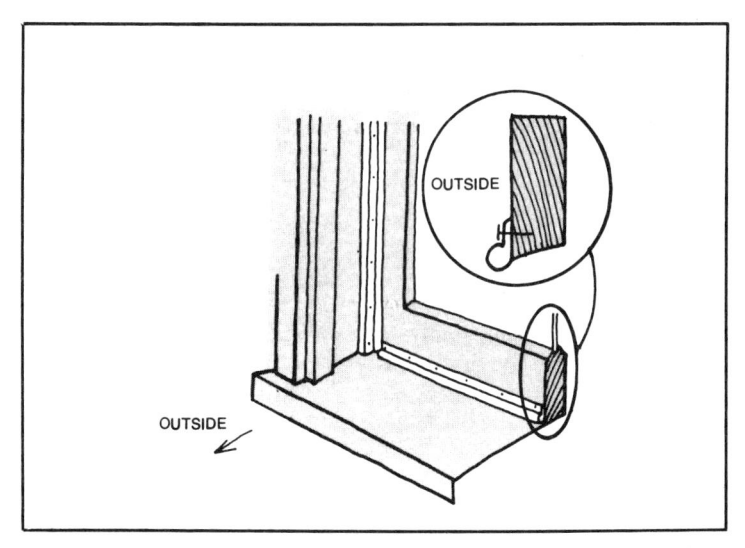

Fig. 4-19. Apply weather stripping on the outside of windows in need of a tighter seal.

Fig. 4-20. Remove broken glass from a window frame. Wear gloves to protect your hands.

putty is commonly available in either white or black. Pick a type that most closely resembles the final trim color of your window frame.

Before installing the new window glass into the frame use a stiff brush to brush out the area where the glass will sit (Fig. 4-22).

Fig. 4-21. Clean old putty out of the frame with a pocket knife.

Fig. 4-22. Brush the inside of the frame clean.

Next, wipe the inside edges of the wooden frame with a rag that has been dampened with turpentine (Fig. 4-23). The turpentine will fill the surface pores of the window frame and prevent the wood from drawing all of the moisture from the new putty. This small step will probably add a few years to the life of the putty.

After the turpentine has been applied, place the new window glass into the frame and hold it in place by pressing angle points next to the glass (all around the window). A standard size window will require two points (Fig. 4-24) per side. For larger windows that are

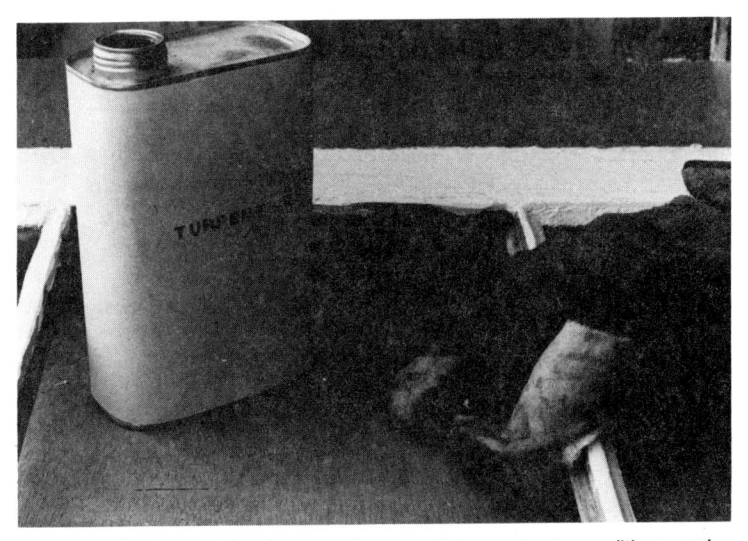

Fig. 4-23. Wipe the inside of wooden frames with turpentine to condition wood.

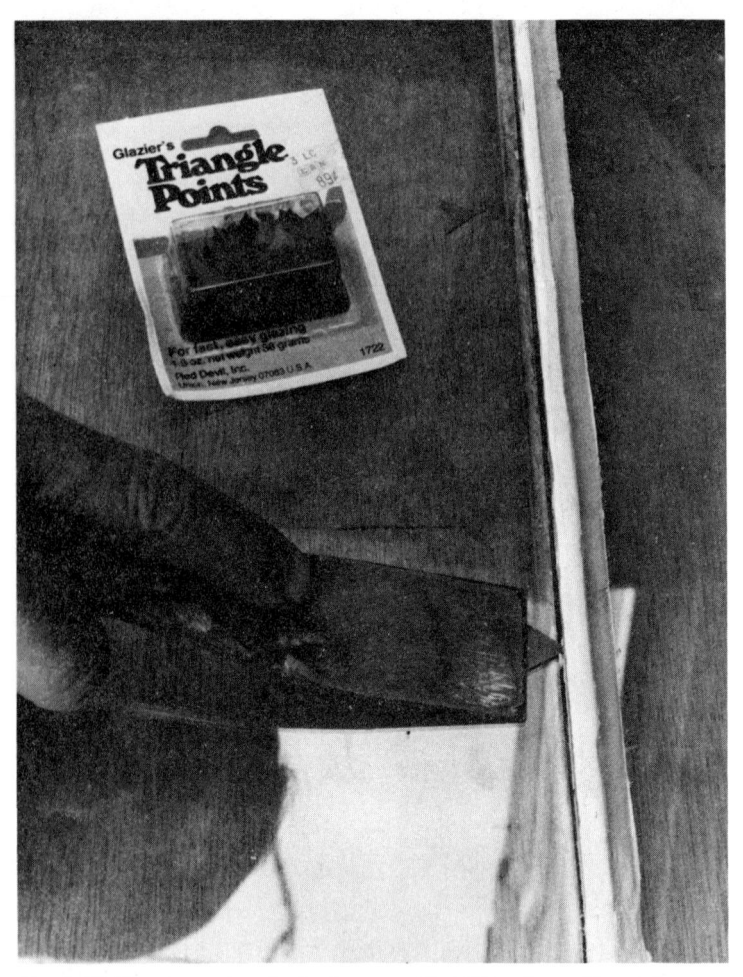

Fig. 4-24. Place new glass in the frame and hold it in place with points.

more than 8 by 10 inches, use more points. Once the glass is held firmly in place, you can start applying the new window putty.

Begin by rolling a ball of window putty between your palms to form a rope about three-fourths of an inch in diameter (Fig. 4-25). Next, starting along one side of the frame, press the putty up against the window glass. Press the putty into its approximate position against the glass along the entire side of the frame you are working on (Fig. 4-26). With a paint scraper or putty knife, press and smooth the new putty into place. Most people find that working from the top of the frame downward is the easiest (Fig. 4-27). Hold the putty knife so that one edge is against the glass while the flat part of the blade rides along the frame at an approximate 45-degree angle to the glass. After one side of the frame has been completed to your satisfaction, do the other three parts of the frame (Fig. 4-28).

Generally, window putty can be painted over as soon as it is applied. It does not generally require a priming or a curing period. Nevertheless, you should check the container label to be sure of this.

In addition to doors and windows, there are a number of other places you should check for caulking around the exterior of your home. Many of these areas are commonly overlooked by the do-it-yourselfer. Two of these areas are where the siding of the house meets the foundation, and where the siding meets the eaves of the house.

The foundation of your home, and the wooden sill that sits on top of it, might not seem like a place to put caulking, but this seam is

Fig. 4-25. Roll new putty into a rope about one-half to five-eighths of an inch thick.

187

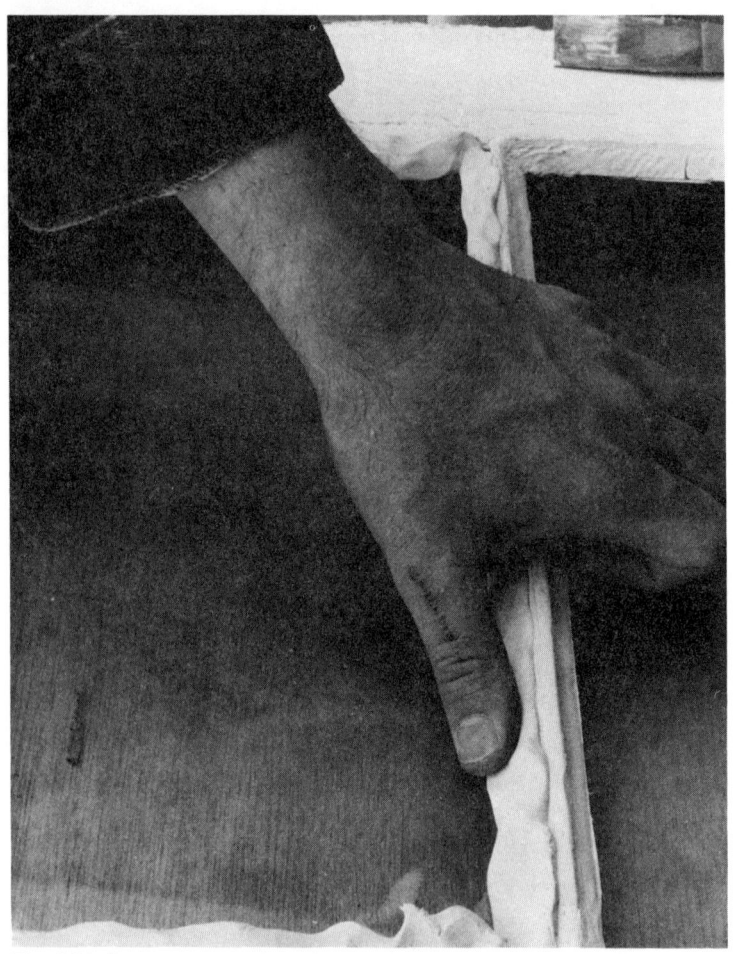

Fig. 4-26. Press new putty into place inside the frame.

one of the longest in your entire house. The problem of air or water leaks is compounded somewhat because siding on a house most commonly covers this area.

To check this seam, it is usually best to work from the interior of the basement. Here the top of the foundation and sill plate will be visible unless you have a finished basement. Assuming that this joint is visible, spend a few minutes looking carefully over the area. In some cases, you will actually be able to see light coming from the outside. In other cases—where the joint is fairly tight—no light will be visible, but an air leak might. To check this area, try holding a lighted candle close to the joint. You might be surprised to see that the flame of the candle actually blows as air from the outside passes through the joint.

There are two basic ways to seal up the joint between your foundation and the sill plate: from the inside, and from the outside.

Fig. 4-27. Smooth the putty with a putty knife.

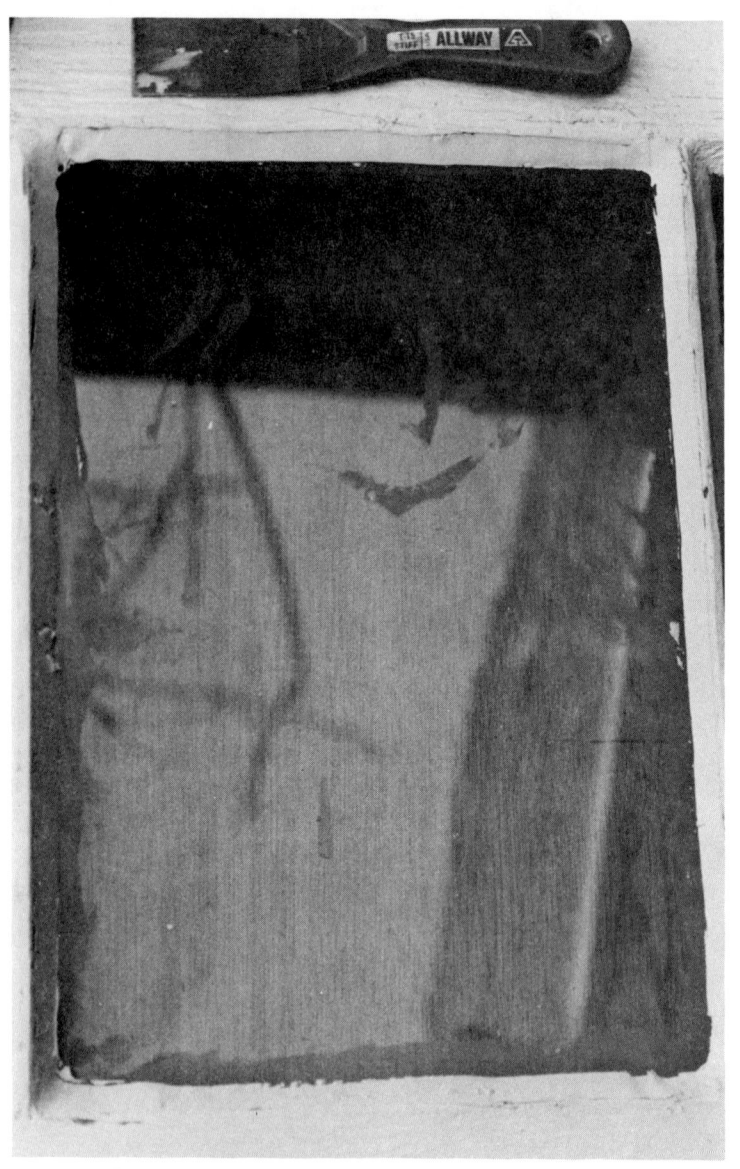

Fig. 4-28. The finished window requires only cleaning of the glass.

In both cases, it might be necessary to pack weather stripping, fiberglass insulation or caulking into the joint area (Figs. 4-29 and 4-30). If at all possible, pack this joint from the exterior. Use a putty knife or other suitable tool for the joint packing. If your exterior

Fig. 4-29. Caulk the foundation sill joint. It is one of the longest joints in your entire home.

siding hangs down more than 4 inches over the sill/foundation joint, you will achieve better results by working from the inside. Pack the joint with weather stripping, fiberglass insulation, or caulking.

Fig. 4-30. If the sill joint is wide, pack it with fiberglass insulation before caulking.

Fig. 4-31. Caulk the eaves/siding joint around your home. If black areas are present you have an air leak.

The area where exterior siding meets the eaves (Figs. 4-31 and 4-32) of your house is another long joint around your home that has the potential for air leaks. If severe leaks are present, they will usually appear as blackish marks along the joint. This is especially true if you heat your home with fuel oil or natural gas. Seal up these areas by either packing with weather stripping, fiberglass insulation, caulking or a combination of these methods.

Other areas to check for caulking includes anything that passes through the siding from the interior to the exterior of your home (Fig. 4-33). Some of the more obvious examples include air conditioners, electrical outlets, water faucets, bath and kitchen vent fans, and even wires for telephone or cable television. Check the joints around all of these areas and use the best means at your

Fig. 4-32. Apply caulking around eaves/siding joint.

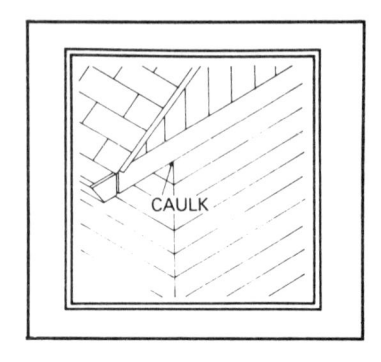

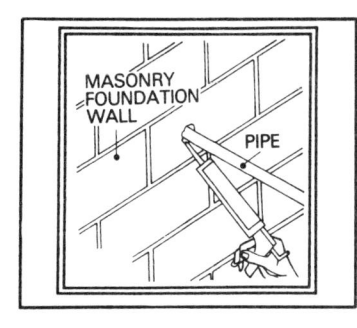

Fig. 4-33. Caulk around outside water-line faucets.

disposal for clean sealing the joint (Fig. 4-34). For small cracks, this will mean a simple application of caulking. For larger spaces, use weather stripping or fiberglass packing.

Do not overlook your roof when you are caulking and sealing the exterior of your house. Areas where two building materials meet have the potential for air leaks. On your roof, there is also the chance that a seam, a joint, a gap or a crack will leak water into the interior of your home and cause untold headaches. Some of the more common areas that you should check (and caulk if necessary) are around plumbing vent pipes (Fig. 4-35), where a chimney passes through a roof, skylights, dormers, and other projections through the roof deck.

If your chimney is located on an exterior wall, you should check the joint where the chimney rests against the wall. Brick reacts

Fig. 4-34. Caulk holes for the telephone line and cable television.

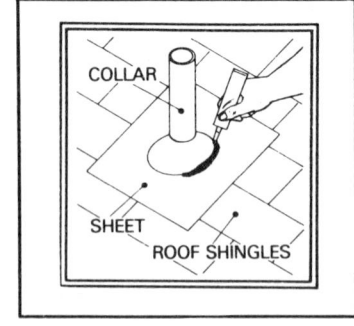

Fig. 4-35. Use caulking to seal around flashing on roof projections.

differently from wooden siding. This joint—on both sides of the chimney—is one that usually requires caulking. In some cases, you also have to pack the joint with fiberglass insulation to really seal the joint effectively (Figs. 4-36 and 4-37).

Fig. 4-36. For wide joints such as where siding meets a chimney, pack with fiberglass insulation.

Fig. 4-37. After packing with insulation, run a bead of caulking to further seal the joint.

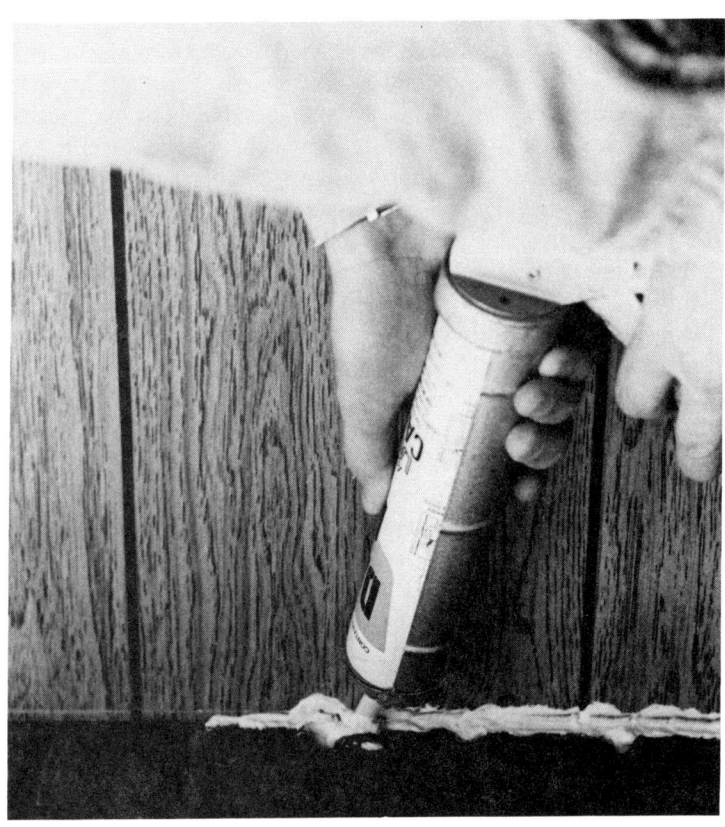

Table 4-1. Caulk Coverage Per 11-Ounce Tube.

Bead Depth in Inches	Bead Width in Inches					
	1/8	1/4	3/8	1/2	3/4	
1/8	96	48	32	24	16	Coverage
1/4	48	24	16	12	8	in
3/8	32	16	11	8	5	Feet

APPLICATION TIPS

Table 4-1 will help you estimate just how much caulking you will require. Another guideline you can use to estimate your caulking needs—and a method often used by professionals—is to estimate that one tube of caulking will be needed for every two windows of average size. One tube will be needed for every door. For long joints such as foundation and side walls, figure on about three to four tubes per long side of the house. As insurance, buy a few extra tubes to cover mistakes and large gaps. This will save you a trip to the store for one or two tubes needed to finish the job. If you buy too many tubes of caulking, you can usually return them for a refund.

While there is nothing particularly difficult about caulking in general, there are a few tricks of trade that are used by professional painters and carpenters that are worth mentioning. These tips will help you to caulk with greater speed and help you to do the work a little better.

To begin with, you must open a tube of caulking before you can use it. The first step is to cut the tip of the tube. The tip should be cut at a 45-degree angle for most caulking tasks. Look closely at the top of the tube of caulking; many are marked with cut lines. Generally, the thinnest bead will result when you cut the tip close to the end. A wide bead will be possible if you cut the tip closer to the actual tube. (Fig. 4-38).

The next step in caulking is to break the inner seal in the tube of caulking. This is most easily accomplished by pushing a long nail (Fig. 4-39) through the end of the cut tip and through the foil seal. The seal is located where the tip meets the actual cartridge of caulking. A common mistake among first-time caulkers is failure to puncture this foil seal. The result is often a burst cartridge and caulking all over the user and gun.

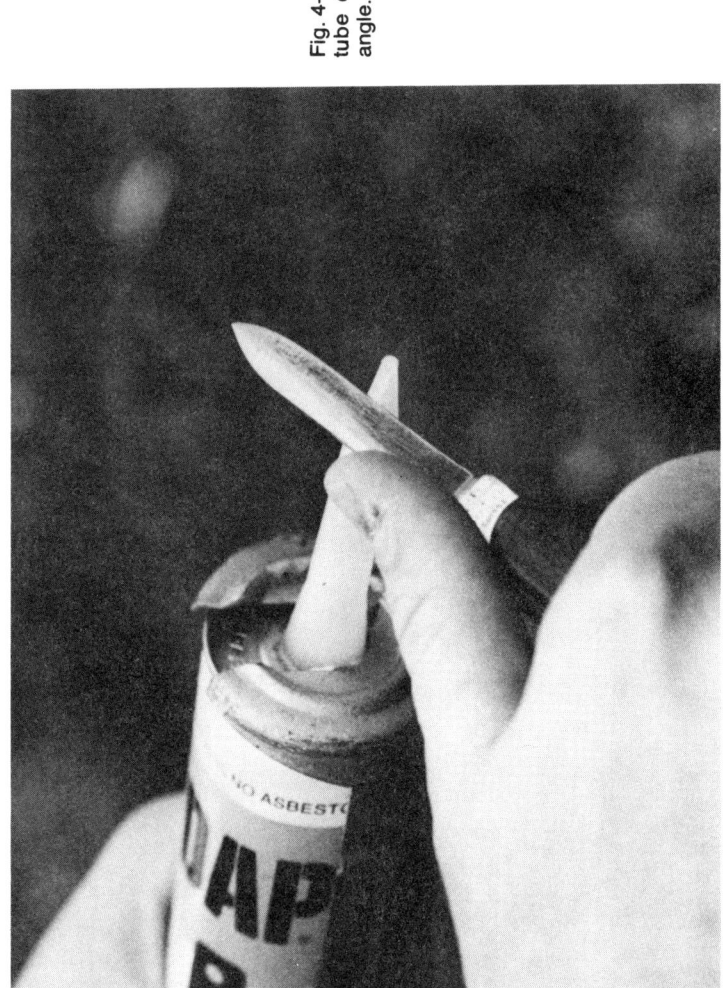

Fig. 4-38. Carefully cut the tip of the tube of caulking at a 45-degree angle.

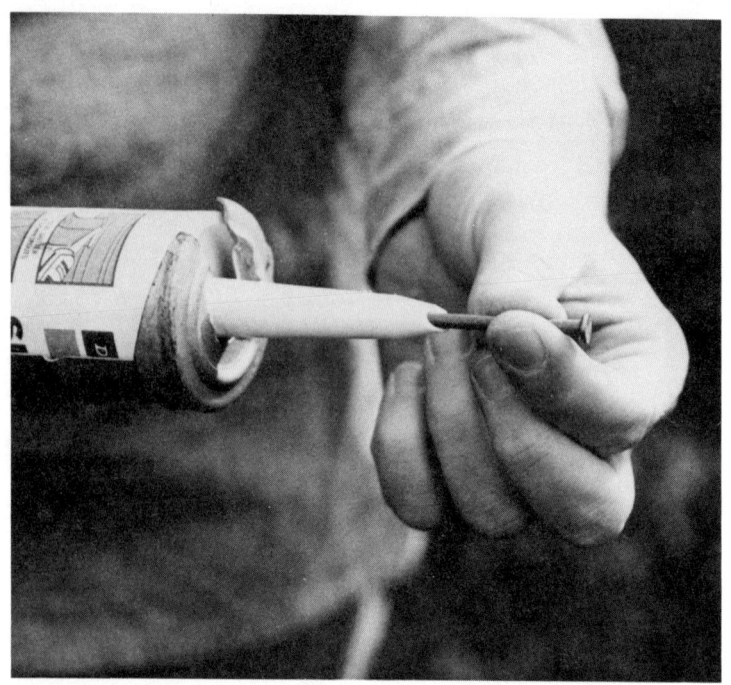

Fig. 4-39. Puncture the inner foil seal with a long nail.

Once the tube of caulking has been cut at the tip and the inner foil seal has been punctured, you are ready to load the tube of caulking into the gun. This is most easily accomplished by first pulling the plunger as far back as possible, then inserting the tube of caulking (rear end first), and then dropping the tube into place (Fig. 4-40).

To start a bead of caulking, turn the plunger handle so that the teeth along the bottom of the shaft can be engaged by the advancing mechanism of the gun. Next give the trigger a few squeezes (Fig. 4-41). This will move the plunger into the back end of the tube and force caulking out of the tip end.

To apply a bead of caulking, first make certain that the area to receive the new caulking is clean and dry. Place the tip of the caulking tube at one end of the joint. Most people find working from the top downward or from right to left to be the most convenient. Squeeze the trigger a few times to start a bead of caulking and start moving the gun and tube along the joint (Fig. 4-42). You will find it necessary to squeeze the caulking gun trigger as you go along. The depth and width of the joint will determine just how much you must

Fig. 4-40. Insert the tube of caulking into the gun.

squeeze the trigger as well as how quickly you can move along the joint.

Most experts agree that the best way to lay down a bead of caulking is in one fluid motion from one end of the joint to the other (Fig. 4-43). This will take a little practice. The tendency for the beginner is to stop and restart before the joint has been completely

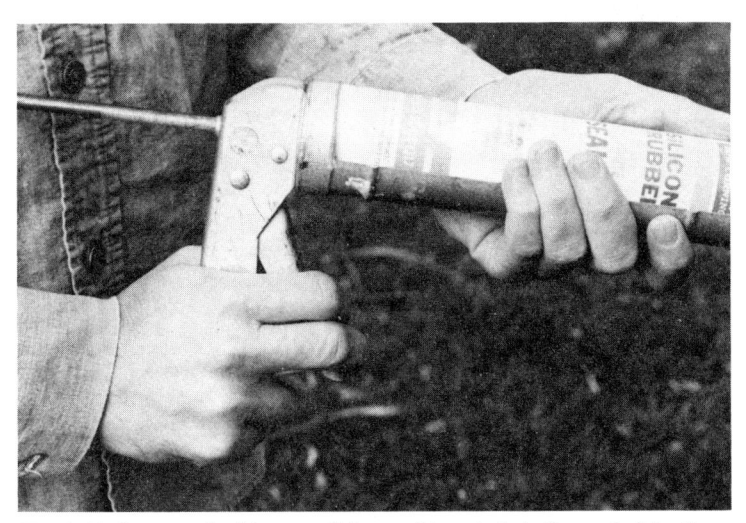

Fig. 4-41. Squeeze the trigger until the caulking starts to flow out of the tip.

Fig. 4-42. Run a bead of caulking along the joint.

filled. After a little practice you will learn just how much trigger pressure and speed are required to produce an even, smooth bead of caulking.

When you empty one tube of caulking, simply insert another opened tube into the gun and continue working. When you finish

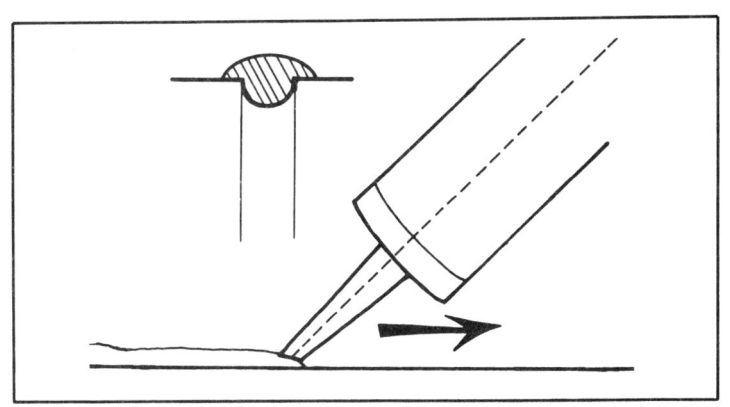

Fig. 4-43. Hold the caulking tube at a 45-degree angle to the joint and let the caulking flow into place. The finished bead should fill the joint well.

caulking, you might find yourself with half a tube of caulking left over. Keep in mind that most caulking tubes can be sealed and reused at a later time. To do this, squeeze a short length of caulking out of the tip (about three-eighths of an inch) and allow this to cure and dry. When you need to reuse the caulking, simply pull out this special caulking plug (Fig. 4-44).

After you finish caulking, you should also clean the gun. Begin by first removing the tube of caulking and storing it standing up in a dry, cool place. Next turn your attention to the gun itself. Clean up

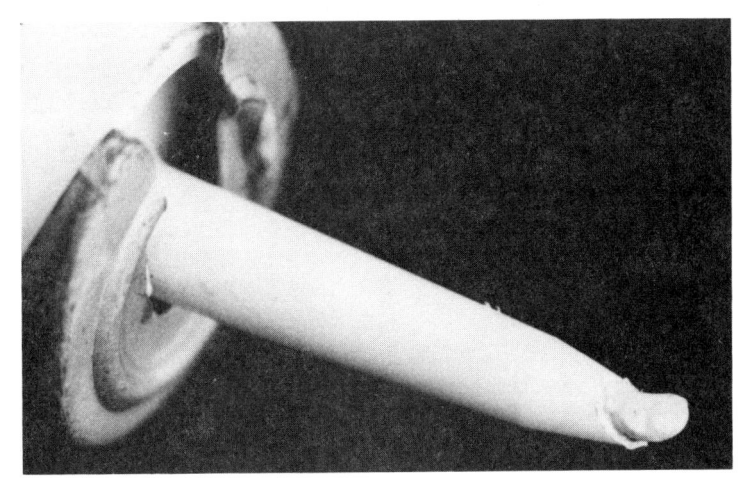

Fig. 4-44. If you still have some caulking left in a tube when you are finished with the caulking project, squeeze a three-eighth inch tag and let this cure. Next time you want to use caulking, simply remove this caulking plug first.

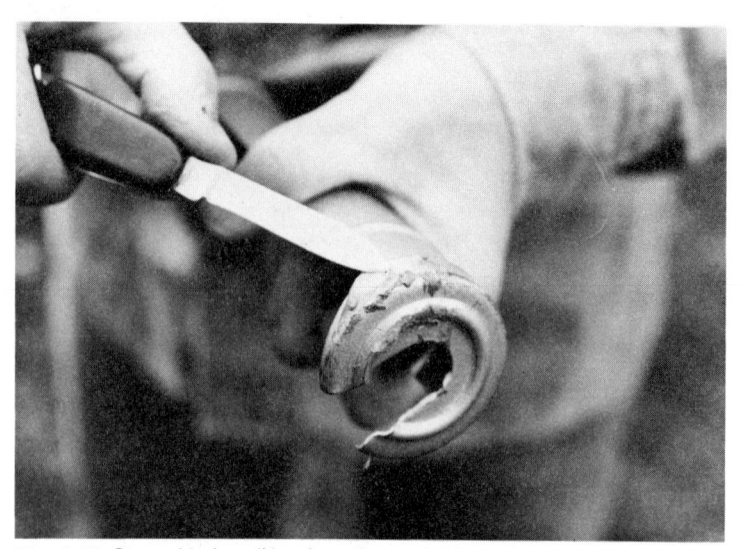

Fig. 4-45. Clean dried caulking from the gun with a pocket knife.

any built-up caulking according to the directions on the tube. In some cases, this will be a simple matter of wiping with a damp cloth (latex caulks, for example), but for other types you will have to use some type of solvent. If the caulking build up has cured and is hard, you can usually clean up the gun with a pocket knife or other suitable tool (Fig. 4-45).

Felt weather stripping is most commonly attached to a surface with either small tacks or staples. Simply position the strip and, beginning at the top, fasten it in place. To be effective, weather stripping must be attached as close to the joint as possible (Fig. 4-46).

Fig. 4-46. Felt weather stripping is commonly tacked or nailed in place.

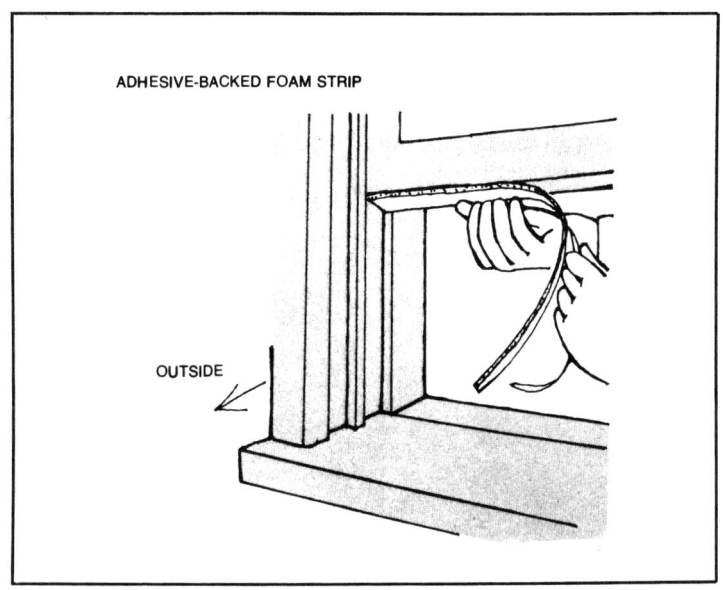

Fig. 4-47. Adhesive-backed foam weather stripping is very easy to apply.

Foam weather stripping (Fig. 4-47) is attached in the same manner as felt weather stripping unless it is adhesive backed. You must exercise care when tacking or stapling foam or it will be compressed and almost ineffective.

Rubber weather stripping most commonly has a special tablike edge that is used for attachment. This is done with either small tacks or staples. As with the other types of weather stripping, close alignment with the joint being sealed is very important (Fig. 4-48).

Putty-type weather stripping (Fig. 4-49) is most commonly available in rope form. The strips of putty rope are placed into the

Fig. 4-48. Rubber weather stripping is tacked or stapled in place.

Fig. 4-49. Putty weather stripping is commonly pressed into place.

joint and pressed for a tight fit. Use a putty knife or other suitable tool for this packing.

Sealing cracks, crevices, and spaces around the exterior of your home with weather stripping and caulking is a project that can usually be done by the average homeowner in one day. There is nothing particularly difficult about the task. Materials are inexpensive and you will make your home more efficient at keeping in the heat and keeping out the cold. A rough estimate for the average-size American home is that you can chop anywhere from $75 to $200 off your annual heating bill (depending on the condition of your home and the part of the country you live in) by caulking all gaps and spaces around the exterior of your home.

Once you have successfully completed a caulking and weather-stripping project, check the areas at least twice a year and repair or replace materials as required. This small effort on your part will easily pay for itself in energy savings. You cannot afford to have a home that is energy inefficient.

Chapter 5

Masonry Repairs and Maintenance

The average American home will have several concrete or masonry surfaces (Fig. 5-1) such as walkways, driveways, steps, porches, sidewalks, a foundation and possibly a garage or carport with a concrete slab floor. When mixed and used in specified proportions of cement, sand, gravel and water, concrete stands up very well to the elements and it can generally be expected to give a lifetime of service with little or no maintenance. The key to a long life for concrete is the mixing.

If a batch of concrete is improperly mixed, there will be a tendency toward some type of failure or breakdown that might take many years to appear. If any of the concrete surfaces around your home are starting to deteriorate (Fig. 5-2), it is too late to start wondering about the cause of the failure. Correct the problem before it becomes worse.

When a small crack or fissure appears on the surface, water can run into the mass of concrete. The first signs of failure usually appear as surface breakdown—peeling or crumbling areas. The problem gets worse as more water is allowed to enter the concrete; freezes and thaws cause widespread concrete breakdown. The first thing that you should do when you start to see signs of concrete breakdown is to patch the area to prevent further deterioration. In most cases, this will save the concrete.

Before we can discuss how to make simple concrete repairs, it might be helpful to mention the tools and materials that are available for the do-it-yourselfer. While there are not very many different types of tools, there are a number of specialized implements

Fig. 5-1. Just about every American home has some type of masonry work.

that will make concrete work go easier and help you to achieve professional-looking as well as enduring results.

TOOLS

The tools you will need for making repairs to concrete are few and simple. Actually, there are only a small number of tools that are specifically designed for concrete work. The others that are mentioned in this section are general-purpose tools that the average do-it-yourselfer will probably have around the workshop.

Fig. 5-2. A crack in any masonry surface will get worse if left unrepaired.

Fig. 5-3. A small sledge hammer is useful for repairs to masonry.

Most concrete repairs begin with removing old and deteriorated concrete from the area. You will need a small sledge hammer and a chisel for this type of work. I have found that a 2½- to 3-pound sledge hammer to be the most useful except for the largest of repairs. It can be used to dislodge old and deteriorating concrete (Fig. 5-3).

Fig. 5-4. A good selection of masonry chisels for repair work.

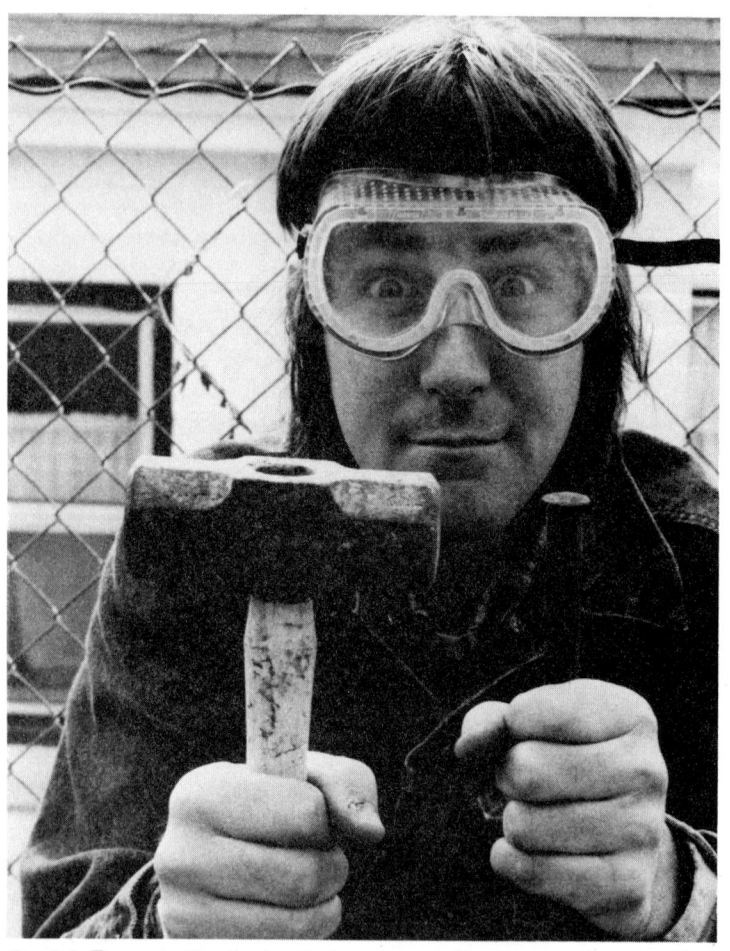

Fig. 5-5. Eye protection is a must when you are chipping away loose concrete with a hammer and a cold chisel.

For shaping joints and cracks so they will be better able to accept a new filling of concrete, a selection of special cold chisels (Fig. 5-4) is very handy. A basic set of cold chisels for concrete work should consist of a thin, star-type chisel and two broader tip chisels such as a 1-inch and a 3-inch wide blade models (Fig. 5-4).

Whenever you are working with striking implements, always wear some type of eye protection. Bits and pieces of concrete are prone to fly in your direction. A small pair of plastic-lens goggles (Fig. 5-5) or even a face shield is more than just a good idea. Flying bits of concrete can seriously damage your eyes.

Fig. 5-6. A wire brush is a good tool for cleaning masonry.

Fig. 5-7. A wheelbarrow is very useful for mixing and moving concrete (courtesy of Sakrete).

After the concrete joint or crack has been cleaned of old and loose concrete, the area should be scrubbed with a stiff brush. The best tool for this is a wire brush (Fig. 5-6).

For mixing concrete, you will find that a wheelbarrow is indispensable. Not only will a wheelbarrow make mixing concrete easier, it will also enable you to move a load of concrete from one area to another quite easily. A good wheelbarrow will have a strong and deep bucket, wooden handles, and an inflatable tire. Such a wheelbarrow will also have some type of guard on the front end that enables the user to easily tip the wheelbarrow forward to dump the contents.

Mixing concrete (Figs. 5-7 and 5-8) is a laborious chore no matter how it is done. Nevertheless, a wheelbarrow will make the work a bit easier. Other tools that make the work less tiring are a special flat-edge shovel and a hoe. It is far easier to mix concrete with a hoe than with any other tool. You can simply pull the ingredients into itself rather than have to lift the ingredients to mix.

Most types of repairs can be accomplished with a float and a trowel. Floats are available in several sizes and construction materials, but probably the most useful for simple repairs is a small wooden-handled, rubber-faced float. You can purchase a wooden float for a few dollars or you can make one from scrap lumber (Fig. 5-9).

A trowel (Fig. 5-10) is specifically designed for working with concrete. For small repairs, you really don't need a special trowel. You can usually do the work with a putty knife or broad knife (the type often used for finishing gypsum panels with joint compound and tape). For medium or larger repairs, you will probably find a special concrete trowel very handy. Keep in mind, however, that a trowel is used primarily for brick and block work and not for smoothing the surface; that is the job of a float.

One other tool that is handy for concrete work is a stiff broom (Fig. 5-11). A broom can be used to add texture to the surface of the concrete before it hardens. This is the type of surface you want to apply on sidewalks and steps. It offers good traction even when wet.

MAINTAINING CONCRETE SURFACES

Most concrete surfaces will last a lifetime with little sign of deterioration. Nevertheless, certain surfaces are prone to staining or get just plain dusty. Part of your periodic home maintenance should include some type of cleaning operation for concrete sur-

Fig. 5-8. A hoe makes mixing concrete easy (courtesy of Sakrete).

Fig. 5-9. A simple wood float can be made from scrap lumber.

faces. The surface of most concrete is rough or textured. This alone is enough to catch and hold dust and dirt. There is also a constant, gradual wearing away of the surface of concrete.

One interesting way to clean a flat concrete surface involves the use of snow. For areas that are notorious for being dusty (such as a garage floor), throw several shovelfuls of snow onto the surface and then sweep or shovel the snow out before it melts. The snow acts like a dirt and dust magnet and it will make your concrete floor practically spotless. If snow is unavailable, or if you find it necessary to clean your concrete surface during the warm months, you can usually do a fair job of picking up the dust and dirt by broadcasting damp sawdust over the floor. Then simply sweep the floor and the dust should come up (Fig. 5-12).

Occasionally a section of concrete will become stained or soiled. If left unchecked this unsightly stain will start to deteriorate the concrete. One common place for this type of staining (Fig. 5-13) is the area under a parked automobile.

The best protection against oil staining—aside from fixing the oil leak—is to place some type of tray in such a way as your parked car will be over it. While this will prevent oil stains in the future, it will not cure the stains that are present. To remove oil stains, you should scrub the area with a strong detergent and warm water (Fig. 5-14). Use a stiff brush and rinse the area with clear water.

Fig. 5-10. A trowel for concrete repairs.

If you are dealing with a puddle of oil, dump a sufficient amount of dry clay bits (kitty litter) on the area first. After a few minutes, sweep the clay up and you should find that just about all of the oil will

Fig. 5-11. A stiff broom is useful for adding texture to the surface of wet concrete.

215

Fig. 5-12. Concrete floors should be swept regularly to keep the dust to a minimum.

have been absorbed by the clay. Then you can scrub the area with water and a detergent to totally remove the stain (Fig. 5-15).

Rust stains on concrete surfaces are common when metal railings are left unpainted for long periods of time. The metal rusts and the rust is carried over the surface by rain water, the result is red stains on the concrete. To cure such a problem, you must do more than just clean the area. First you must correct the rust problem. It is usually best to begin by wire brushing the metal surface to remove all traces of rust. In extreme cases, you will have to rent special equipment such as a disk sander to help you remove the rust. The metal must be primed with a special metal primer, and then painted with a special metal paint. See Chapter 3 for additional information.

Once the origin of the rust problem has been cured, you can turn your attention to the rust stains on the concrete. Probably the best way to remove rust from concrete is to scrub the surface with a solution of tri-sodium phosphate and water—1 pound per gallon of

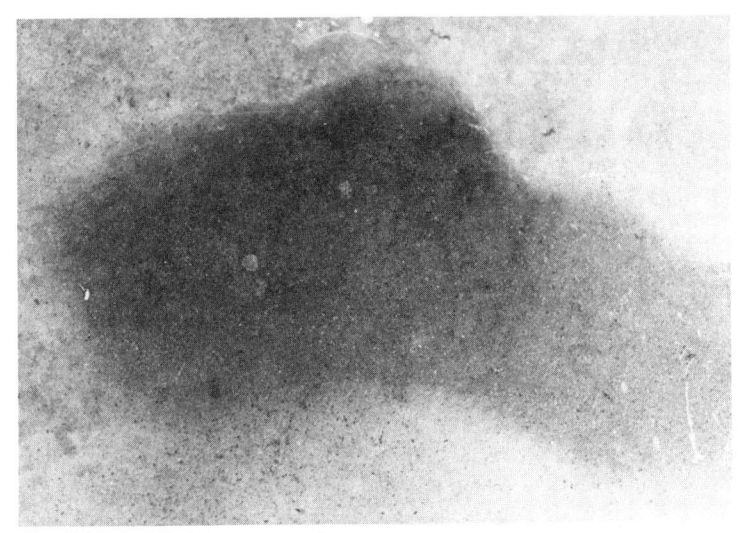

Fig. 5-13. An oil stain on concrete.

warm water—and a stiff wire brush. To totally remove the rust stain, you will find it necessary to first soak the area well, and then apply lots of elbow grease to the scrub brush. Make sure you rinse the area with plenty of clear water, after the scrubbing, to remove all traces of the cleaner (Fig. 5-16).

HOW TO PATCH CONCRETE SURFACES

Once deterioration of a concrete surface begins, it will accelerate into advanced stages rather quickly. This is especially if freez-

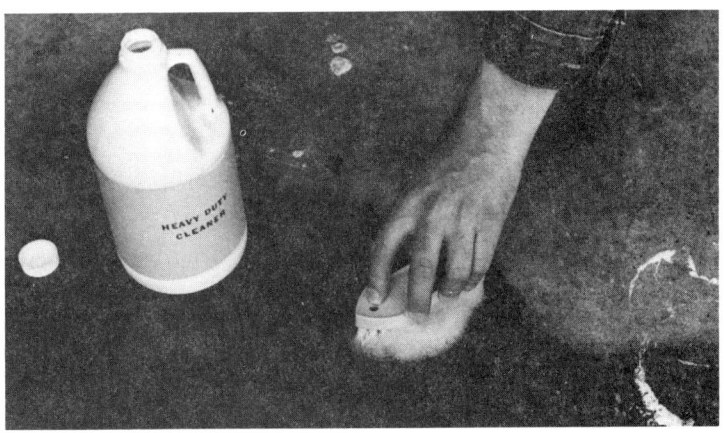

Fig. 5-14. Clean concrete with a heavy duty cleaner and scrub brush.

Fig. 5-15. Use clay bits to pick up fresh oil puddles.

ing and thawing weather is common for your area. Once you discover an area of concrete that is starting to or is deteriorating, you must first make an assessment of the extent of the breakdown. You must ask yourself if the area can be repaired or if the section must be removed and an entirely new section poured.

Generally, a section of concrete can be repaired with a patch if it is not in an advanced stage of deterioration. Problems that can be repaired with a patch include small cracks that have not caused the section of concrete to buckle and surfaces that are peeling or coming loose from the main body of concrete (Fig. 5-17).

Once you have determined that the problem can be solved with a patch of concrete, begin by removing all loose or broken concrete from the crack (Fig. 5-18). In most cases, you will find that a cold chisel and a hammer or a sledge will be the best tools for this type of work. Work carefully and try not to enlarge the crack more than

Fig. 5-16. Wet down concrete before cleaning to remove rust stains.

necessary to, as this will mean you will have to use more of the patching concrete than necessary to do the job (Fig. 5-18).

The next step is to scrub the crack with a wire brush to remove small particles of old concrete. Wash the crack with water or blow it

Fig. 5-17. Small cracks in concrete should be repaired before they become large cracks.

219

Fig. 5-18. Remove all loose concrete with a hammer and a cold chisel.

out with compressed air to remove all traces of dust (Fig. 5-19). Dampen the crack with water so that when you apply the patching concrete the old concrete will not cause the new material to dry out too quickly. It is important that you do not apply too much water at this point. Water should not puddle - but you should thoroughly wet the area. (Fig. 5-20).

Next you must mix up the patching concrete. The standard mix for repairs is 1 part cement, 2 parts sand, and 2 parts pea gravel. For very narrow cracks, you can eliminate the gravel and use a mixture of 1 part portland cement and 3 parts sand. Use only enough water (in either case) so that the mixture is very stiff. This will enable you to tightly pack the crack with the repair concrete.

One very good alternative to mixing sand, cement, and gravel is to purchase ready-mixed concrete. There are a number of brands of prepared concrete mixes such as Sakrete (the most popular and widely marketed). Part of the beauty of these mixes is that you only have to add water to the dry ingredients before use. For most repairs around the home, this is the best choice for the do-it-yourselfer (Fig. 5-21).

Once the patching concrete is mixed to a stiff consistency, pack it into the joint using a trowel. Most concrete shrinks slightly as it dries. For this reason, you should overfill the crack with the patching concrete. A little common sense is called for here. Keep in mind that your intention is to overfill the crack with just a bit more than is called for so that, when the concrete patch is dry, it will be at about the same height as the original material (Fig. 5-22).

After the patch is in place, smooth the surface with a trowel or a float for larger areas. The next step is to make the patch blend in with existing concrete. If you are working on a sidewalk, for example, you can usually blend in the new concrete with a broom. Simply

Fig. 5-19. Clean out the crack with wire brush.

Fig. 5-20. Wet down the surface before patching.

brush the surface in the same direction as the other concrete is brushed. If the surface is to be smooth, use a steel-bladed trowel for finishing (Fig. 5-23).

After you are satisfied with the patch, the next step is to cover the area with a piece of vapor-tight material. Clear plastic sheeting (Fig. 5-24) works well for this. The purpose of the sheeting is so that the patch won't dry too quickly and the covering material will effectively lock in the moisture and prevent it from drying out too fast. For most concrete repairs, a five-day curing period is about right. Check the area once a day. If it appears to be drying too quickly, spray the patch with only enough water to dampen the patch and the surrounding area.

The other type of repair that you might have to make in concrete is to a veneer-like covering on a wall. One example is stucco. Occasionally, this material will come away from the wall surface to which it was attached. In addition to being unsightly, this type of concrete deterioration also opens the door to more extensive breakdowns in the concrete. Water will run down an exterior wall and get behind the surrounding area and cause it to come undone as well.

Before you can repair stucco, you must first remove all loose concrete around the area. The best tools for this are a hammer, a

Fig. 5-21. Mix only enough concrete for the repair, and only after all surface preparation has been completed.

chisel and a wire brush. Totally clean the area and then brush it to remove any dust. Next, wet down the area with a fine spray from a garden hose (Figs. 5-25 through 5-28).

Fig. 5-22. Overfill the crack slightly. Pack wet cement tightly into the joint.

Fig. 5-23. Smooth to blend in with surrounding masonry.

Good material for patching stucco is a mortar mix of 1 part cement, 3 parts sand and just enough water to make the mixture workable. A somewhat easier mixture is a bag of ready-mixed mortar, such as Sakrete, mixed to the same consistency.

Apply the patching material to the damp area with a trowel. Work the material into the area and feather the edges so the patch will blend in well with the surrounding area. You must prevent a stucco patch from drying out too quickly. To accomplish a slow drying, cover the area with plastic material. You can usually hold the plastic in place with tape; duct tape works fine for this. After a few days, the patch should be thoroughly cured (Figs. 5-29 and 5-30).

LARGE REPAIRS TO CONCRETE

If repairs are not made to concrete in the early stages of deterioration, the breakdown will advance rather quickly. The re-

Fig. 5-24. Cover with plastic sheeting to allow slow curing.

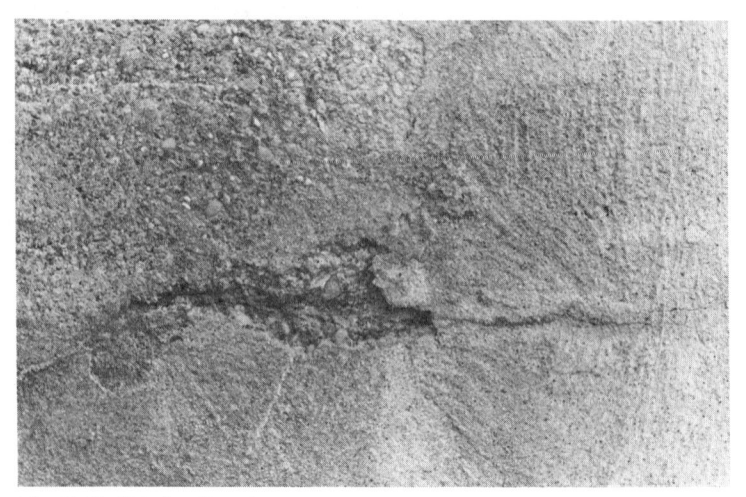

Fig. 5-25. Deteriorating stucco.

sult will be an entire section that is beyond repair (Fig. 5-31). Because repairs are too late at this point, it is always best to remove all broken parts and repour the damaged section.

Because a bad section of concrete is most commonly well defined, you can easily see what must be done. All of the deterior-

Fig. 5-26. Remove all loose and crumbling stucco.

Fig. 5-27. With a wire brush, remove all dust and loose stucco.

Fig. 5-28. Wet down the area before patching.

ated concrete must be removed. A sledge hammer and a chisel are the best tools for this type of work. Once this has been accomplished, the next step is to build forms to hold the new concrete in place as it cures. These can be easily made from dimensional

Fig. 5-29. Pack the patch and feather to blend in well with the surrounding area.

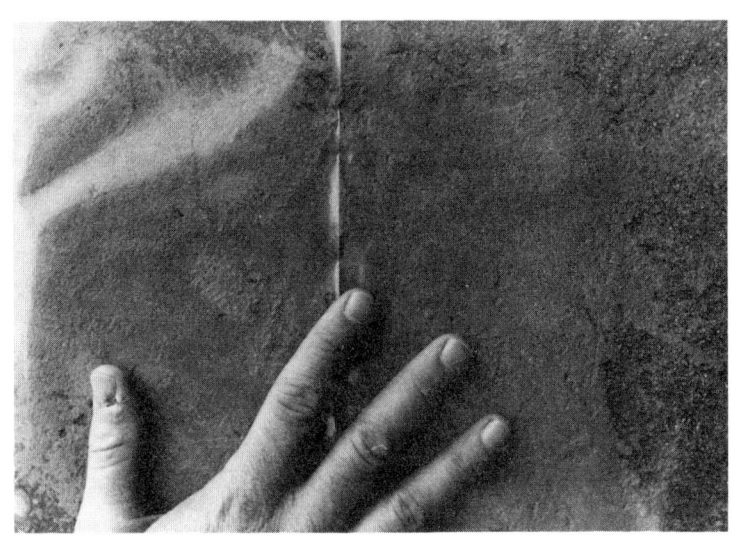

Fig. 5-30. Cover the patch with plastic to allow slow curing.

lumber (such as 2 by 4s or 2 by 6s) or from exterior grade plywood. Keep in mind that your intention is to recreate the damaged section and to do this you can use existing (and undamaged) concrete in the area as a guide. Build the forms strong and drive pegs into the ground outside the frame to hold it in place (Fig. 5-32).

If the section of concrete you are replacing was damaged because of excessive weight on the area—such as a parked automobile—it will be a good idea to reinforce the new concrete so that the problem will not recur in the future. Concrete reinforcing wire is designed for this purpose and it should be used.

After you have removed all old and broken concrete, built the forms, and added reinforcing rod or wire, the next step is to estimate how much new concrete you will need for the replacement. To do this, you must first determine the square footage of the new section. Table 5-1 will give you a good indication of how much concrete will be needed for a given section.

Generally, if you are repairing a large section of concrete, consider purchasing transit mix for the project. Keep in mind that the current cost is about $40 per square yard of concrete. It might be worth the extra cost if you have a number of sections of concrete to replace.

If the section of concrete you are replacing is small, I suggest that you use premixed concrete. Simply add water, mix thoroughly and pour into the form. If you are reinforcing the new section, it is

Fig. 5-31. A bad section of sidewalk must be removed, and filled with new concrete.

important that the reinforcing wire or bar, not lay in the bottom of the new section. To be effective, the reinforcement should be suspended in about the middle layer of the slab. You can usually hold it at about this height with small stones (Fig. 5-33).

After the form has been filled with wet concrete, the next step is to tamp it to remove air bubbles. Use a float for this and begin smoothing the surface as you work. If the new section is a piece of sidewalk, brush the surface with a broom to achieve a slightly roughened finish. Make the new section blend in as well as possible with the other sections of sidewalk in the vicinity (Figs. 5-34, 5-35, and 5-36).

After you are satisfied with the finish on the concrete, you must cover the new section to let it cure slowly. Plastic sheeting is a good choice for this covering. One added benefit of the plastic is that it will deter children from scratching their initials or anything else into the new concrete.

If the new section of sidewalk is in an area that receives much foot traffic, you should put a few saw horses around the section to

Fig. 5-32. Build a concrete form to contain wet concrete (courtesy of Sakrete).

keep people off until it has cured sufficiently. After about 24 hours, you should be able to walk over the new section. Do not park vehicles on it for at least one week. This is also about how long you should leave the plastic on the new section. Check the drying every day. If you discover that the new concrete is drying too quickly, give the area a spray of water from a garden hose. Don't apply too much—just enough to dampen the surface—and then recover with plastic.

Table 5-1. Estimating Concrete.

		\multicolumn{7}{c	}{Length (in feet) (Depth 4 inches)}
		1	1.5	2	2.5	3	3.5	4
Width	6" 12" 18" 24"	.17 .33 .5 .66	.25 .5 .75 1.0	.33 .66 1.0 1.33	.42 .83 1.25 1.66	.50 1.0 1.5 2.0	.58 1.17 1.75 2.33	.66 1.33 2.0 2.66

Fig. 5-33. Dump the mixed concrete into the form (courtesy of Sakrete).

Fig. 5-34. Screed the wet concrete with 2 by 4 lumber to level (courtesy of Sakrete).

Fig. 5-35. Finish the surface with a float (courtesy of Sakrete).

While working with concrete is not particularly difficult, it is laborious—to say the least. Done properly, however, most concrete repairs and patching should last. Now I would like to pass along a number of masonry tips that are used by professionals. Pick and choose those helpful hints that will aid you in your concrete repairs.

☐ When mixing concrete, keep in mind that excess water will weaken the concrete. Use only enough water to make the concrete workable.

☐ When working with sand, cement, gravel, mix the ingredients thoroughly before adding water. This will ensure a uniform mix of concrete. You should also dry mix the ingredients in ready-mix concrete (such as Sakrete) before adding water.

☐ Break big concrete repair jobs into small ones that can be handled by one person. One or two sections of sidewalk repair a day is plenty of work for one person.

☐ If you are using concrete forms, to repair a section of sidewalk, remove them within 24 hours. Then scrape and wash them with a garden hose to remove all traces of the concrete.

☐ Steel reinforcing wire or bar can be used to strengthen concrete. In many cases, wire mesh or bar will enable you to use less concrete for the project (from one-third to one-half). For moderate-size projects, this will mean possibly thousands of pounds less material that you must handle.

☐ Position reenforcing wire as you pour the concrete and not after it is poured. You can usually hold the wire or bar in the approximate position of the slab with small stones. Make sure that you pack the wet cement under and around the wire, however, or you might create air pockets.

☐ Mix concrete in a specially designed wheelbarrow so that it is easy to move to the pour sight. Concrete can also be mixed on almost any flat surface (Fig. 5-37) such as a sheet of plywood or concrete slab. Wash the area with clear water after mixing to avoid a

Fig. 5-36. Finish the edges of the concrete with an edging tool (courtesy of Sakrete).

Fig. 5-37. Small batches of concrete can be mixed on any flat surface (courtesy of Sakrete).

buildup of new concrete. Mix small batches of concrete in a plastic pail.

☐ The ingredients in any concrete mix will quickly remove oils from your hands. To avoid this, wear work gloves when working with concrete.

☐ Store unopened sacks of concrete in a cool, dry area (preferably under cover). Opened and partially used concrete should be put into a container that can be closed or the relative humidity will render it useless in about one month.

☐ Wash all tools used for concrete work before the concrete on them dries. A strong stream of water from a garden hose will usually be sufficient for this.

☐ The area that is to be repaired should have all surface preparation work completed before you mix the cement. Because cement starts to setup and cure almost from the minute water is added, you will want to work quickly. This rules out any surface preparation after the cement is mixed.

☐ Do not plan to work on a cement repair or patching project if the weatherman calls for a freezing spell. The project will turn out poorly if the cement freezes before it cures thoroughly (at least five days).

☐ Always wear eye protection when you are chipping away at deteriorated concrete. This includes all work with a sledge hammer a hammer and a cold chisel.

☐ If you are doing much concrete work such as building a sidewalk or a driveway, consider having ready-made transit mix delivered to the job site. For smaller projects and those that are done on a budget, consider renting a cement mixer.

Chapter 6

Insulation and Ventilation

Excessive moisture in some form is usually the cause of problems around the exterior of the home. Many of these moisture-related problems originate inside the home as a result of the passage of water vapor through interior walls and ceilings. The results are added maintenance costs such as the need for more frequent painting, and increased heating costs. The best way to deal with these problems is to provide adequate ventilation, to install vapor barriers, and to increase the insulation in your home.

CONDENSATION

In the Northern sections of the United States, especially where the January temperature averages 34 degrees F, or lower, the first signs of spring might appear as dark stains on exterior siding, peeling paint (Fig. 6-1) and, in extreme cases, the beginning of rot on sections of siding. These signs are very real indications that some type of cold-weather condensation problem is present. If icicles or ice dams form along the eaves after a heavy snowfall, this indicates still another type of moisture problem that must be corrected.

Water vapor originating within a house, when unrestricted, can move through interior walls and ceilings during the heating season and come to rest on a cold surface—the wall cavity side of exterior siding—where it condenses and forms frost or ice. During warm periods, this ice and frost melts. During severe conditions, the water from melting ice in unvented attics might drip down to the ceiling (Fig. 6-2) below and cause damage to the interior finish

Fig. 6-1. Excessive peeling paint is a sure sign of water vapor passing through the siding.

materials. Moisture can also soak into the roof sheeting or rafters and set up ideal conditions for decay of these materials. When ice melts inside interior walls, the water can run out through the siding joints and this will cause stains, blisters, and peeling paint.

Framing materials and siding materials can also absorb moisture and as they do they often bow, cup, or buckle. In addition, the thermal insulation installed in wall and ceiling cavities becomes wet and provides far less resistance to heat loss. Masonry walls are not exempt from moisture-related problems. They too have the capability of absorbing moisture from condensation. Efflorescence, cracks, and general deterioration are sure signs that masonry walls are suffering from an excess of moisture probably originating inside the home.

After World War II, changes in design, materials and building techniques brought about homes that were easier to heat, less expensive to build, and more comfortable to live in. Many new building materials and methods were first used on a large scale and many of the new materials increased the potential for condensation problems. New types of weather stripping, storm sash, and sheet material for exterior siding (as well as interior wall coverings), and other modern building materials all help to create very tight structures that restrict the entrance of air into homes. At the same time, these materials inhibit the escape of moisture that has been generated inside the home.

A typical family of four converts approximately 3 gallons of water into water vapor per day. Unless this excess water vapor is removed in some way (most commonly by some type of ventilation system), it will either increase the humidity of the home or condense on cold surfaces such as window panes. In more serious cases, this excessive water vapor will condense inside wall, roof, and floor cavities. Heating systems equipped with winter air conditioning systems compound the problem by further increasing the humidity inside the home.

Conventional building practices call for from 2 to 3½ inches of thermal insulation inside walls and at least 6 inches in ceilings. Unfortunately, the more efficient the insulation is in retarding heat transfer, the colder the outer surfaces can become. Unless moisture is restricted from entering the wall or ceiling, the greater the potential becomes for moisture condensation. Moisture migrates toward cold surfaces and it will condense or form frost or ice on these surfaces.

The stage is set for condensation any time the temperature drops below the dewpoint (100 percent saturation of the air with

Fig. 6-2. Mildew or rot on the inside of roof sheeting indicates a condensation problem.

water vapor at a given temperature). Commonly, under such conditions some surface accessible to the moisture in the air is cooler than the dewpoint and the moisture condenses on that surface. See Fig. 6-3.

Condensation can also occur in crawl spaces under unheated or unoccupied rooms. This area usually differs from those on the interior of the house and in the attic because the source of the moisture is most commonly from the soil or from warm, moisture-laden air that enters through foundation ventilation systems. Moisture condenses on the cooler surfaces in the crawl space. These conditions usually occur during warm periods in the late spring.

An increase in the relative humidity of the interior atmosphere will also increase the potential for condensation on inside surfaces. For example, when the inside temperature is 21 degrees C, surface condensation will occur on a single glass window when the outside temperatures is at or below −23 degrees C and the inside relative humidity is 10 percent. When the inside relative humidity is 20 percent, condensation can occur on the single glass when outside temperatures are at about −14 degrees C. When a storm window is added or insulated glass is used, surface condensation will not occur until the relative humidity has reached 38 percent when the outdoor temperature is −23 degrees C. The above conditions only apply where storm windows are not tight. Where lower temperatures are maintained in such areas as bedrooms, condensation will occur at a higher outside temperature.

Condensation in concealed areas, such as wall spaces, often is first indicated by stains on the exterior siding and peeling paint. Water vapor moving through permeable walls and ceilings is normally responsible for such damage. Water vapor also escapes from houses by constant leakage through cracks and crevices, around doors and windows, and by ventilation. But this moisture vapor loss is usually insufficient to eliminate condensation problems.

Increases in relative humidity inside the home are a result of moist air that has entered the structure or is generated by the occupants. Ordinary household tasks that generate significant amounts of moisture into the internal environment include dishwashing, cooking, bathing, laundry work, as well as human respiration. The average human gives off about 1 pint of water just while sleeping during an 8-hour period. Even evaporation from houseplants is a factor. Other common sources of moisture include unvented or poorly vented clothes dryers and central winter air conditioners or humidifiers.

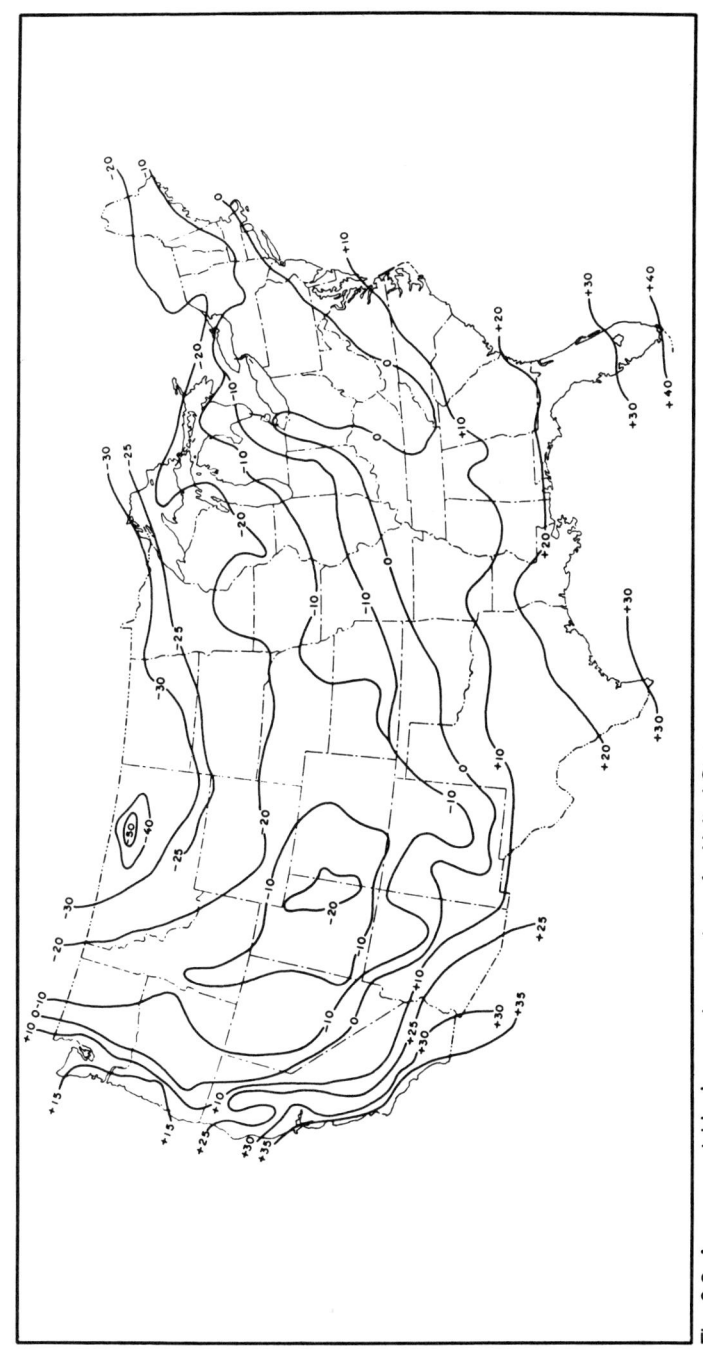

Fig. 6-3. Average outside January temperatures for United States.

Water vapor from the soil of crawl spaces under houses does not usually affect the occupied areas. However, without good construction practices or proper precautions, water from this area can be a factor in causing moisture problems in exterior walls over the area as well as in the crawl space itself. It must be assumed, therefore, that crawl spaces can be another source of moisture-related problems and some steps should be taken to correct the problem.

Other sources of moisture, often unsuspected, can cause condensation problems in the home. One such source is a gas-fired furnace. It is desirable to maintain flue-gas temperatures within the recommended limits throughout the appliance (in the flue, the connecting vent, and other areas). Otherwise excessive moisture problems can result. If all sources of excessive moisture have been exhausted in trying to determine the reason for present condensation problems, it is a good idea to have the heating system examined by a specialist.

In all homes, a distinct relationship exists between indoor relative humidity and outside temperatures. The humidity is generally high indoors when outdoor temperatures are high and it decreases as outdoor temperatures drop. In an exceptionally tight modern house, where moisture buildup is a problem, it is a good practice to introduce air from the outside—via cold air return ductwork—to reduce the relative humidity of the house.

Inexpensive methods of preventing condensation problems are widely available. They mainly involve the proper use of vapor barriers and good ventilating practices. It is far simpler, less expensive, and much more effective if these methods are employed during the construction stage of the home rather than adding them at some point in the future.

Many materials used as interior coverings for exposed walls and ceilings, such as plaster, drywall, wood paneling, and plywood, permit water vapor to pass slowly through them during cold weather. Temperatures of the sheeting or siding of the house are often low enough to cause condensation of water vapor within the cavities of a framed wall. When the relative humidity inside the house is greater than within the wall, water vapor will migrate through the plaster or other finish material into the wall cavity. There it will condense if it comes in contact with surfaces colder than its dewpoint temperature. Vapor barriers are used to resist this movement of water or moisture in various areas of the home.

The amount of condensation that can develop within a wall depends on three factors.

☐ The resistance of the intervening materials to vapor transfusion.

☐ Differences in vapor pressure, interior versus exterior.

☐ Time.

Plastered walls or ordinary dry walls offer little resistance to vapor movement. When these same surfaces are painted with an oil base paint, their resistance to passage of water vapor is increased. High indoor temperatures and relative humidities result in high indoor vapor pressures. Low outdoor vapor pressures always exist at low temperatures. A common combination of high inside temperatures and humidities and low outside temperatures will normally result in vapor movement into a wall cavity if no vapor barrier is present. Long periods of severe weather will result in condensation problems.

Generally, vapor barriers are used in three areas in the home to help minimize condensation and moisture problems.

☐ walls, floors and ceilings.

☐ under concrete slabs.

☐ as crawl space soil covers.

Vapor barriers are a common feature in modern buildings. They will greatly reduce the movement of water vapor through building materials and, therefore, almost eliminate condensation problems if some type of ventilation is provided to exhaust moisture-laden air. Materials for this type of vapor barrier should have a "perm value" of 0.025 or less to be most effective. This material can be part of the insulation or a separate film. Some of the more common vapor barrier materials include asphalt-coated or laminated papers, Kraft-backed aluminum foil, and the very popular plastic films such as polyethylene. Foil-backed gypsum board and various coatings also serve as good vapor barriers. Oil-base paints, aluminum-base paints, or similar coatings can be used in older homes that might not have had vapor barriers installed during their original construction (Fig. 6-4).

Vapor barriers are also installed under concrete slabs and they greatly reduce the movement of moisture from the soil through the slab and into the living area. Materials used for this should have a perm value of at least 0.50 and be strong enough to withstand damage from pouring and the mass weight of the concrete. Some of the materials currently being used for vapor barriers under con-

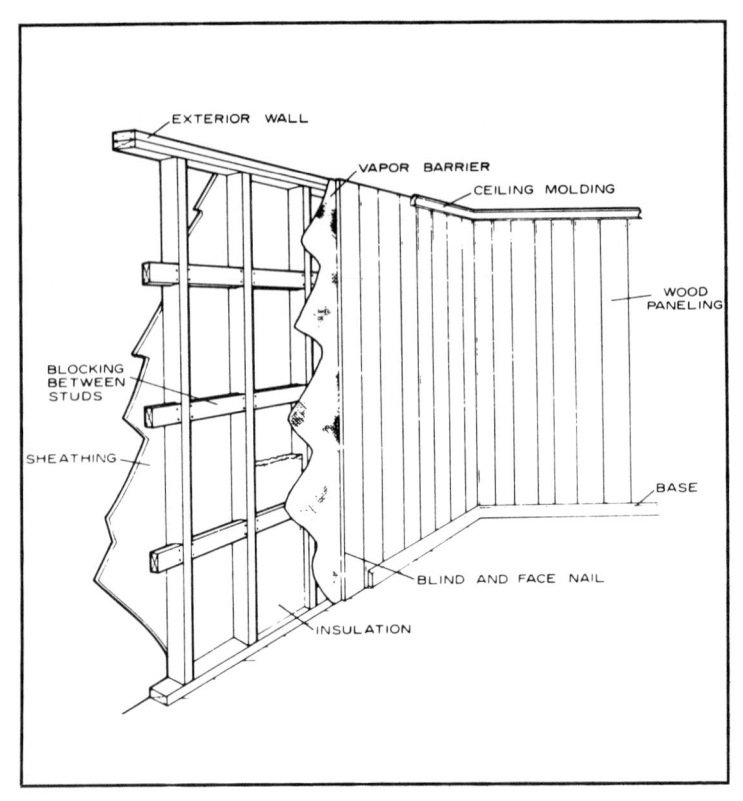

Fig. 6-4. A vapor barrier should be installed on the warm side of your walls to eliminate the passage of water vapor.

crete include heavily laminated asphalt papers, roll roofing, and heavy plastic films such as thick polyethylene (Fig. 6-5).

Vapor barriers are also installed over the soil in crawl spaces to prevent the movement of water vapor from the soil upward. A material with a perm value of 1.0 or less is considered sufficient for this type of vapor barrier. Polyethylene film is probably the most common soil cover in crawl spaces at this time.

VENTILATORS

When used in proper amounts and locations, ventilation is a recognized means of controlling condensation in modern homes. Inlet and outlet ventilators in attic spaces, ventilation of rafters spaces in flat roofs, and crawl space ventilation, all aid in preventing an accumulation of condensation in these areas. By introducing fresh air into living quarters during the winter, some humid air is forced out of the house while the incoming air has a low water vapor content. Well-insulated vapor barriers can increase the need for ventilation in living quarters because little of the moisture generated can escape.

The use of both inlet and outlet ventilators in attic spaces aids in keeping the air moving and preventing the accumulation of frost or condensation on roof boards in cold areas. "Dead" air pockets in the attic can normally be prevented by good distribution of inlet ventilators in the soffit areas. Nevertheless, there is still a need for vapor barriers in the ceiling as ventilation alone will not prevent condensation problems. A good vapor barrier is especially important under the insulation in a flat roof where ventilation is not generally possible (Fig. 6-6).

Crawl space moisture, which results in high moisture content of wood framing members (joists, sill plates, subflooring, etc.), can be almost entirely eliminated by a vapor barrier over the soil. When such protection is used, the need for ventilation is reduced to about 10 percent of that required when no soil cover is used (Fig. 6-7).

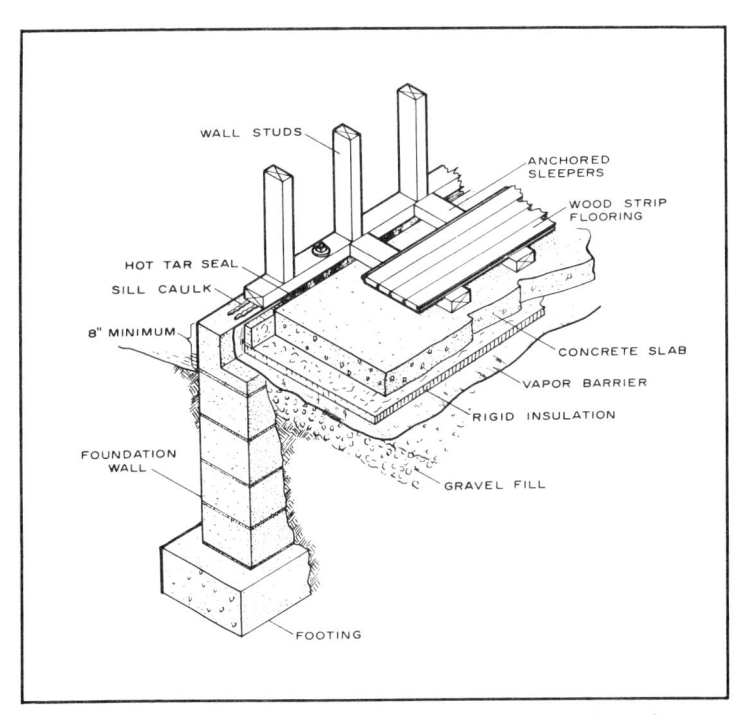

Fig. 6-5. A vapor barrier, installed under a concrete slab, will cut down on moisture problems. This barrier must be installed before concrete is poured.

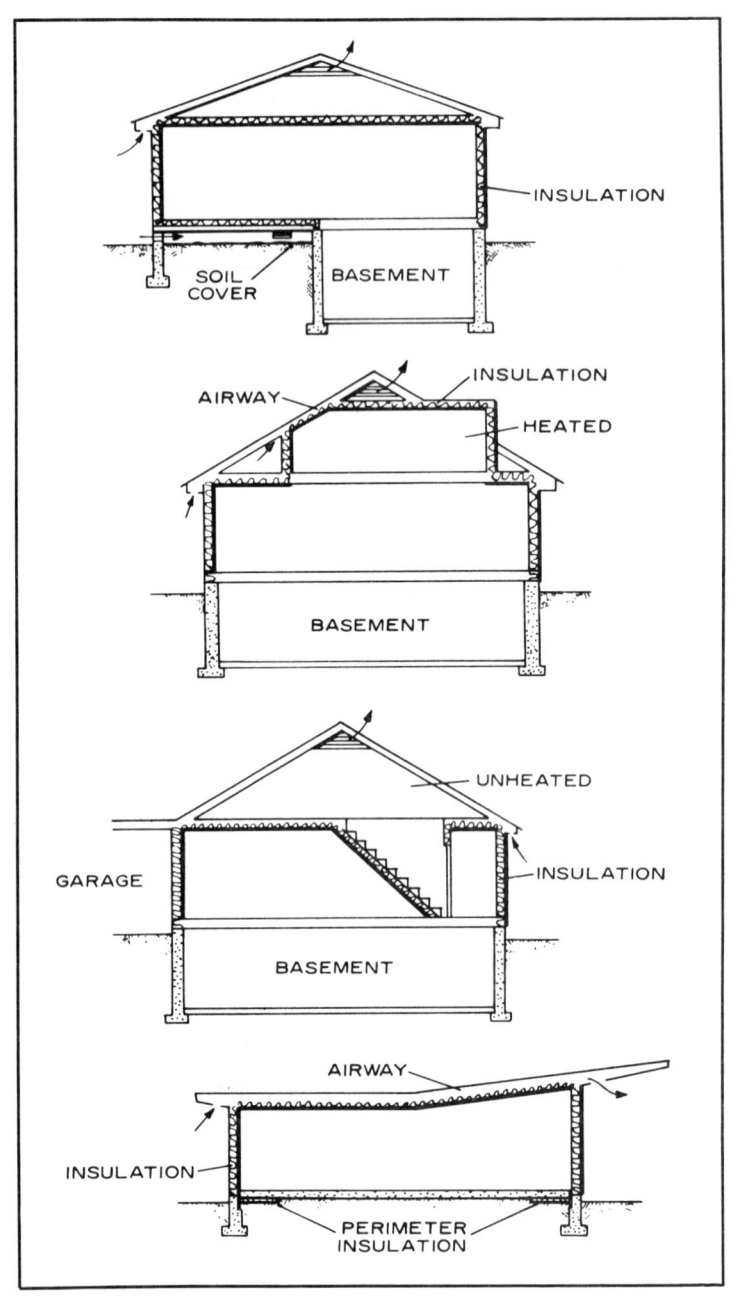

Fig. 6-6. Insulation and vapor barriers are all important components in reducing condensation problems.

During warm, damp periods in late spring, moisture often condenses on basement walls or around the perimeter of the floor in concrete slab houses. Soil temperatures in the northern part of the United States remain quite low until summer, and surface temperatures of the floor or wall are often below the dewpoint. When the concrete reaches normal temperature and the atmosphere changes, such problems are normally reduced or eliminated. Until they are, however, ventilation should be used to decrease the overall dampness.

INSULATION

The control of condensation through the use of vapor barriers and ventilation should be practiced regardless of the type of insulation used. To achieve complete protection from condensation problems in unheated crawl spaces, a combination of ground cover, thermal insulation (attached between the floor joists), and foundation ventilators are normally used. Foundation wall ventilators are most effective when they are installed near the top of the masonry wall (Fig. 6-8). Special vents the size of a block, are available for foundation walls that are constructed of concrete blocks

The amount of ventilation required for an unheated crawl space is based on the total area of the space and assumes that a soil cover (vapor barrier) is present. This soil cover must be placed in such a way as to have all seams overlapped—by at least 3 inches—and held in place with weights to prevent movement of the cover. Bricks and stones are commonly placed on seams and around the perimeter of the soil cover for this purpose.

The most common type of insulation used in crawl spaces is fiberglass batting (Fig. 6-9). These are fastened to the flooring

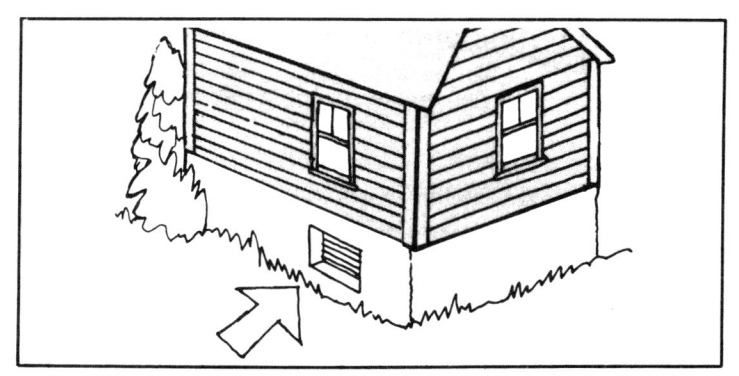

Fig. 6-7. Crawl spaces should be ventilated.

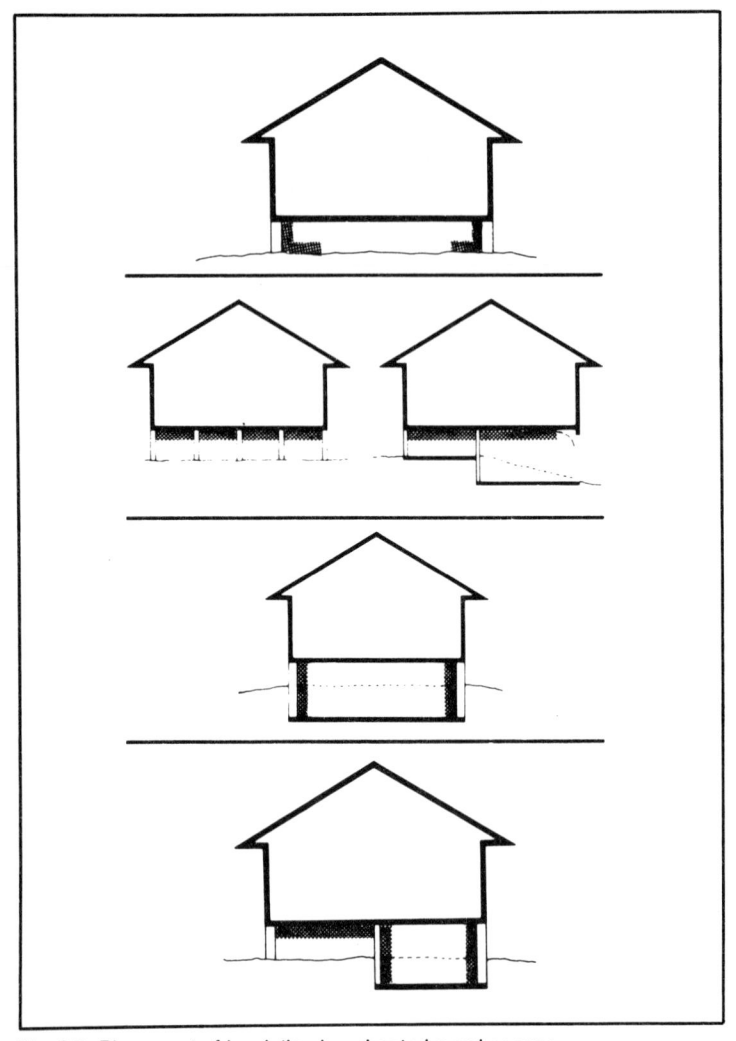

Fig. 6-8. Placement of insulation in unheated crawl spaces.

joists (from above in new construction) before the subflooring is installed. If insulation is being installed after the subflooring has been fastened in place, the insulation is usually stapled from below.

One common problem with insulation is unheated crawl spaces is that, in time, this material always seems to droop or fall out of place. At least part of the problem lies in how the insulation was installed between the joists: with staples. One sure cure for this problem is to hold the insulation up between the joists by applying a layer of large mesh wire to the bottom side of the joists. Chicken wire is often used for this and it works quite well (Fig. 6-10).

A different approach to condensation problems is required when a crawl space is heated. One method of heating crawl spaces employs the crawl space as a plenum chamber. Warm air is forced into the crawl space, which is somewhat shallower than those normally used without heat, through wall and floor chambers around the outer walls, and into the rooms above. When such a system is used, insulation is placed along the perimeter walls. A vapor barrier must be placed over the soil, and flexible insulation with the vapor barrier facing the interior is placed between the joists. In most cases, this type of crawl space is not vented except when the heating system requires fresh air from the outside.

A full basement—with concrete walls and floor—can also benefit from the addition of thermal insulation and a vapor barrier. This is most commonly done by constructing a stud wall around the perimeter. Fiberglass insulation, with a vapor barrier face, is fastened between the studs. The vapor barrier face (most commonly foil) is placed toward the room. The last step is to apply a finish wall over the studs. One good combination is gypsum panels that is followed by decorative paneling. See Figs. 6-11, 6-12 and 6-13.

Interior walls are commonly insulated with blanket or batt-type insulation. In recently built homes, you can figure that the walls are insulated and that there is a vapor barrier in place as well. Usually this is accomplished by stapling fiberglass batt insulation between the studs (vapor barrier facing the living area) before the finish wall covering is attached. Many contractors, in addition to the above, also apply a layer of polyethylene plastic film over the studs,

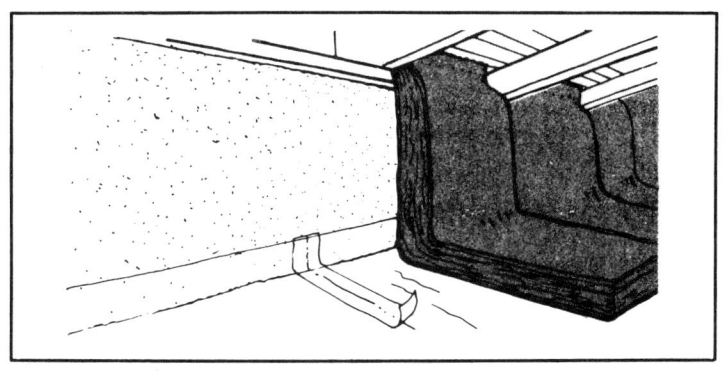

Fig. 6-9. A soil cover (plastic film) and insulation should be installed in unheated crawl spaces.

Fig. 6-10. Use chicken wire attached to floor joists to hold insulation batts in place.

just prior to nailing up gypsum panels. This insures that the wall will not permit the passage of water vapor. If you are considering building your own home, you should do this as well.

Older homes will have inadequate or, in some cases, no insulation in the walls. When energy was relatively inexpensive, this was a common practice and it resulted in homes that were less expensive to build. Uninsulated walls now account for 15 to 25 percent higher heating costs than insulated walls.

One very good way to determine if your home has insulation in the walls is to remove a light switch or electrical outlet cover on an exterior wall. Shine a flashlight into the space around the outlet and look for evidence of insulation. If there is any insulation in the wall, this test should reveal it.

As you can well imagine, installing insulation inside walls that presently have a finish covering is no easy task—to say nothing of the expense. Insulation can be blown into the wall cavity by a professional (Fig. 6-14). Various types of fill materials are being used for this. If you discover that there is no insulation in your walls,

Fig. 6-11. Build a stud wall around the perimeter of your masonry foundation walls.

and you decide that you would like to add some, look in your telephone directory to find a few contractors who specialize in this type of work. Get several estimates, and then make your final decision.

Fig. 6-12. Attach insulation with the vapor barrier facing the interior of basement.

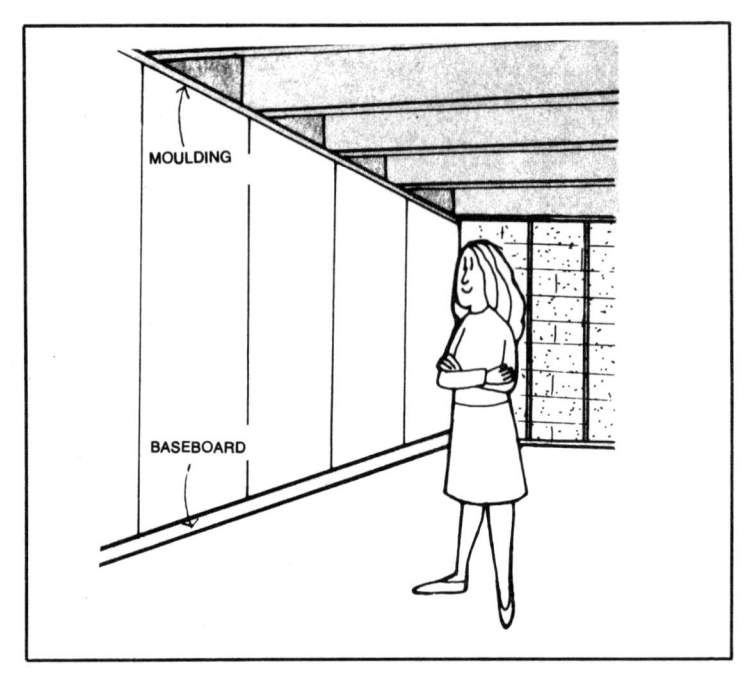

Fig. 6-13. Cover insulated stud walls with finish material such as gypsum boards or wood paneling.

Keep in mind that no insulation blown into wall cavities provides any type of vapor barrier. To achieve tight walls, however, there are two things that you can do. First you must seal all openings on interior walls where moisture might pass. These include areas around all windows, doors, and appliances that pass through an exterior wall (ventilators and air conditioners are examples). Another thing you can do is paint all interior walls with a low permeability paint such as high-gloss enamel or other finish. Ask your paint dealer for more information.

One additional thing to consider before you decide on having your walls filled with insulation is the type of insulation that will be used. Some of the more popular types of blown-in insulation are glass fiber, rock wool, and cellulosic fiber. Ureaformaldehyde is suspected of being a cancer-causing agent. Carefully consider the choices before making your final decision.

If your home has an attic space, it should be insulated and ventilated to reduce heating costs and to prevent condensation problems. Ventilation of attic spaces and roof areas is important in minimizing water vapor buildup. There is still a need for vapor barriers in ceiling areas. This is especially true for the flat roof or low-slope roof where only a 1-inch to 3-inch space above the insulation might be available for ventilation.

In houses with attic spaces, the use of both inlet and outlet ventilation is recommended. Placing inlet ventilators in soffit or friezeboard areas of the cornice, and outlet ventilators as near the ridge line as possible, will insure air movement through a "stack" effect. The difference in height between inlet and outlet ventilators normally assures air movement even on windless days or nights.

Generally, fiberglass batt or blanket insulation is used in unfinished attic spaces. In older homes, loose fill such as rock wool, cellulosic fiber, vermiculite or perlite is more common. Blankets and batts are laid into place between the joists; loose fill is poured into place. Whichever is used, it is important that ventilation systems not be blocked. This material should not be placed closer than three inches from any light fixture (for the room below) or overheating of the fixture will result. See Figs. 6-15, 6-16, and 6-17.

A vapor barrier should also be installed in the attic space. This should be placed below the insulation. Polyethylene sheeting can be

Fig. 6-14. If your existing walls do not contain any insulation, consider having insulation blown in by a contractor.

255

Fig. 6-15. Loose insulation fill is a good choice for unfinished attics.

used for loose-fill insulation or batts without vapor barrier backing. If foil-faced insulation is used, this side should be placed down (Fig. 6-18).

The minimum amount of attic or roof-space ventilation required is determined by the total ceiling area. The use of both inlet and outlet ventilators is recommended whenever possible. Divide the total ceiling area by the number of ventilators used to find the recommended square foot area of each. For example, a gable roof with inlet and outlet ventilators has a minimum required total inlet and outlet ratio of 1-to-900 of the ceiling area. If the ceiling area of the house is 1,350 square feet, each net inlet and outlet ventilating area should be 1,350 divided by 900, or 1½ feet.

If ventilators are protected with number 16 mesh screen and plain metal louvers, the minimum gross area must be 2 by 1½, or 3 square feet. When one outlet ventilator is used at each gable end, each should have a gross area of 1½ square feet (3 divided by 2). When distributing the soffit inlet ventilators to three on a side, for a small house, each ventilator should have a gross area of one-half square feet. For long houses, use six or more ventilators on each side (Fig. 6-20).

Fig. 6-16. Blanket or batt insulation is simply laid between joists.

Inlet ventilators in the soffit can consist of several designs. It is a sound practice to distribute them as much as possible to prevent "dead" air pockets in the attic where moisture might collect. A

Fig. 6-17. Do not place insulation any closer than 3 inches from any lighting fixture.

Fig. 6-18. Install a vapor barrier between joists in the attic space before adding insulation.

continuous screened slot satisfies this requirement. Continuous slots or individual ventilators between roof members should be used for flat roof houses where roof members serve as both rafters and ceiling joists. Locate the openings away from the wall line to

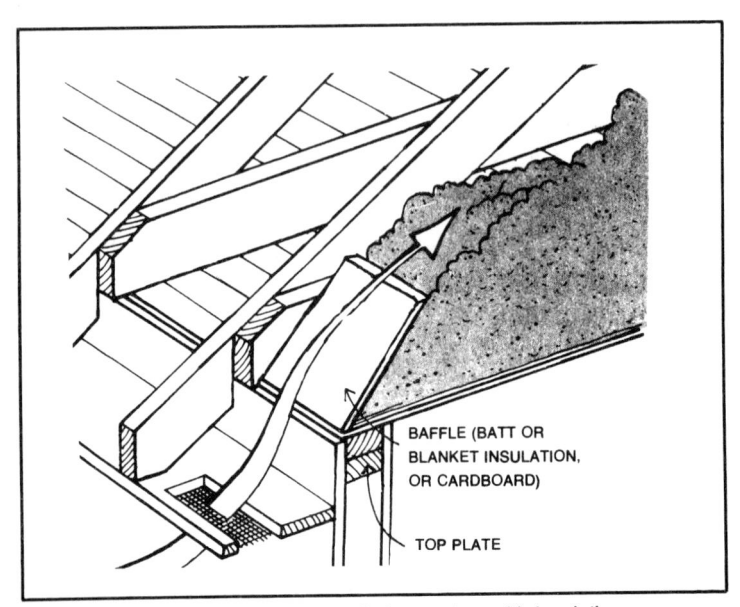

Fig. 6-19. Do not cover the attic ventilation system with insulation.

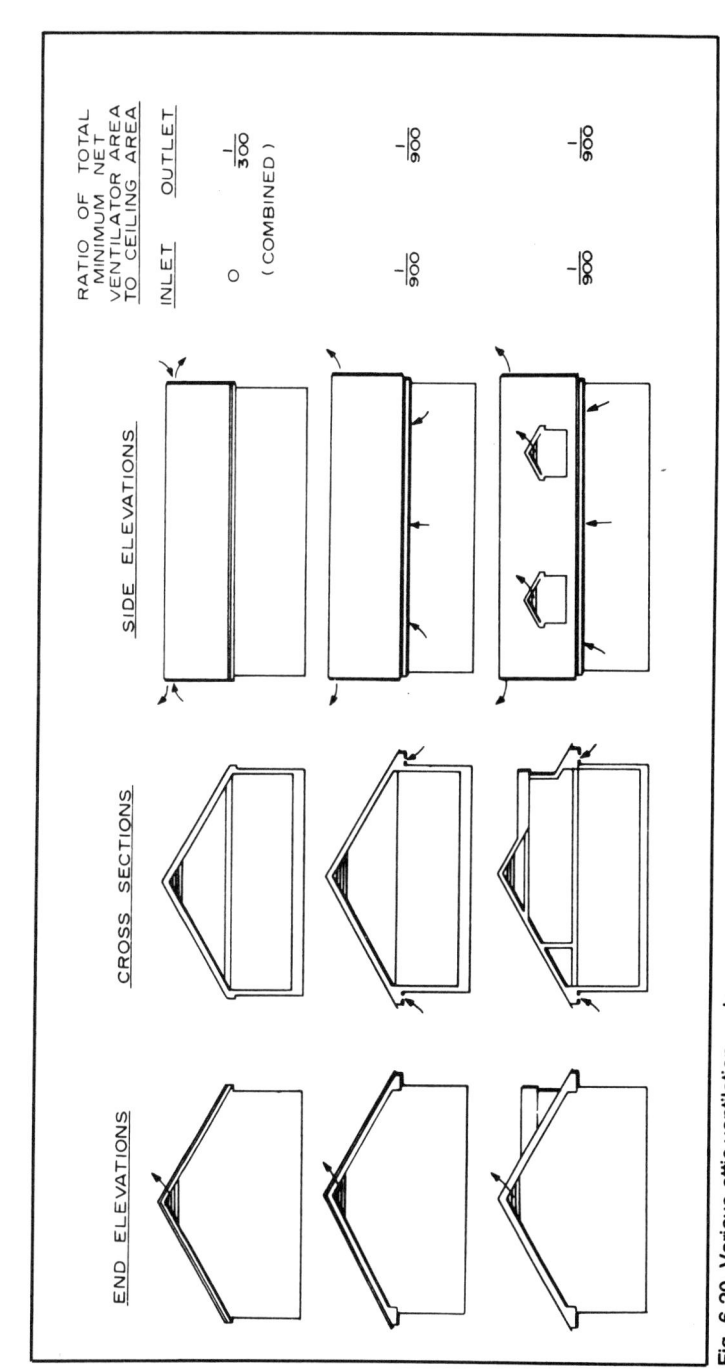

Fig. 6-20. Various attic ventilation systems.

Fig. 6-21. Remember that your attic must have inlet vents (along eaves) and outlet vents (as high as possible) to create good air circulation.

minimize the possible entry of wind-driven snow or rain. A soffit consisting of perforated hardboard can also be used to advantage, but the holes should be no larger than one-eighth of an inch in diameter. Small metal frames with screened openings are also available and they can be used in soffit areas. For open cornice design, the use of a friezeboard with screen ventilating slots should be satisfactory. Perforated hardboard might also be used for this purpose. The recommended minimum inlet ventilation ratios should be followed in determining total net ventilating areas for both inlet and outlet ventilators (Fig. 6-21).

To be most effective, outlet ventilators should be located as close as possible to the highest portion of the roof ridge. They can be placed in the upper wall section of a gable roofed house in various forms. In wide gable-end overhangs with ladder framing, a number of screened openings can be located in the soffit area of the lookouts. Ventilating openings to the attic space should not be restricted by any type of blockage.

Outlet ventilators on gable or hip roofs might also consist of some type of roof ventilator. Hip roofs can have a venting gable (commonly called a modified hip). Protection from blowing snow and rain must be considered. This often restricts the use of a continuous ridge vent.

Locate the single roof ventilators along the ridge toward the rear of the house so they are not visible from the front of the house. Outlet ventilators can also be located in a chimney as a false flue that has a screened opening in the attic area.

ICE DAMS

Water leakage into walls and interiors of homes in the snow belt areas of the country is sometimes caused by ice dams. This is often mistaken for a condensation problem. Such problems occur after heavy snowfalls where there is sufficient heat loss from the living quarters to melt the snow along the roof surface. The water moves down the roof deck to the colder overhang of the roof where it then freezes. This causes a ledge of ice over the eaves and backs up additional melting snow from above. This water then works its way up under the finish roofing and often into the attic space below. In extreme cases, this water will drip down and damage framing members and finish ceiling materials (Fig. 6-22).

Ice dam problems can be almost entirely eliminated by following modern construction practices of vapor barriers, insulation, and ventilation. By reducing attic temperatures by installing adequate insulation and venting the space, rapid snow melt is reduced and the run off that does occur, through the action of the sun and a rise in outdoor temperatures, will pass over a roof deck that is approximately the same temperature. Good insulation—an R value of at least R-30—for homes in the northern sections of the country greatly reduces heat loss from the house proper. Adequate ventilation, in turn, tends to keep attic spaces dry with temperatures only slightly above outdoor temperatures. A combination of good ventilation and insulation is the solution to ice dam problems (Fig. 6-23).

Another protective measure is provided by the use of a flashing material. A 36-inch wide strip of 45-pound, mineral-surfaced roll roofing can be installed along the eaves line. See Chapter 1.

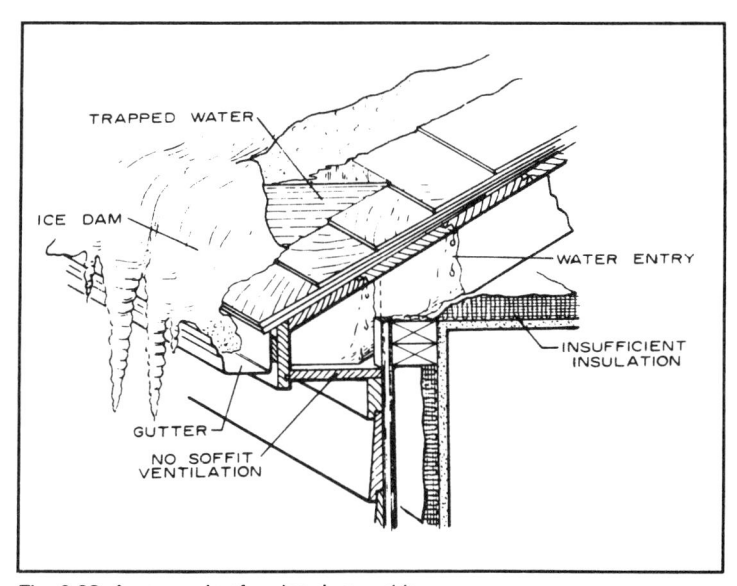

Fig. 6-22. An example of an ice dam problem.

Condensation or frost on protruding nails, on the surfaces of roof boards, or other members in attic areas normally indicates the escape of excessive amounts of water vapor from the heated rooms below. If a vapor barrier is not already present, place one between the joists and under the insulation. Make sure the vapor barrier fits tightly around ceiling lights and exhaust fans. Caulk where necessary. In addition, increase both inlet and outlet ventilators to conform to the minimum recommendations covered earlier in this chapter. Decreasing the amount of water vapor produced in the living areas is also helpful.

Walls and doors to unheated areas such as attic spaces should be treated to resist water vapor movement as well as to minimize heat loss. This includes the use of insulation and vapor barriers on all wall areas adjacent to the cold attic. Vapor barriers should face the warm side of the room. In addition, some means should be used to prevent heat and vapor loss around the perimeter of the door into the attic space. One method is to attach weather stripping around the door and to attach a sweeper type seal along the bottom of the door. The door itself will be more effective if it is given several coats of paint or varnish to further help reduce the passage of both heat and water vapor (Fig. 6-24).

Reducing high relative humidities within the house to permissible levels is often necessary to minimize condensation problems. Discontinue the use of room-size humidifiers or reducing the output

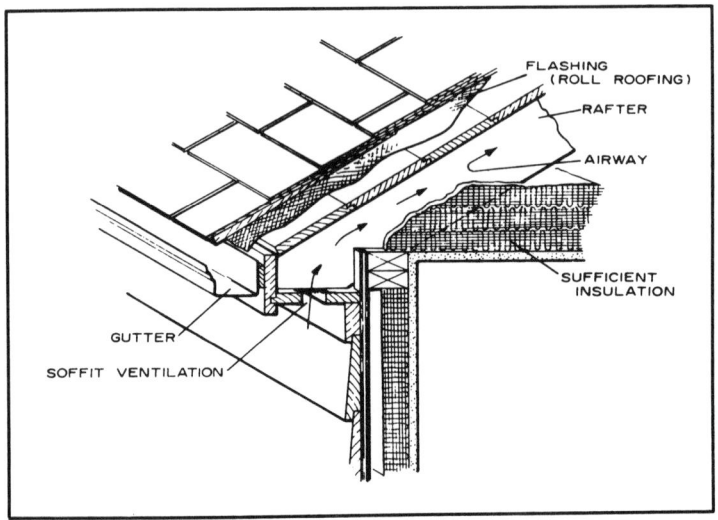

Fig. 6-23. Ventilation and insulation is a sure cure for ice-dam problems.

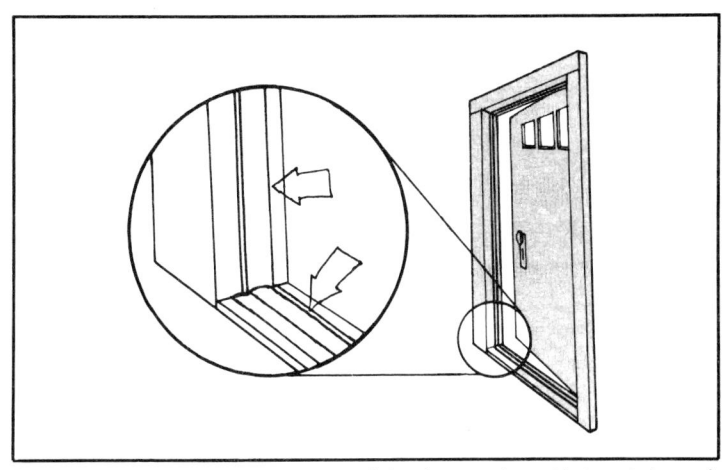

Fig. 6-24. Use weather stripping around the doorway into attic to cut down air leaks.

of automatic humidifiers until conditions are improved is also helpful. The use of exhaust fans and dehumidifiers are also helpful in reducing the high humidity problem in some houses. Exhaust fans are very helpful for high humidity areas such as the kitchen, bathrooms and, the laundry. This is especially true for homes with electric heat.

Concealed condensation takes place within a component such as a wall cavity when a condensing surface is below the dewpoint. In cold weather, condensation often forms as frost. Such conditions can cause staining of siding, peeling of paint, and possibly decay in extreme cases. These problems are usually not detected until spring. Solutions to these problems should be taken care of before repainting or residing is attempted. Some solutions to the problem are:

☐ Reduce or control relative humidity in the home.

☐ Add a vapor-resistant paint coating to interior walls and ceilings.

☐ Improve the vapor resistance of the ceiling by adding a vapor barrier between ceiling joists in the attic space.

☐ Improve attic ventilation.

Chapter 7

Building Materials

Anyone who plans to attempt any project around the home should not only have a knowledge of construction techniques and the use of tools, but also know how to choose the proper material for a particular project. Therefore, this chapter will deal with building materials, masonry materials, choosing grades and types of lumber, fasteners, wood preservatives, etc.

LUMBER

Wood is used for such basic building materials as solid lumber, plywood, particle board and hardboard. All of these materials are useful for projects around the home, but the handyman must know how to select and order these basic materials.

Select Lumber

☐ 1 and 2 Clear: Highest quality lumber—generally clear and free from defects. Suitable for natural finishes and fine cabinetwork.

☐ C select: Might have minor imperfections. One side might be without blemish.

☐ D select: Lowest finishing grade. Has minor defects and blemishes, but ideally suited for painted finishing.

Common Lumber

☐ No 1: Might have small, sound knots. Takes paint well. Usable with minimum waste.

☐ No. 2: Utility grade. Has larger and more numerous knots. Often used for knotted paneling.

Table 7-1. Grades and Uses of Exterior Plywood.

Grade	Uses
A-A	Outdoor, where appearance of both sides is important.
A-B	Alternate for A-A, where appearance of one side is less important.
A-C	Siding, soffits, fences. One "good" side grade.
B-C	For utility uses such as farm buildings, some kinds of fences, etc.
C-C	Excellent base for tile and linoleum, backing for wall covering.
C-C	Unsanded, for backing and rough construction exposed to weather.
B-B	Concrete forms. Re-use until wood literally wears out.

☐ No. 3: Numerous defects. Some waste in use.
☐ No. 4: Lowest grade usable in building.
☐ Bottom quality. Suitable only for crating, rough concrete forms, etc.

PLYWOOD

Plywood is probably the most versatile wood that the homeowner can buy. Douglas fir is used extensively for plywood; it is the least expensive type manufactured. Other kinds include hardwood-faced plywood, that are available in many beautiful hardwoods.

All plywoods have their own grading system and it is important to know these when ordering material. Interior plywood, for example, should be used only in dry locations, while exterior plywood is for use in damp (or wet) locations. The laminated layers will not come apart on exterior plywood even when placed in boiling water. Tables 7-1 and 7-2 give the various grades of fir plywood—for both interior and exterior use.

HARDBOARD

Hardboard is a dense wood sheet material that can be used for wall paneling and many other projects. It can be cut with hand saws

Table 7-2. Grades and Uses of Interior Plywood.

Grade	Uses
A-A	Cabinet doors, built-ins, furniture where both sides will show.
A-B	Alternate of A-A—one side high standard, the other, solid and smooth.
A-D	Good one side for paneling, built-ins, backing, underlay, etc.
B-D	Utility grade. Has one good side. Backing, cabinet sides, etc.
C-D	Underlay for tile, linoleum, and carpet and similar uses.
C-D	Sheathing and structural uses such as temporary enclosures, subfloor.
B-B	Concrete forms, re-use until wood wears out.

or power saws and can be nailed, screwed, drilled, routed, planed, sanded, etc.—just like any other wood product.

Because hardboard is entirely free from grain, it won't split or crack. Furthermore, it will bend around framework or take self-supporting bends. However, it requires that nails or screws be secured to some other material because the hardboard, itself, will not hold nails or screws.

When cutting hardboard, use a colored pencil to mark the cutting line. The dark surface will hide conventional lead pencil marks. Use a fine-tooth crosscut or combination blade (8 to 12 points to the inch); hold the hand saw at a flat angle and bend the hardboard slightly to overcome saw "buckle."

The rough edges from a cut can be smoothed with a file or rasp or rounded with a small plane. Always use a shallow set on the plane and then sandpaper it. You might also want to apply a wash-coat of shellac before final dressing. Then, practically any finish normally applied to wood surfaces can be used to finish the hardboard.

FASTENINGS

The basic types of nails are wire nails, box nails, finishing nails, and casing nails as shown in Fig. 7-1. Common wire nails are used

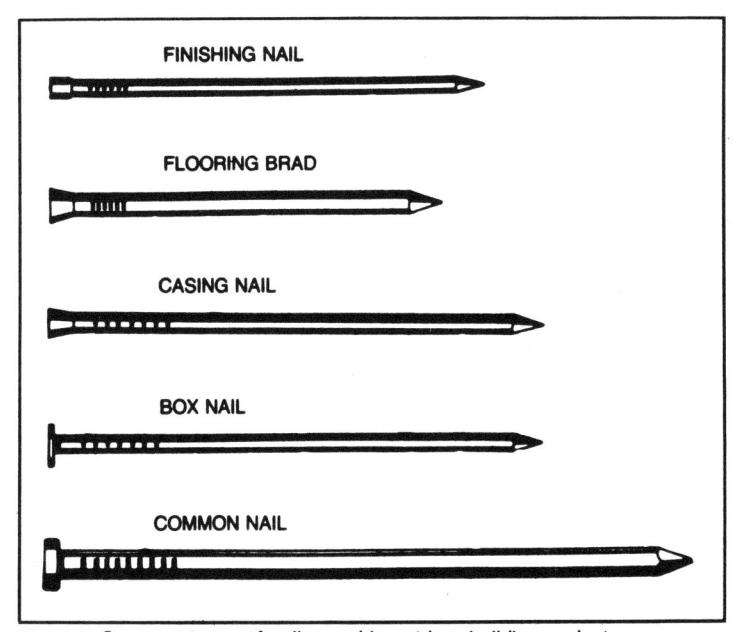

Fig. 7-1. Common types of nails used in outdoor building projects.

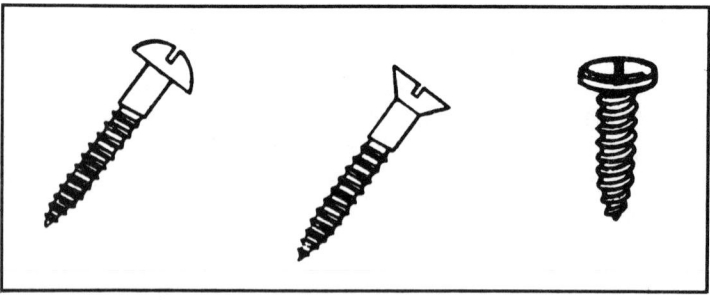

Fig. 7-2. Common screw types.

for rough, heavy work. Box nails are thinner and therefore will not split the wood as easy as common nails, but are used for the same purpose. The small head on finishing nails can be set below the surface. Casing nails are used for trim.

Common screw types include the flathead, which is set flush with the surface; oval head, which is more decorative; and the roundhead, which does not require countersinking. All of these types are shown in Fig. 7-2.

Some nails—like gypsum-board fasteners—have tapered threads and broad flat heads for better holding (see Fig. 7-3). Masonry nails are threaded and made of high-carbon steel for driving into masonry; they are good for anchoring items to foundations, walls, and so forth. See Fig. 7-4.

Machine bolts have heads while a carriage bolt has a square collar that locks it against turning in wood as shown in Fig. 7-5. The machine bolt is normally used in metal and the carriage bolt in wood.

Lag screws (Fig. 7-6) have square heads for turning with a wrench or pliers and coarse threads for pre-bored holes in wood.

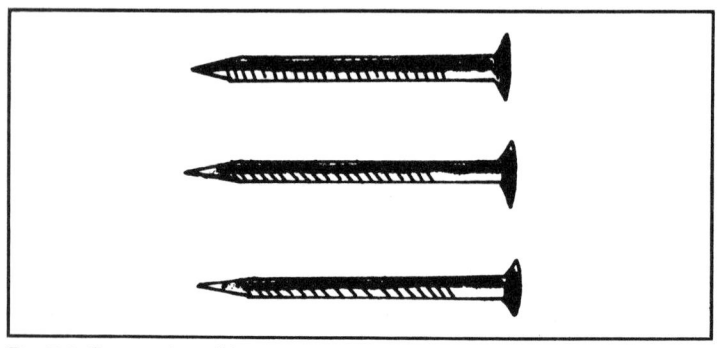

Fig. 7-3. Gypsum-board fasteners have tapered threads and broad, flat heads for better holding.

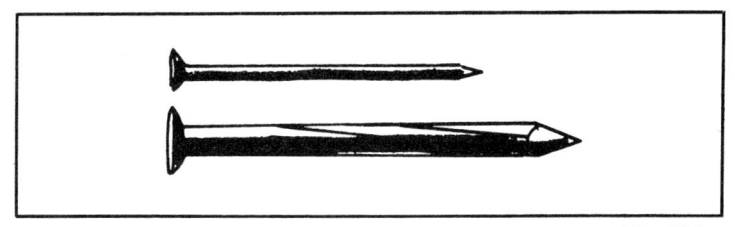

Fig. 7-4. Masonry nails are threaded and made of high-carbon steel for driving into masonry.

These screws are excellent for securing wood members when a hole can't be bored clear through to accept a carriage bolt.

Hooks and eyes have a variety of uses for outdoor projects. A U-bolt, for example, is a very strong "eye" that can be used to secure a hammock, clothesline, etc. A hook and eye is also very handy for securing wood members in place that will frequently have to be removed. For example, the roof of a dog house might have to be removed periodically to clean the interior. Four hooks and eyes placed at the corners of the roof where it attaches to the lower structure will hold the roof in place and also make it easy to remove when necessary.

CONCRETE

Ready-mixed concrete is easy for the handyman to use; all that is necessary is to add water according to directions. Basically, there are three types available: mortar mix, sand mix, and gravel mix.

For large jobs, the homeowner will save money by mixing his own concrete. In general, use 1 part cement to 2 parts sand and 3 parts gravel. However, the job will determine the best mix to use. The following mixes are recommended for the homeowner:

Fig. 7-5. A machine bolt.

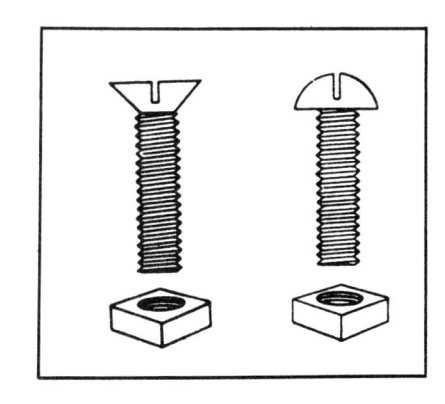

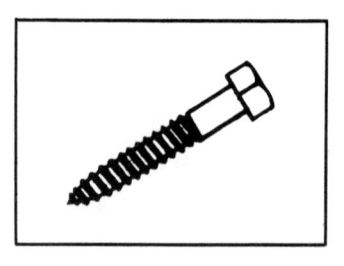

Fig. 7-6. A typical lag screw.

☐ Footings and Foundations: The mix should consist of 1 bag of cement to 3 cubic feet sand and 5 cubic feet of gravel with the maximum aggregate size 1½". You will need from 5 to 7 gallons of water per bag of cement, depending upon the dampness of the sand.

☐ Columns, chimneys, retaining walls, etc.: Mix proportions of cement to sand and gravel at 1:3:4; that is, one bag of cement, 3 cubic feet sand, and 4 cubic feet of gravel with 1½" being the largest aggregate size. The amount of water will range between 4¾ gallons to 6¼ gallons—depending upon the dampness of the sand.

☐ Watertight wall, swimming pools, etc.: Mix proportions of cement to sand and gravel at 1:2:3 respectively. The amount of water will range between 4¼ to 5½ gallons.

☐ Driveways, terraces, tennis courts, steps, etc.: You will need 1 bag of cement to 2½ cubic feet sand and 3½ cubic feet of gravel with the aggregate size no larger than 1 inch.

☐ Topping for pavement, steps, tennis courts, etc.: mix 1 bag of cement to 1 cubic feet sand and 1¼ cubic feet of gravel—¾" maximum aggregate size—and about 4½ gallons of water.

☐ Posts, garden furniture, tanks, bird baths, etc.: You will want to use a 1:2:2 mix with about 3¾ gallons of water. The largest gravel size should be ½".

You can see that concrete ingredients consist of cement, sand, gravel and water. You can mix the ingredients on any flat, hard surface or platform. Unless you have or rent a concrete mixer, a

Table 7-3. Materials Needed for Concrete.

Mix Formula	Cement (bags)	Sand (cu. ft.)	Gravel (cu. ft.)
1:3:5	4½	15	22
1:3:4	5	15	20
1:2½:3½	6	15	21
1:2:3	7¼	14¼	21
1:2:2	8	16	16

standard wheelbarrow is hard to beat for mixing small batches of concrete around the home. Mix all the dry ingredients first and then sprinkle water over the concrete. Let it soak a minute or two before thoroughly mixing with a concrete hoe.

Once you have worked with concrete for a while you will be able to accurately judge the water needed by the way the material handles. However, never use more than indicated in the formulas. A little less won't hurt anything, but never use more water.

When planning your concrete project, calculate the amount of concrete needed in cubic yards. Then determine the amount of materials needed to obtain the required amount of ready-to-pour concrete.

Fig. 7-7. Bird & Son, Inc., of East Walpole, MA, manufactures two kinds of horizontal siding. Both come in double 4-inch or single 8-inch clapboard widths. Panels are available with or without fiber or foam polystyrene backing for acoustical and thermal insualtion.

Fig. 7-8. Vinyl siding never needs painting, and it will not dent, pit, peel, or corrode. Solid vinyl gutters and downspouts, and soffit and facia systems complete a low-maintenance exterior. Polystyrene shutters add a finishing touch (courtesy of Bird & Son).

Fig. 7-9. Vinyl sidings and vinyl accessories offer the look of wood without the work. They never need painting, and a spray from a garden hose keeps them clean and new looking year-round (courtesy of Bird & Son).

Fig. 7-10. When installed by a qualified contractor, aluminum siding is suitable for many architectural styles (courtesy of Alcoa Building Products, Inc.).

Fig. 7-11. Rugged durability and ease of application makes vinyl siding popular with homeowners and contractors.

Fig. 7-12. One of the best ways to find an aluminum siding contractor is to talk with neighbors who are satisfied with remodeling work done on their homes (courtesy of Alcoa Building Products, Inc.).

SIDING

Aluminum, vinyl, asbestos-cement, and wood are the materials most commonly installed on the exterior walls of American homes. In the Southwest and the West Coast areas, stucco or a cement plaster finish, preferably over a wire-mesh base, is often used. For homeowners who want a minimum of problems with siding maintenance, vinyl and aluminum provide almost maintenance-free exterior coverings. See Figs. 7-7 through 7-12.

Nonwood materials do not have the problems associated with repeated painting, blistering, peeling, or rotting. Aluminum and vinyl can do more than save on home-maintenance costs. Polystyrene fiber panels or polystyrene foam can be installed with the siding to acoustically and thermally insulate a home.

Chapter 8

Siding

The proper installation of siding requires skill and a considerable investment in tools and equipment. Aluminum siding manufacturers recommend that homeowners hire professional applicators to install aluminum siding. The illustrations, instructions, and procedures in this chapter have been adapted from the *Aluminum Siding Application Manual* courtesy of the Aluminum Association and the Architectural Aluminum Manufacturers Association.

The sections of this installation chapter are designed to guide you through every step of the job with practical advice based on years of industry practice and experience. Please note, however, that this information is designed to help the qualified siding installer.

The techniques discussed in this chapter are illustrative of the procedures covered. They are not intended to be fully exhaustive and definitive. Other methods and techniques are used by qualified installers with full success. The best method depends on the specific construction of the building worked on, the brand and type of siding used, and the particular skills of the applicator.

SIDING STYLES

8-Inch Horizontal. The most commonly used siding today, featuring an 8-inch clapboard appearance resembling wood lap siding. Eight-inch horizontal (Fig. 8-1) is available in both smooth and wood-grain embossed textured surfaces. A large selection of colors is available in addition to ever-popular white.

Fig. 8-1. Eight-inch horizontal siding.

Double-4 and Double-5 Horizontal. The double 4-inch siding panel is installed the same way as 8-inch horizontal, but it has the appearance of two individual 4-inch boards. The style is often chosen for homes of colonial design. The double 5-inch siding gives a 10-inch exposure while appearing as two individual 5-inch panels. These sidings are generally available with smooth finishes and with a variety of embossed textures. See Fig. 8-2.

Insulated Siding. It is available with factory-laminated backing in both polystyrene and fiberboard. In addition, separate drop-in backer board is available which can be combined with the siding panels at the time of installation. Laminated and drop-in backer board thicknesses vary from ⅜ inch to ½ inch and can be used with 8-inch, double-4, double-5 siding. More selection is usually available for 8-inch horizontal siding. See Fig. 8-3.

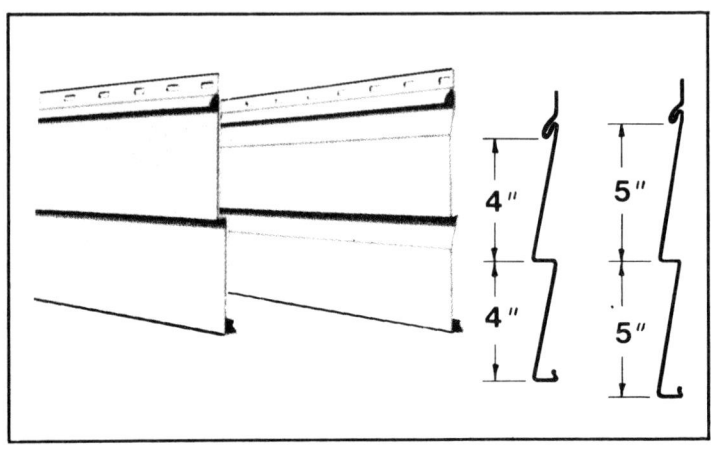

Fig. 8-2. Double-4 and double-5 horizontal siding.

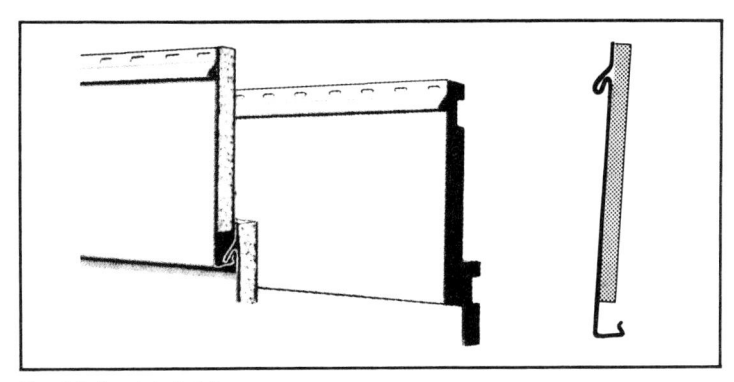

Fig. 8-3. Insulated siding.

Vertical Siding. This is similar in appearance to board-and-batten or V-groove siding (Fig. 8-4). Vertical is often used for accent on gable ends, or for breaking up a long, horizontal sweep. Most common is the 12-inch exposure width, although 16-inch vertical siding is offered by some producers. It is available in a wide range of colors in both embossed wood-grain textures and smooth finishes.

ACCESSORIES

Starter Strip. Base-line accessory that secures the first course of siding to the wall (Fig. 8-5). Used with horizontal and vertical siding. Nail 12 inches O.C. (on center).

J-Channels. Used for receiving siding on all sides of windows and doors, at rake edges of gables and in other miscellaneous

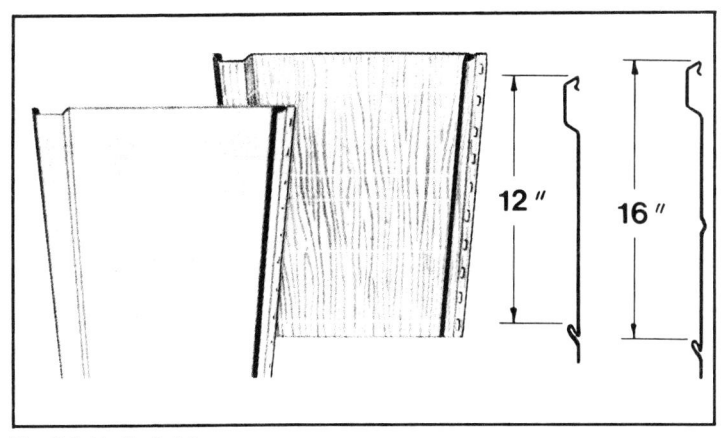

Fig. 8-4. Vertical siding.

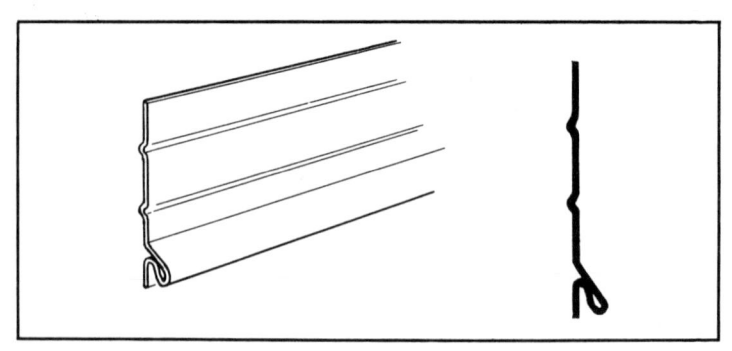

Fig. 8-5. Starter strip.

situations (Fig. 8-6). Deeper J-channels are for insulated siding, and narrower J-channels for non-insulated siding. Nailed 12 inches O.C.

Window Head Flashing. Possible alternative to J-channel to receive siding over doors and windows and as base flashing on vertical siding installations (Fig. 8-7). Nailed 12 inches O.C.

Inside Corner Post. Provides a means of joining at inside corners where siding butts from both sides. Deeper posts are for insulated siding, and narrower posts for non-insulated siding (Fig. 8-8). Nailed 12 inches O.C.

Outside Corner Post. Provides neat appearance outside corners for horizontal (8-inch, double 4-inch, double 5-inch) and vertical sidings. Receives siding from both sides. Deeper post is used with insulated siding, and narrower post with non-insulated siding. Both flanges are nailed 12 inches O.C. See Fig. 8-9.

Individual Outside Corner Cap. A possible alternative to outside corner post when installing 8-inch horizontal siding. Maintains continuity of siding courses in traditional clapboard style. Make sure nails are long enough. See A of Fig. 8-10.

Fig. 8-6. J-channels.

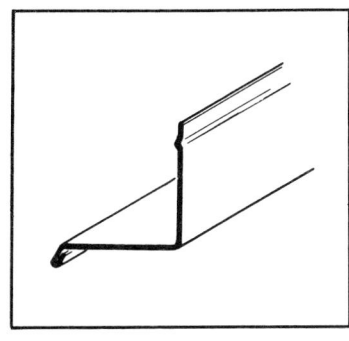

Fig. 8-7. Window-head flashing.

All-Purpose Trim. Used to finish off ("trim") job-site cuts on siding, as under windows, at eaves, and at porch floor locations. May also be used to receive vertical siding at corners and window jambs. See B of Fig. 8-10.

Backer Tab. Provides support for non-insulated 8-inch siding at panel overlaps (joints), and behind panels at corners to assure a smooth installation. See C of Fig. 8-10.

TOOLS REQUIRED

The siding applicator's job can be made much easier with the proper tools. Here is a list of the most essential:

Carpenter's Metal Square
Carpenter's Folding Rule
2-Foot Level (minimum)
Caulking Gun
Steel Measuring Tape
Fine-Tooth File
Power Saw (Optional) with Aluminum-Cutting Blade 1/16 Inch Thick—Minimum 10 teeth per inch

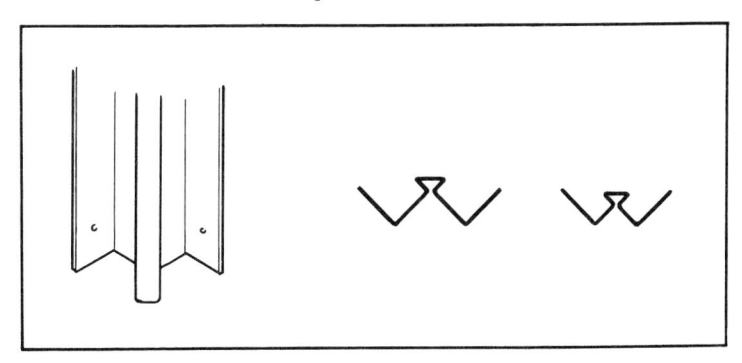

Fig. 8-8. Inside corner post.

279

Fig. 8-9. Outside corner post.

Claw Hammer
Chalk Line
Screwdriver
Pliers
Tinsnips: Duckbill Type
Aviation Shears: Double-Acting
Carpenter's Saw: Crosscut
Safety Goggles
Steel Awl
Metal-Cutting Hacksaw: Fine-Tooth (24 teeth per inch)
Utility Knife
Line Level
Putty Knife: 3-Inch
Hard Hat

Additional materials required for the installation of siding are shown in Fig. 8-11. These are: a *gutterseal mastic* (1); *Trim sheet* (2) that is available in various widths such as 10-inch, 14-inch, 18-inch and 24-inch; *aluminum breather foil* (3) is usually sold in 36-inch

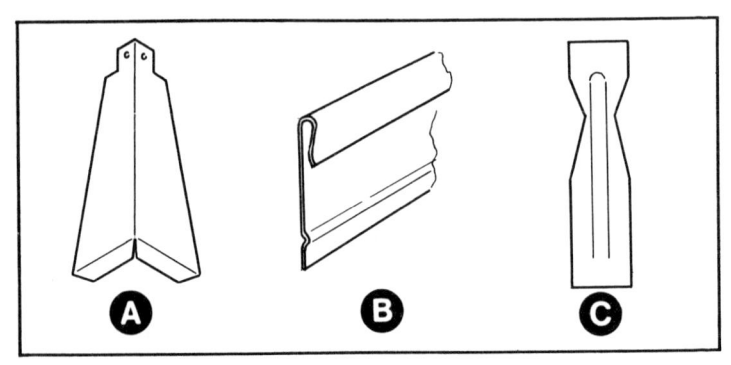

Fig. 8-10. Individual outside corner cap (A), all-purpose trim (B), and backer tab (C).

wide rolls; *touch-up paint* (4) in colors to match siding (for kitchen fans, service cables, etc.); *caulking* (5) should, preferably, be a butyl caulk; *aluminum nails* (6) should be 1½ inch for general use, 2-inch nails for re-siding, 2½-inch (or more) through insulated siding into soft sheathing, and 1-inch to 1½-inch trim nails (colored to match siding).

Note: A minimum penetration of ¾ inch, excluding point of nail, into solid lumber is required for nailing to be effective with plain shank nails. Screw shank nails could be used through ½-inch plywood for similar effectiveness.

EQUIPMENT

Ladders and Scaffolds. Proper ladders and scaffolds are necessary. The pump jack is widely used to provide a working platform. The posts upon which the pump jacks move are normally two 2-by-4's nailed together to form a 4-by-4 post. With a pump jack platform, the distance from the building facade remains the same from the bottom to the top. Exact specifications on spacing dimensions, planking, permissible heights and loads, etc., are contained in the OSHA Construction Safety and Health Regulations under sections 1926.450 and 1926.451 covering ladders and pump jacks. Contact your local OSHA office.

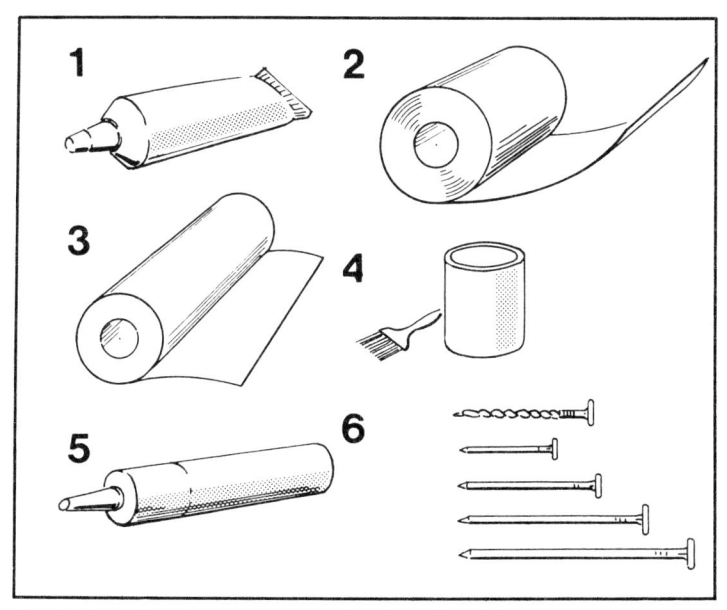

Fig. 8-11. Additional material required for installing siding.

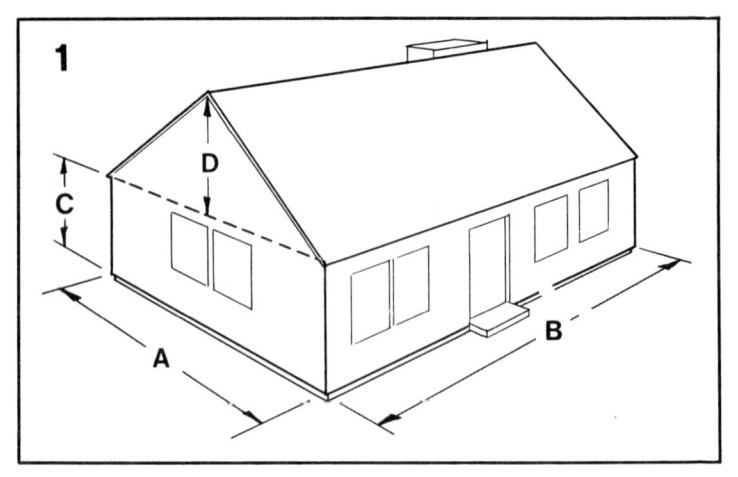

Fig. 8-12A. Houses can be divided into a series of rectangles and triangles.

Cutting Table. For a more efficient and professional operation, specialized equipment is available. A valuable time-saver is the portable cut-off table or trim table that allows a standard portable circular powersaw to be mounted in a carrier, and stood off from the work to avoid damaging the siding. These tools can help measure and cross-cut, as well as help make miters and bevels. The units are constructed of light-weight aluminum and can be easily set-up on the job-site by one man.

Portable Brake. For job-site bending of custom-trim sections, such as facia trim, window casing and sill trim, a portable metal-bending machine (brake) is extremely useful. Using white or colored coil stock, precision bending involving multiple bends can be accomplished. These machines are lightweight and can be carried to the job site and set in place. Various sizes and brake styles are available.

ESTIMATING MATERIAL

Siding. In order to arrive at the amount of siding necessary to cover a house, the measuring operation can be reduced to simple steps. Virtually all houses are made up of a series of rectangles or triangles, or a combination of both, regardless of how broken up the face of a wall appears to be Fig. 8-12A. Using the formula shown in Fig. 8-12B, measure the height (excluding gables) and width of each side of the house (including windows), and arrive at the area in square feet for each. Now compute gable triangle areas by using the formula in illustration 3 of Fig. 8-12B. Total all these areas. Win-

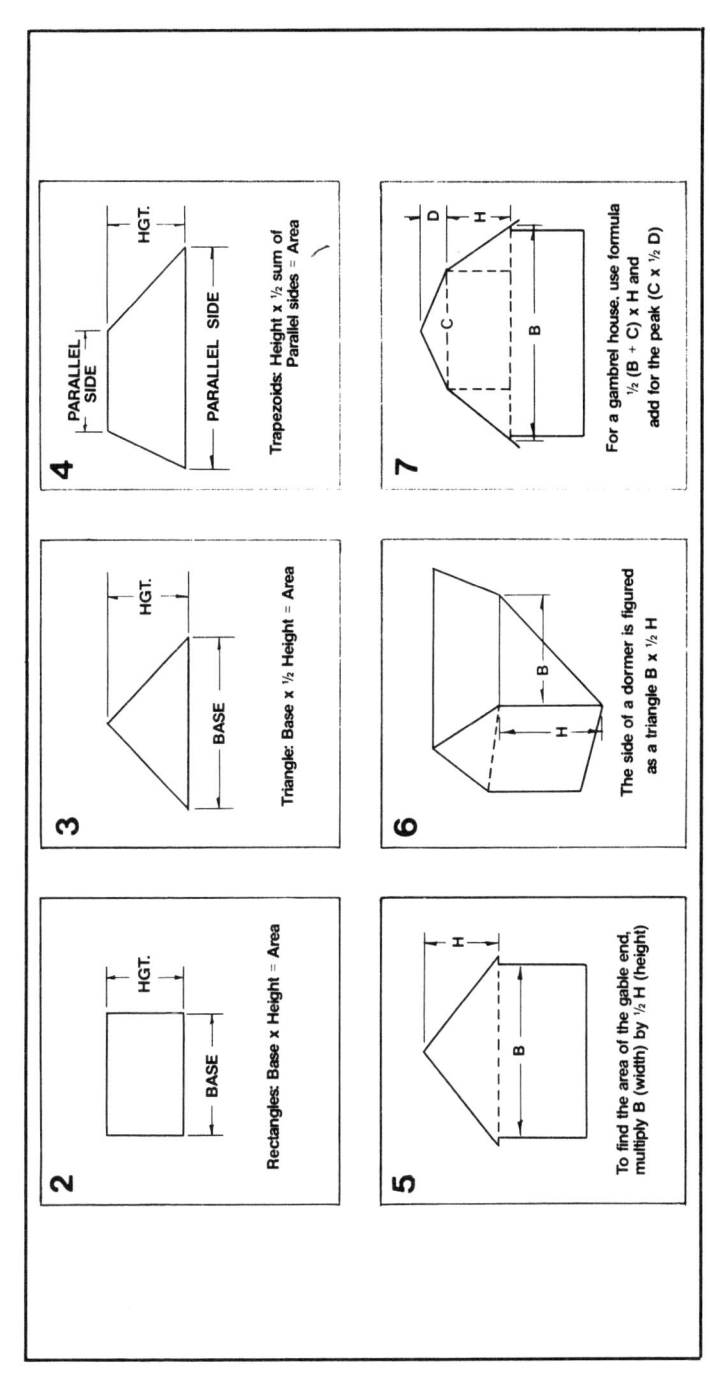

Fig. 8-12B. Estimating the amount of siding required to cover the exterior of a house.

dows and door areas are generally not deducted, as including them in the wall area figures will provide an allowance factor for waste. If these window and door areas are extremely large (such as garage doors or sliding glass doors), some deduction might be made. Dormers and gables are traditionally prone to material waste due to cutting and fitting; to compensate, add 1 foot in height to the original measurements to allow for waste.

Accessories. For amount of starter strip required, measure the lineal feet around the entire base of the building to be covered. For corner posts and accessories, also measure in lineal footage. Measure lineal footage and add a factor of approximately 10 percent to allow for waste. Furring estimates might also be required. See the section on wood furring.

SAVING ENERGY

Today's concern with energy saving has brought about a vastly increased interest in better insulation of house sidewalls. Insulated aluminum siding offers a convenient, economical method of reducing heating and cooling costs. Homeowners who have already decided on aluminum siding can realize fuel cost savings by upgrading to the additional insulation techniques described in the accompanying diagrams. Aluminum siding installed with aluminum breather foil, furring strips, or insulation board sheathing can substantially increase the insulation value of typical uninsulated wall constructions. The additional costs of any of these added insulation systems will probably be recoverable within a few heating seasons through annual heating savings.

Construction materials are measured by thermal resistance values (R-values) and the higher the number the better the insulation properties.

The accompanying diagrams give the R-values that can be realized by following the specific constructions described. These values are in addition to the existing wall (that might or might not have good insulation properties). Air spaces, aluminum breather foil, and furring all contribute to incrased R-values. For instance, if aluminum foil is used with ¾-inch wood furring strips, the R-value will be more than triple that of ¾-inch furring strips alone.

The shiny surface of the foil should always face toward an air space, but it makes no difference which side of the air space the polished surface faces. Aluminum reflector foil reflects heat waves back when it is on the cold side of an air space, and when it is on the warm side, it retains heat. For remodeling work, always use perforated ("breather") aluminum reflector foil (with a "perm rating" of at least 10) to prevent condensation that can be caused by warm air vapor migrating through the wall and condensing on the cold foil.

A study and comparison of the diagrams clearly indicates the gains possible through added insulation techniques. (Installation over old wood lap siding is assumed). Another companion insulation option for the homeowner at this time could be the contracting for blown-in-the-wall insulation (such as mineral wool or cellulose). The drilled access holes in the old siding, required for this process, will be covered up by the new siding.

A — Furring, ¾" Airspace, Existing wall, Polystyrene backerboard
2 sheets of aluminum reflector foil, *both* polished surfaces facing either inside *or* outside
R = 5.5-6.0

B — Existing wall, Hollowbacked siding, ½ in. Isocyanurate (both sides foil)
R = 5.0

C — ¾ in. T&G extruded Polystyrene
R = 4.7

D — Furring, 3/8" Airspace, Existing wall, Foil faced Polystyrene Backerboard
Aluminum reflector foil with polished surface facing *inside*
R = 4.5

E — Existing wall, Polystyrene backerboard, Aluminum reflector foil (polished surface facing outside)
R = 2.5-3.0

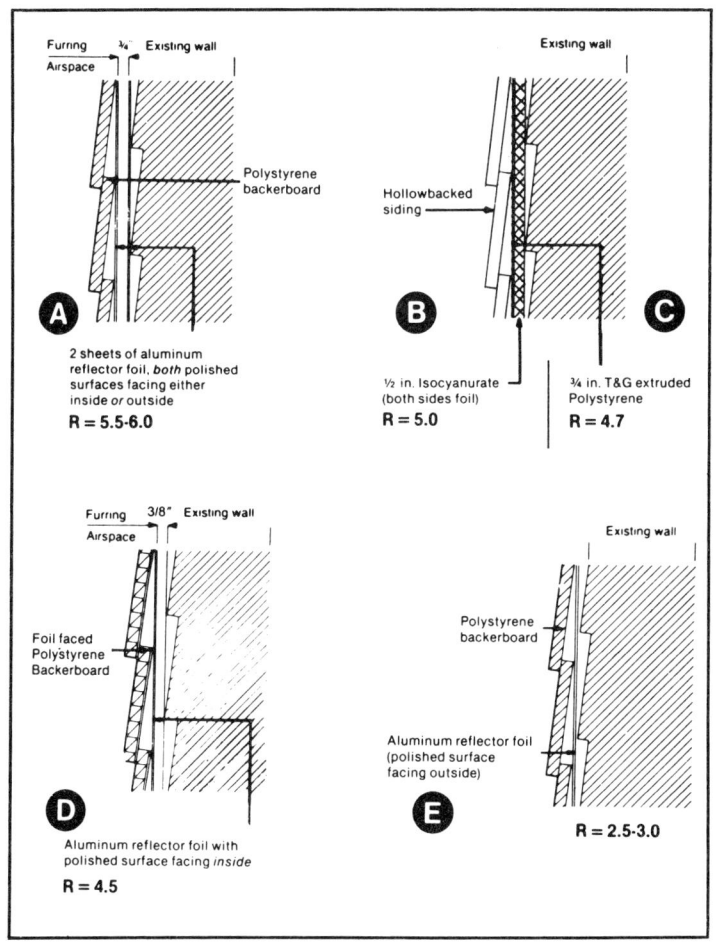

Fig. 8-13. Use "breather" (i.e., perforated) aluminum reflector foil, except on backerboard, to vent wall vapor through siding vent holes.

Fig. 8-14. Cut off window sill extensions.

SURFACE PREPARATION

The quality of the finished job depends on good preparation of the work surface. Check for low places in the plane of the wall and build out (shim out) if required. Prepare the entire building a few courses at a time. Securely nail all loose boards and loose wood trim. Replace any rotted boards. Scrape away old paint buildup, old caulking, and hardened putty. This is especially important around windows and doors where it might interfere with the positioning of new trim. New caulk should be applied to prevent air infiltration.

Remove downspouts and other items that would interfere with installation of new siding. Tie back shrubbery and trees from the base of the building to avoid damage to the landscaping.

Window sill extensions (Fig. 8-14) can be cut off so that J-trim can be installed flush with window casing. Alternatively, to maintain the original window design, coil stock can be custom-formed around the sill instead of cutting away the sill extensions.

FURRING AND INSULATION TECHNIQUES

Wood Furring. Furring is building out from the wall surface to provide a smooth even base for nailing on the new siding. Lath strips ⅜-inch thick are most commonly used. Lumber strips 1″ × 3″ are often used over brick and masonry. Furring is not usually necessary in new construction, but older homes often have uneven walls. Furring out low spots, or shimming, can help prevent a wavy appearance to the siding installation. Insulation value can be added by furring out an entire wall. Furring should be installed vertically 16 inches on center for horizontal siding, and the air space at the base of siding should be closed off with strips applied horizontally. Window, door, gable, and eaves trim might have to be built out to match the thickness of the wall furring.

Vertical Siding. Furring for vertical siding is essentially the same as for horizontal siding, except the wood strips are securely nailed horizontally into structural lumber on 16 to 24 inch centers. When using 1″ × 3″ furring, be sure to check what effect the additional thickness might have on trim situations.

Aluminum Foil Underlayment. Aluminum reflector foil is a good insulator and it can be used advantageously as an underlayment to siding. It can be stapled directly to the existing wall, or over ¾-inch furring strips to provide an additional air space and better insulation. Reflector foil for remodeling must be of the perforated or "breather" type to allow passage of water vapor. The foil should be installed with the shiny side facing the air space (outward with no furring, inward if applied over furring). Foil is generally available in 36-inch-wide rolls and 48-inch-wide rolls. Nail or staple just before applying siding. When applying foil over furring, be careful not to let the foil collapse into the air space. Place foil as close as possible to openings and around corners where air leaks are likely to occur, and overlap side and end joints by 1 to 2 inches.

Underlayment Board. Underlayment board is often used instead of furring strips. It is available in large sheets and in accordian-fold panels that can be nailed or stapled to the old wall. Some versions are faced two sides with perforated aluminum foil; that provides a considerable increase in insulation value. The core constructions vary from cellular kraft to polystyrene. The board should have a vapor permeance of at least 10 perms.

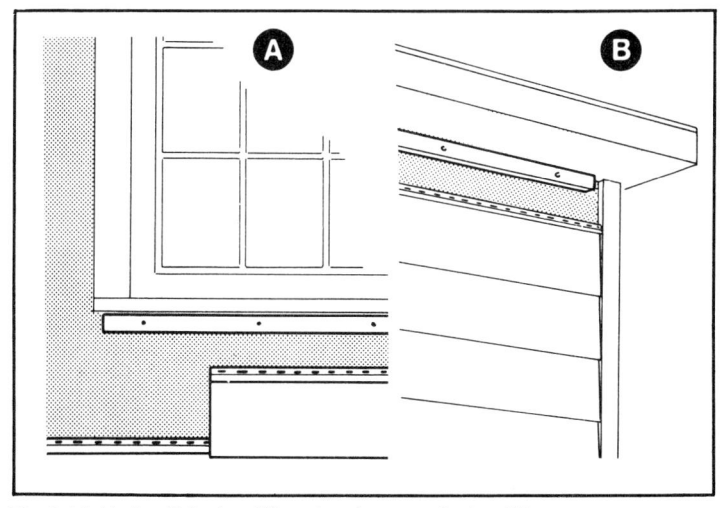

Fig. 8-15. Undersill furring (A) and undereaves furring (B).

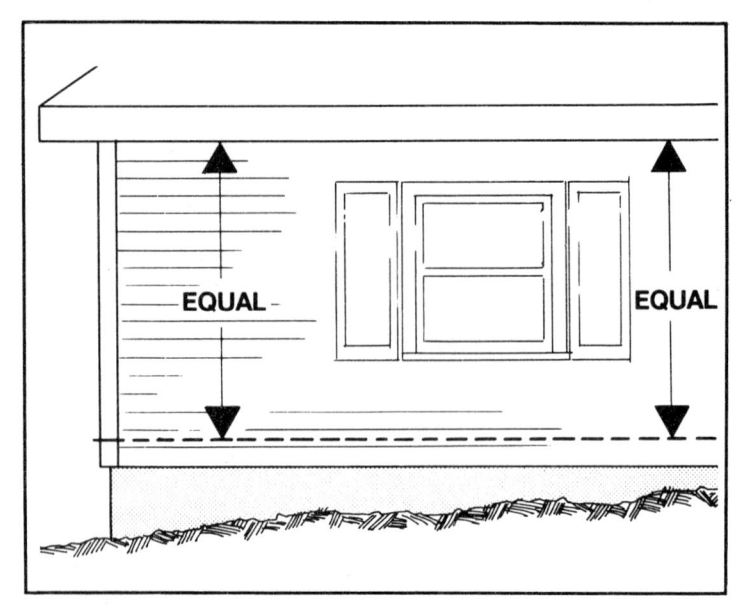

Fig. 8-16. A straight-line reference.

Windows and Door Build-Out. Some trim build-out at windows and doors might be required to maintain the original appearance of the house when using furring strips or underlayment board. This is particularly true when using furring strips or underlayment board more than ½-inch thick. Thicker furring and underlayment generally provide added insulation value, and are usually a good investment for the homeowner. This is particularly true if the home is uninsulated. When estimating the labor and materials required for installing furring and underlayment, be sure to include an estimate on window and door build-out. Longer siding nails will be needed to compensate for added thickness of insulation board.

Undersill Furring. Building out below window sills (A of Fig. 8-15) is often required in order to maintain the correct slope angle if a siding panel needs to be cut less than full height. The exact thickness required will be apparent when the siding courses have progressed up the wall and reached this point. See the section on panels at windows and doors.

Undereaves Furring. For the same reason, furring is usually required to maintain the correct slope angle of the last panel where it terminates at the eaves. (B of Fig. 8-15). This panel usually has to be cut to less than a full height, thus requiring back-up furring and a special piece of trim for capping. See section on fitting under eaves.

BASE CHALK LINE

Straight Line. The key element in a successful siding installation is establishing a straight reference line upon which to start the first course of siding (Fig. 8-16). The suggested procedure is to measure equal distances downward from the eaves or windows. This insures that the siding appears parallel with the eaves, soffit, and windows regardless of any actual settling of the house from true level.

Find the lowest corner of the house. Partly drive a nail about 10 inches above the lowest corner, or enough to clear the height of a full siding panel. Stretch a taut chalk line from this corner to similar nail installed at other corner. Re-set this line based upon measuring down from points of equal dimension from eaves or windows. Repeat this procedure on all sides of the house until the chalk lines meet at all corners. Before snapping chalk lines, check for straightness. Be particularly alert to sag in the middle if line is more than 20 feet long. If you prefer, lines can be left in place while installing the starter strip, as long as they are checked periodically for excess sag.

Level. If the house is reasonably level, an alternative is to use a level to set the chalk line approximately 2 inches (or the width of the starter strip) from the lowest point of the old siding, and locate the top of the starter strip to that line. Be careful when using a standard carpenter's level because the progressive measurements could increase the possibility of error. The level should be at least 2

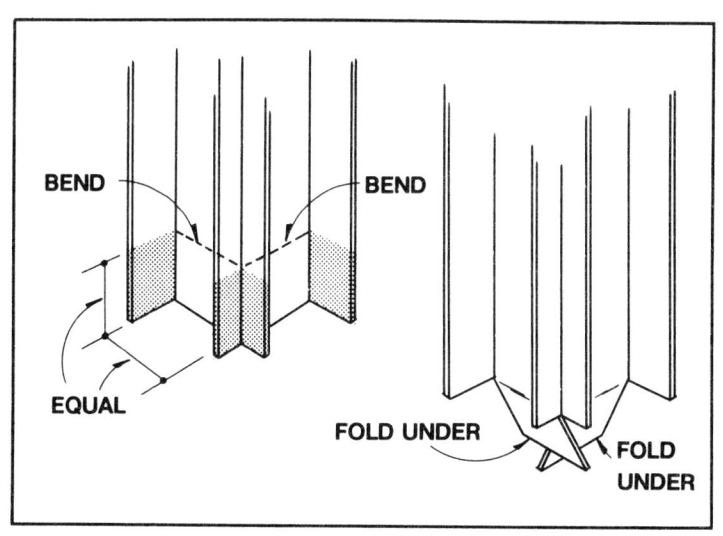

Fig. 8-17. Bottom cap.

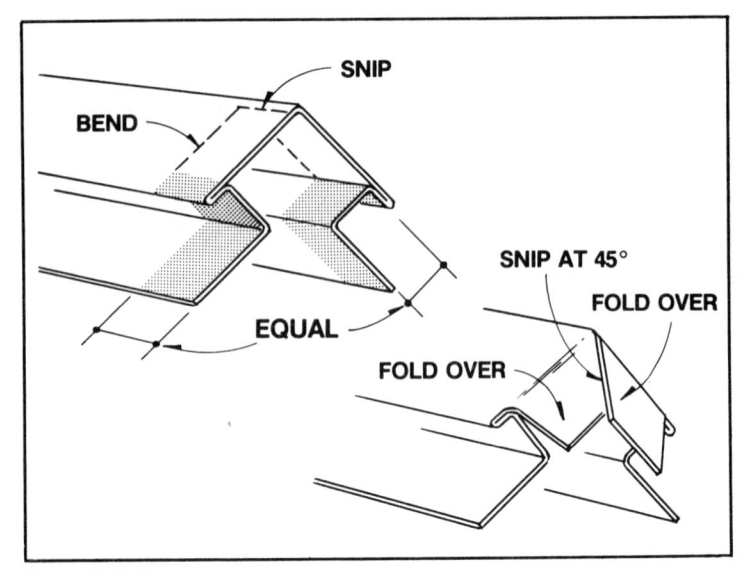

Fig. 8-18. Bottom cap.

feet long, and preferably longer. Take level reading at center of chalk line for best results.

INSIDE CORNER POSTS

Bottom Cap. To help prevent unwanted air infiltration and to keep out insects, cap the bottom of corner post before installation. Cut the post at the end as shown in Fig. 8-17. Remove unwanted material (shaded areas of diagram) with tinsnips, and fold remaining tabs 90° back to complete the closure.

Installation. Inside corner posts are installed before the siding is hung. Deeper or narrower posts might be required, depending on type of siding (insulated or non-insulated). The post is set in the corner full length, reaching from ¼-inch below bottom of starter strip up to eaves or gable trim. Nail approximately every 12 inches on both flanges with aluminum nails. Make sure the post is set straight and true. Flanges should be nailed securing to adjoining wall, but do not over-drive nails so as to cause distortion. If a short section is required, use a hacksaw to cut. If a long section is required, posts should be overlapped (with the upper piece outside).

Expansion Allowance. The siding is later butted into the corner and nailed into place allowing approximately 1/16-inch space between the post and the siding for expansion purposes. For more information on expansion and contraction requirements, see the section on installing the siding.

OUTSIDE CORNER POSTS

Bottom Cap. Using tinsnips, cut away unwanted material (shaded area in Fig. 8-18) and then fold remaining tabs 90 degrees back to close the cavity. If the corner post is not covered by eaves, the top of the corner post might have to be similarly closed off.

Installation. The outside corner post produces a trim appearance and it will accommodate the greatest variety of siding types (including double-4 and double-5). Most outside corner posts are designed to be installed before the siding is hung, in a manner similar to the inside corner post. If desired, old corner posts can sometimes be removed. Set a full-length piece over the existing corner running from ¼-inch below the bottom of starter strip to the underside of the eaves. If a long corner post is needed, overlap corner post sections with the upper piece outside.

Nailing. Nail every 12 inches with aluminum nails on both flanges. Make sure flanges are securely nailed, but avoid distortion caused by over-driving nails (Fig. 8-19). Use a hacksaw to cut short sections if required. If insulated siding is being used, wider corner posts are needed.

Note: Individual corner caps can be used on 8-inch, horizontal-lap siding instead of outside corner posts. See the section on individual corner caps for an explanation.

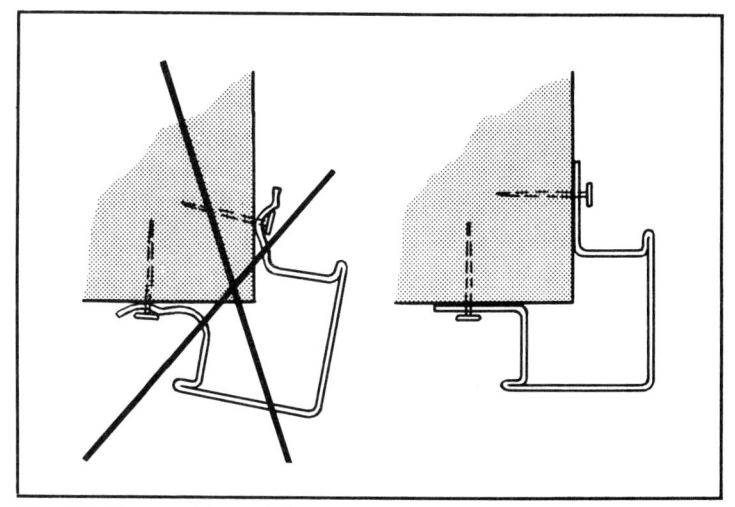

Fig. 8-19. Proper nailing techniques are shown on the right.

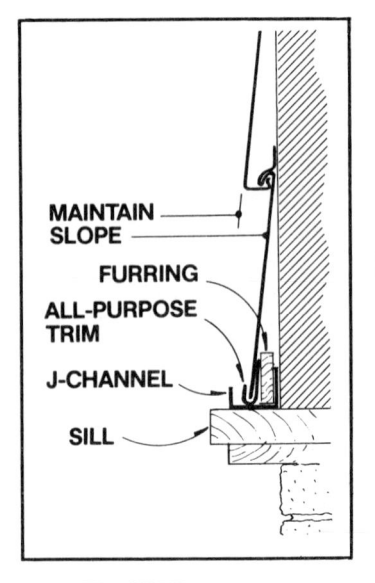

Fig. 8-20. An alternative course starter.

STARTER STRIP

Horizontal Siding. Using the chalk line previously established as a guide, take equal distance measurements and install starter strip all the way around the bottom of the building. If insulated siding is used, the starter strip should be furred out the thickness of the backer (see the section on insulated siding). It is extremely important that the starter strip be straight and meet accurately at all corners, because it will determine the line of all siding panels installed. Where hollows occur in the old wall surface, shim out behind the starter strip to prevent a wavy appearance of the finished siding application.

Vertical Siding. A plumb line should be used when you are applying starter strip in a vertical position. See the section on vertical siding.

Nailing. The starter strip should overlap the corner post flanges to help reduce air infiltration. When using individual corner caps, install the starter strip up to the edge of the house corner. Use aluminum nails spaced not more than 8 inches apart to securely fasten the starter strip. Nail the started strip as low as possible. Be careful not to bend or distort. Do not over-drive nails. Cutting lengths of starter strip is best accomplished with tinsnips. Butt sections together.

Alternatives. Starter strip might not work in all situations. Other accessory items such as J-channels or all-purpose trim might work better in starting siding courses over garage doors and porches, or above brick, for instance. These unusual situations must be handled on an individual basis as they occur. See the section on special situations.

WINDOW AND DOOR TRIM

Coil Stock. For a superior job in remodeling work, the old window sills and casings can be covered with aluminum coil stock, bent to fit, on the job site. The advantage is freedom from maintenance.

Sometimes window and door casings need to be built out to retain the original appearance of the house, or to improve the appearance. To do this, use appropriate lengths and thickness of good-quality lumber, and nail securely to existing window casings. Remove storm windows before covering casings with aluminum coil-stock sections custom-formed on the job-site.

Forming aluminum sections to fit window casings is done with a portable brake as follows. Door casings are handled similarly.

1. Sill Cover. Form aluminum trim to dimensions of wood sill being covered. For flashing purposes, snip and fold upright tabs at jamb locations and sill ends as shown in Fig. 8-21. Install with small head trim nails and/or adhesive.

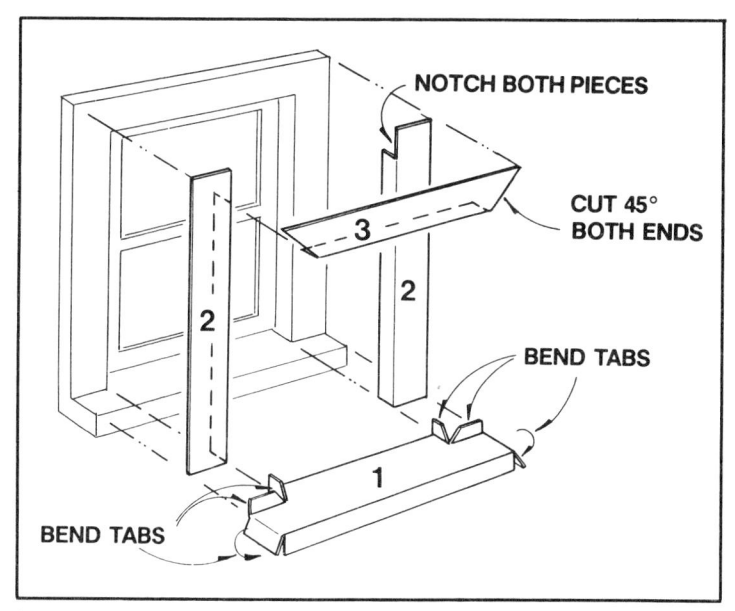

Fig. 8-21. Sill cover procedures.

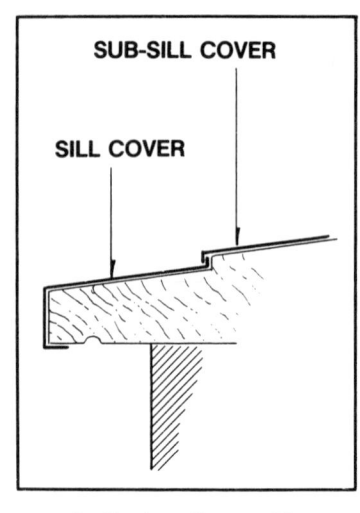

Fig. 8-22. Covering a two-piece sill.

2. Casing Cover. Form aluminum casing trim to dimensions of wood jamb being covered. Install over vertical flashing tabs of sill cover trim. Fasten in place as above.

3. Window Head Cover. Form aluminum to dimension of wood head being covered. Miter corners (as shown in Fig. 8-21) on both sides. Install so as to lap over casing trim pieces and fasten in place.

4. Caulk. Caulk where necessary to prevent water penetration behind trim pieces.

Two-Piece Sill. If there is a step in the wood sill, it can be covered best by bending two separates sill cover pieces as shown in Fig. 8-22. Let the flanges lap over for best water run-off.

Sill Ends. By using tinsnips and bending flanges on the job, the old sill ends can be boxed-in to provide a neat appearance and to prevent water penetration. See Fig. 8-23.

WINDOW AND DOOR TRIM; GABLE-END TRIM

Trim. J-channel is used around windows and doors to receive siding. Side J-channel members are cut longer than the height of the window or door, and notched at the top as shown in Fig. 8-24. Notch the top J-channel member at a 45 degree angle and bend tab down to provide flashing over side members. Caulking should be used behind J-channel members to prevent water infiltration between window and channel. See Fig. 8-24.

Flashing. To further prevent water from getting behind siding, a flashing piece is cut from coil stock and slipped under the base

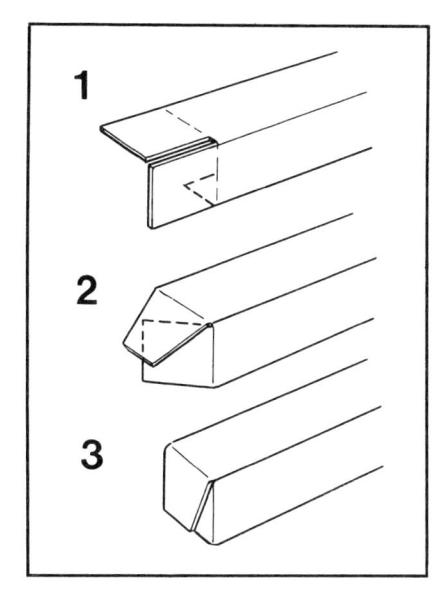

Fig. 8-23. Covering sill ends.

of the side J-channel members, and positioned so as to lap over the top lock of the panel below. See Fig. 8-25.

Gable Ends. Before applying siding, J-channel should be installed to receive siding at the gable ends (Fig. 8-26). Where the left and right sections meet at the gable peak, let one of the sections

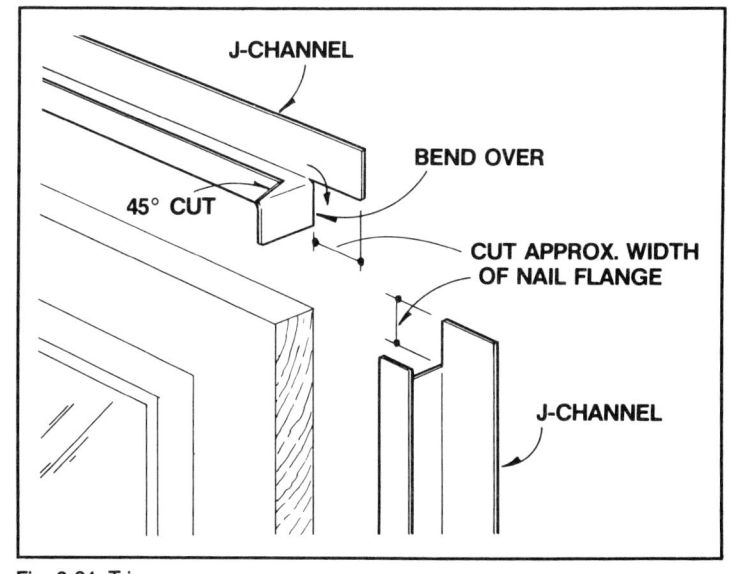

Fig. 8-24. Trim.

295

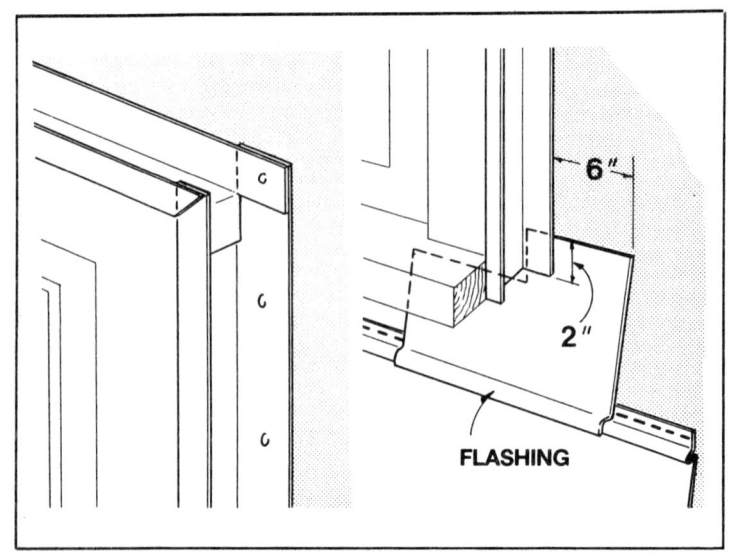

Fig. 8-25. Flashing.

butt into the peak with the other section overlapping. A miter cut is made on the face flange of this piece for better appearance. All old paint build-up should be removed before installing J-channels. Nail every 12 inches with aluminum nails.

CUTTING PROCEDURES

Power Saw. For precision cutting, a power saw is most convenient. Cutting one panel at a time is recommended. A special work-table jig that will keep the saw base clear of the work is preferred to prevent damage to panels. Use a minimum 10-point, aluminum-cutting blade. A bar of soap can be rubbed on the blade to produce a smoother cut on the siding panel and prolong blade life. Feed the saw through the work slowly to prevent flutter against the blade. *Caution:* Safety glasses should be worn at all times while operating a power saw.

Tinsnips. Individual panels can be cut with tinsnips. Start by drawing a line across the panel using a square. Begin cutting at the top lock first and continue toward the bottom of the panel. Break the panel across the butt edge and snip through bottom lock. Use a screwdriver to re-open a lock that might have become flattened by tinsnips. Aviation shears are sometimes used to cut the top and bottom locks and a utility knife is used to score and break the face of the panel. For straight cuts, the best choice is duckbill snips.

Score and Snap Method. The utility knife is useful for cuts lengthwise as well as cuts across a single panel. A heavy score is made on the panel and the piece is bent back and forth until it snaps cleanly along the score line. On window cut-outs, the combination of utility knife and tinsnips is most efficient. See the section on panels at windows and doors.

Accesories such as all-purpose trim, J-channel, and starter strip can best be cut using duckbill tinsnips. Use a hacksaw to cut accessories like corner posts.

INSTALLING THE SIDING

First Course. Extra care must be taken on the first course of siding applied; this course establishes the base for all other courses. Apply a panel by hooking the bottom lock of the panel into interlock bead of starter strip. Make sure lock is engaged. Do not force or jam; that might cause distortion of the panel and result in an undesirable shadow line. Double-check for continuous locking along the panel before proceeding further. Particularly check for alignment at corners.

At corner posts, slide panel into recess first, then exert upward pressure to lock the panel into place along its entire length. Allow clearance for expansion as necessary. See the section on expansion and contraction. If individual corner caps are being used, keep the panels back from corner edges ¾-inch for non-insulated siding (¼-inch for insulated) to allow for later fitting of the individual

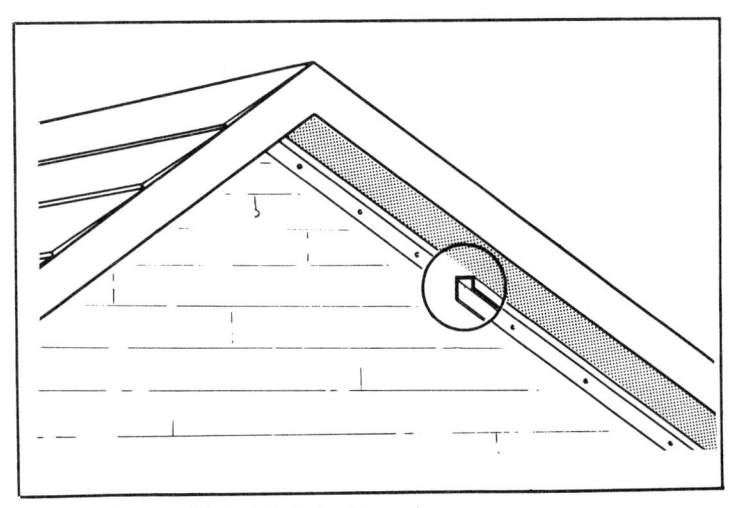

Fig. 8-26. J-channel is installed at gable ends.

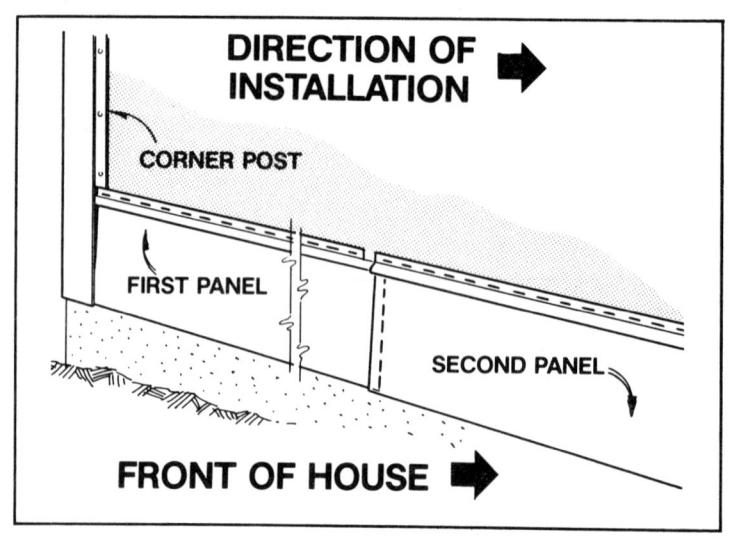

Fig. 8-27. Overlapping.

corners. Panels must be hung with aluminum nails through the center of the factory-slotted holes every 16 to 24 inches along their entire lengths. Nails must be driven into sound lumber, such as: ¾-inch penetration into house framing with plain shank nails or through ½-inch plywood with screw shank nails.

Lapping. On the sides of the building, start at the rear corner and work toward the front, so that the lapping will be away from the front and less noticeable. On the front of the building, start at the corners and work toward the entrance door for the same reason. When lapping, factory-cut ends of panels should be on top of field-cut ends for best appearance.

Overlapping. Panels should overlap each other by approximately ½ inch (Fig. 8-27). A maximum of ⅝ inch and a minimum of ⅜ inch is a good rule of thumb. Thermal expansion requirements need to be considered in panel overlaps. Avoid short panel lengths of under 24 inches, and make sure factory-cut ends are always on top of field-cut ends. The job should start at the rear of the house and work toward the front.

Expansion and Contraction. Aluminum will expand when heated and contract when cooled. The expansion can amount to approximately ⅛ inch in a 10 foot length for every 100 degrees of temperature change. Allowance for this expansion or contraction should be made when installing siding. If siding is installed in hot weather, the product is already warm and at least partly "expanded." Therefore, less room will be required to allow for temperature expansion. With the product stored in a hot sun area, the applicator could apply an aluminum siding panel against a corner post with minimum clearance (say 1/32 to 1/16 inch). In cold weather, assuming the aluminum product was stored in the outside cold, the applicator should allow between 1/16 and 1/8 inch space between areas of possible restriction, such as at a corner post. Using this expansion and contraction "common sense," the applicator should be able to install the products properly for good appearance, and thus avoid unnecessary waves or buckles that could occur with temperature change.

Proper Staggering of Panels. For visual appearance, the staggering of joints should be well-planned. Many applicators plan their joining so that any two joints in line vertically will be separated by at least two courses (see Fig. 8-28). At a bare minimum, separate panel overlaps on the next course by at least 2 feet. Joints should be avoided on panels directly above and below windows. Shorter pieces that develop as work proceeds can be used for smaller areas around windows and doors.

Improper Staggers of Panels. A poor arrangement of panel overlaps detracts fromt the appearance of the installation. See Fig. 8-29.

Backer Tabs. Backer tabs are used with 8-inch horizontal, non-insulated siding only. They insure rigidity, evenness of installation, and tight end-laps. They are used at all panel overlaps and behind panels entering corners. Slip the backer tab behind the panel with the flat side facing out, after the panel has been locked in place. The backer tab should be directly behind and even with the edge of

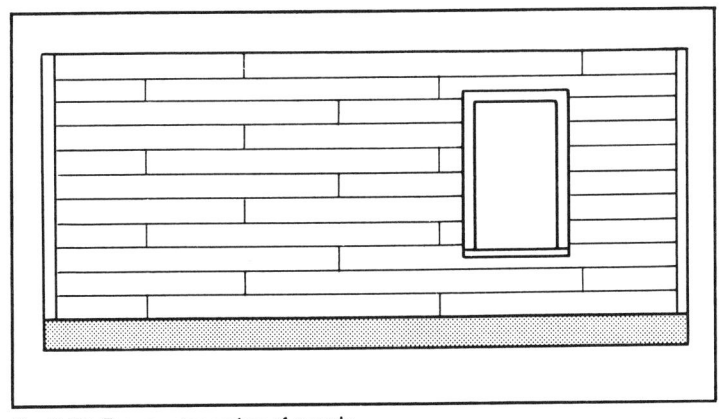

Fig. 8-28. Proper staggering of panels.

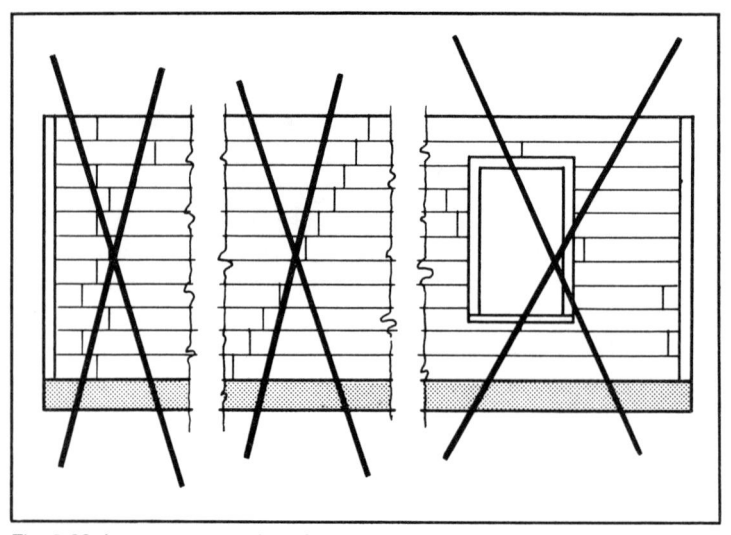

Fig. 8-29. Improper staggering of panels.

the first panel of the overlap. Nail the backer tab to keep it in place. See Fig. 8-30.

NAILING POINTERS

Hanging the Siding. Siding is hung on the nails (not nailed to the wall). When nailing, drive the nail through the center of the factory-slotted hole to within 1/32 inch of the nailing flange—snug but not tight. The slots are elongated to permit the siding to contract and expand freely. Siding nailed too tightly will not be able to move with temperature changes and could also produce an unattractive wavy appearance. Expansion requirements vary with the seasons. An application installed in the hot summer requires less allowance. An application installed in winter might require as much as ⅛ inch expansion allowance per panel. See the section on expansion and contraction.

Nails. When you are nailing siding and accessories, always use aluminum nails. Nails should be driven straight and level (Fig. 8-31). They should never be slanted up or down so as to possibly cause distortion of the panel. Use 2-inch nails (or longer) for insulated siding and 1½-inch nails (or longer) for non-insulated siding, as well as most trim accessories. AAMA specification No. 1403.2-1975 (Installation Specifications for Residential Aluminum Siding) recommends a minimum ¾ inch penetration into studs with plain shank nails, or penetration through ½ inch plywood with screw

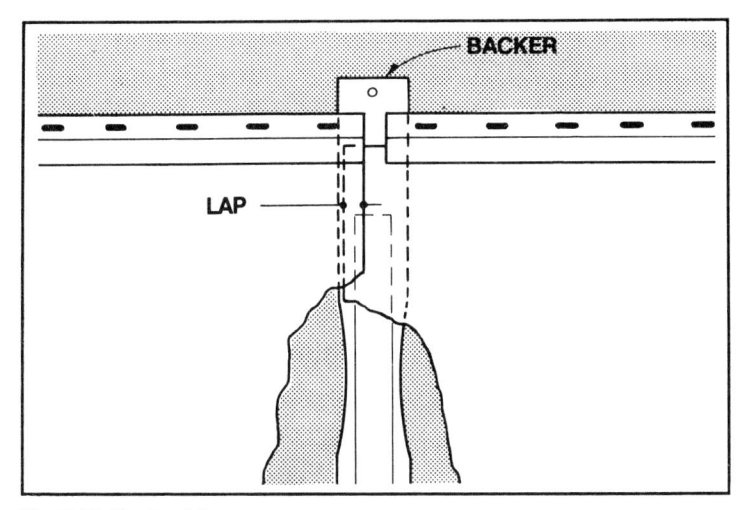

Fig. 8-30. Backer tabs.

shank nails. Where visible nails are required, use trim nails that match the siding or accessory.

Nailing Centers. Siding nails should be spaced on approximately 16-inch centers (maximum of 24 inches), and should not be driven closer than 6 inches from panel overlaps. Where low spots are encountered in a wall, drive the nails on both sides of the low spot and allow the panel to float over the low spot to maintain a

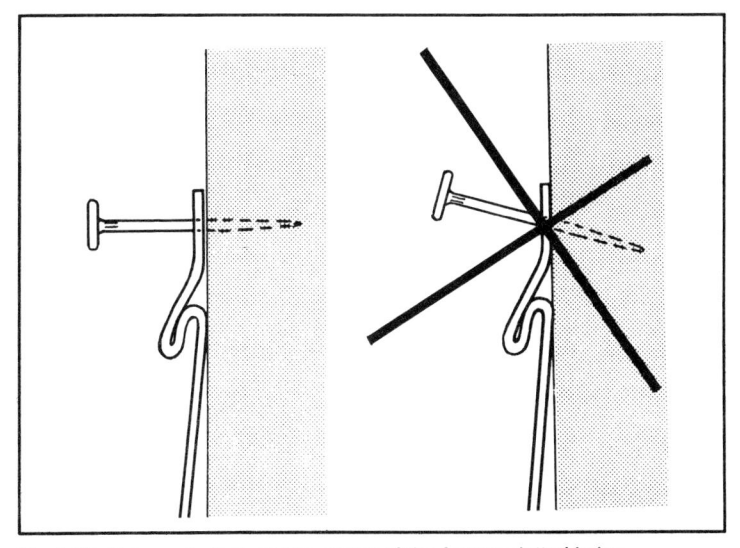

Fig. 8-31. Drive nails through the center of the factory-slotted holes.

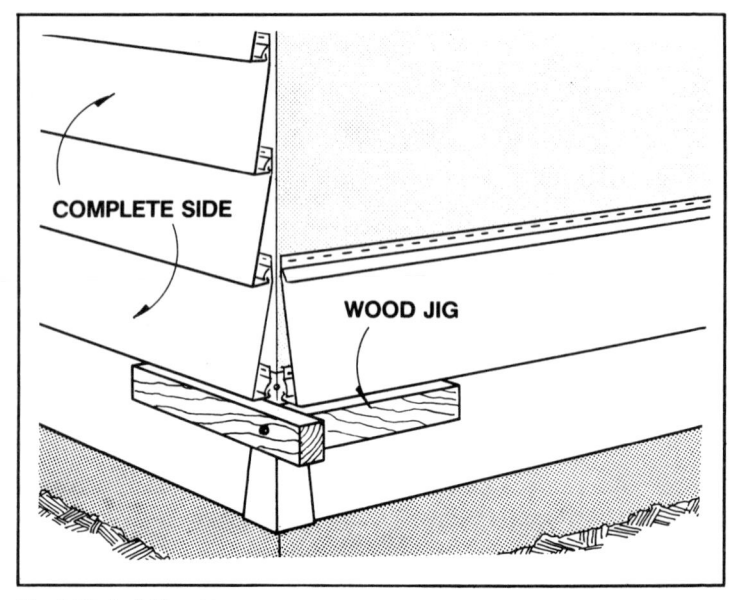

Fig. 8-32. Installing corner caps.

straight shadow line. On new construction, nail into the studs on 16-inch centers. Do not skip studs. In remodeling, when siding is installed over old wood, be sure that rotted or broken boards are not used as the nailing base.

INDIVIDUAL CORNER CAPS

Individual corner caps can be used for 8-inch horizontal lap siding instead of outside corner posts. The siding courses on adjoining walls must meet evenly at the corners. to allow room for the cap, install siding with ¾-inch clearance from the corner (¼-inch clearance for insulated siding).

Installation. Complete one wall first. On the adjacent wall, install one course of siding, line the course up, and install the corner cap. Each corner cap must be fitted and installed before the next course of siding is installed. A jig can be constructed to facilitate the alignment, or a special tool can be purchased for this purpose. See Fig. 8-32.

Install by slipping bottom flanges of corner cap up under the butt of each siding panel. Slight steady pressure should be used to press the cap in place. If necessary, insert a putty knife between the panel locks; pry slightly outward to allow room for the flanges to slip in. Gentle tapping with a rubber mallet and wood block can also be helpful. When the cap is in position, secure with 2- or 2½-inch nails, or long enough for ¾ inch penetration into solid wood or sheathing. Nail through at least one of the pre-punched nail holes in the top of the corner cap. Note: Before securing corner, make sure butts or corner cap and siding panels are flush.

PANELS AT WINDOWS AND DOORS

Measuring. As siding courses reach a window, a panel will probably need to be cut narrower to fit the space under the window opening. Plan this course of siding so that the panel will extend on both sides of the opening. Hold the panel in place to mark for the vertical cuts. Use a small piece of scrap siding (A of Fig. 8-33) as a template; place it next to the window and lock it into the panel below. Make a mark on this piece ¼-inch below the sill height to allow clearance for all-purpose trim. Do the same on the other side of the window, because windows are not always absolutely level.

Cutting. The vertical cuts are made with duck bills, tinsnips, or power saw from the top edge of the panel. The lengthwise (horizontal) cut is scored with the utility knife one time, and bent back and forth until the unwanted piece breaks out. See B of Fig. 8-33.

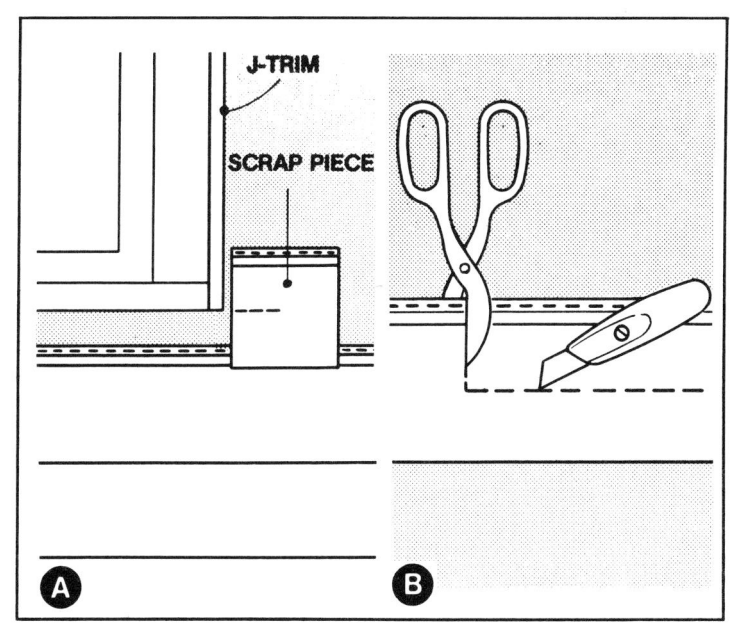

Fig. 8-33. Measuring and cutting techniques.

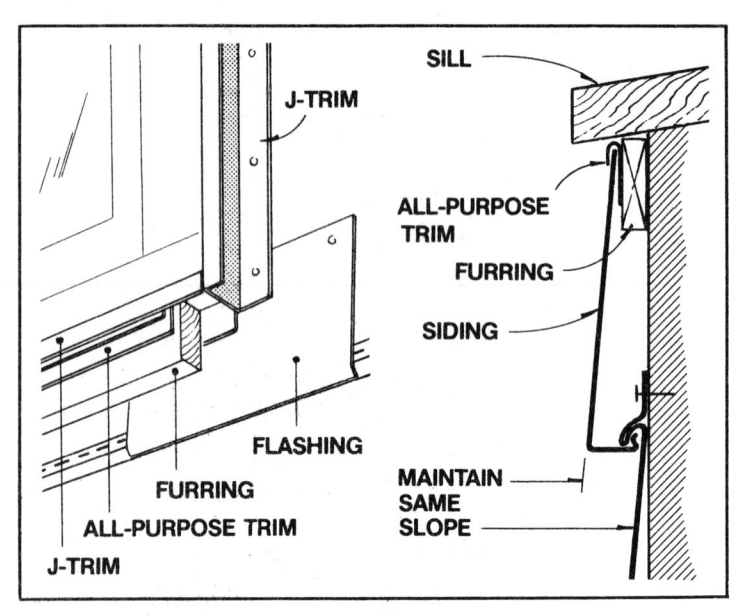

Fig. 8-34. Installing trim and furring strips.

Trim and Fur. The raw cut edge of the panel should be trimmed the exact width of the sill with all-purpose trim. First determine if furring is required behind the cut edge to maintain slope angle with adjacent panels. Nail the correct thickness of furring under the sill and install all-purpose trim over it—with aluminum nails—close up under the sill, for a tight fit.

Install. Slide the panel upward so as to engage the all-purpose trim, the J-channels on window sides, and the lock of the panel below. See Fig. 8-34.

Measuring and Cutting. Fitting panels over door and window openings is almost the same as making undersill cut-outs, except that clearances for fitting the panel are different. The cut panel on top of the opening needs more room to move down to engage the interlock of the siding panel below (on both sides of the window). Mark a scrap piece template without allowing clearance, and then make saw cuts ¼ to ⅜ inch deeper than the mark. This will provide the necessary interlock clearance. See Fig. 8-35.

Furring. Check the need for furring over the top of window or door in order to maintain slope angle. Install furring strips if they are needed.

Trim. Cut a piece of all-purpose trim the same width as the raw edge of a cut panel, and slip over this cut edge in the panel before

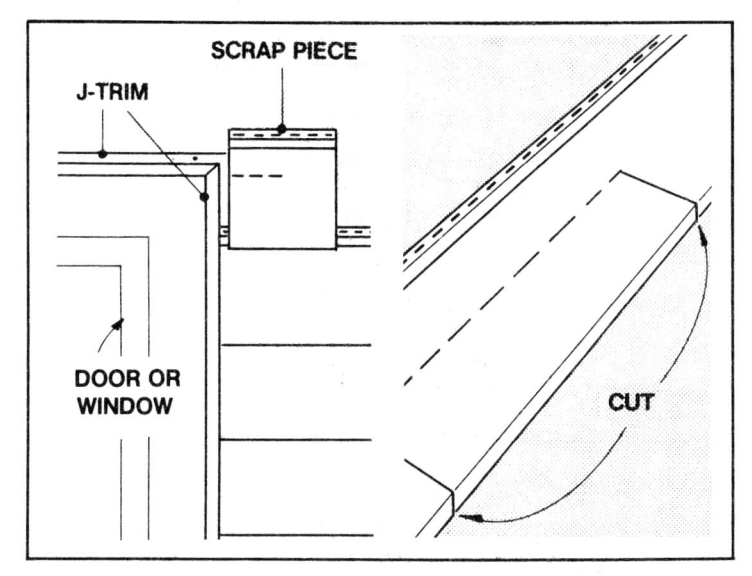

Fig. 8-35. Installing trim over a door.

installing. Drop the panel into position engaging interlocks on siding panels below. All-purpose trim can now be pushed downward to close any gap noticeable at the juncture with the J-channel. See Fig. 8-36.

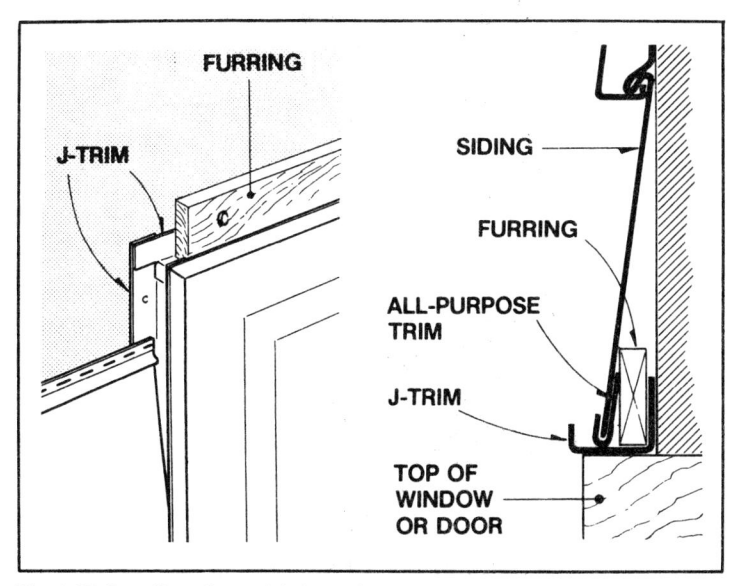

Fig. 8-36. Installing trim and J-channel.

305

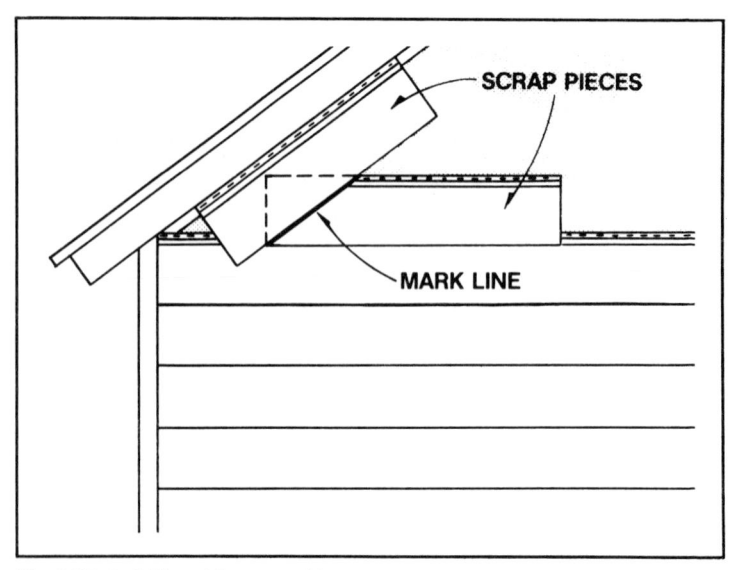

Fig. 8-37. Installing siding on gables.

FITTING AT GABLE ENDS

Measuring and Cutting. When installing siding on gables, diagonal cuts will have to be made on some of the panels (Fig. 8-37). To make a pattern for cutting panels to fit the gable slope, use two short pieces of siding as templates. Interlock one of these pieces into the panel below. Hold the second piece against the J-channel trim on the gable slope. Along the edge of this second piece, scribe a line diagonally across the interlocked panel and cut along this line with tinsnips or power saw. This cut panel is a pattern that can be used to transfer cutting marks to each successive course along the gable slope. This pattern should be checked on each course for accuracy because the slope is not always straight. All roof slopes can be handled in the same manner as gable-end slopes.

Installation. Slip the angled end of panel into J-trim previously installed along gable edge. Lock the butt into interlock of the panel below. Remember to allow for expansion or contraction where required. If necessary, face nail with 1¼ inch (or longer) painted head aluminum nail in the apex of the last panel at the gable peak (Fig. 8-38). Touch-up enamel in matching siding colors can also be used for exposed nail heads.

Do not cover existing louvers. Attic ventilation is necessary in summer, to reduce temperatures, and in winter to prevent the accumulation of moisture.

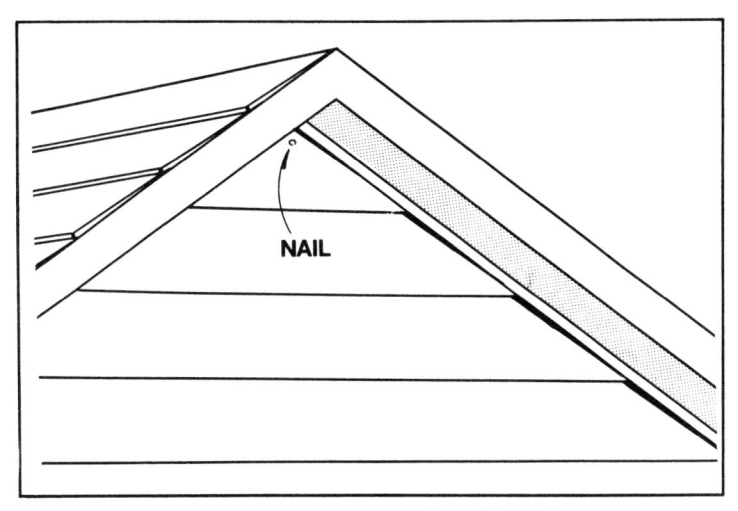

Fig. 8-38. If necessary, nail the last panel at the gable peak.

FITTING UNDER EAVES

Furring. The last panel course under the eaves will almost always have to be cut lengthwise to fit in the remaining space (Fig. 8-39). Usually, furring will be needed under this last panel to maintain correct slope angle. Determine proper furring thickness and install the furring. Nail all-purpose trim to the furring with aluminum nails. Trim should be cut long enough to go the length of the wall.

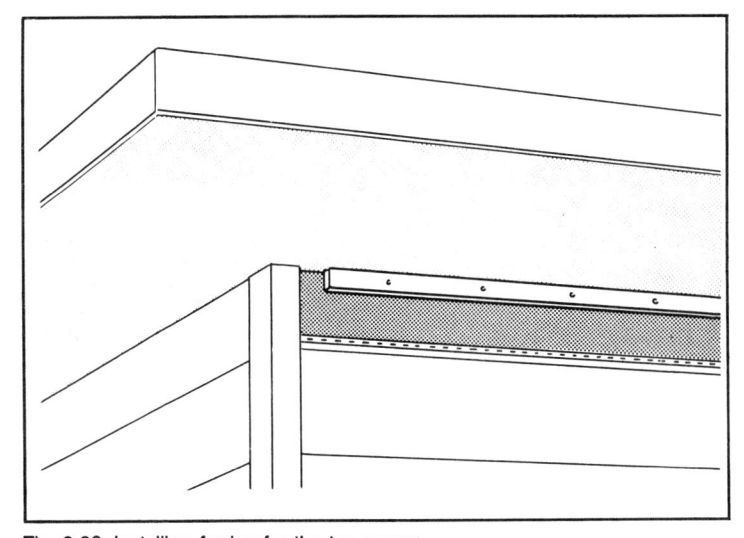

Fig. 8-39. Installing furring for the top course.

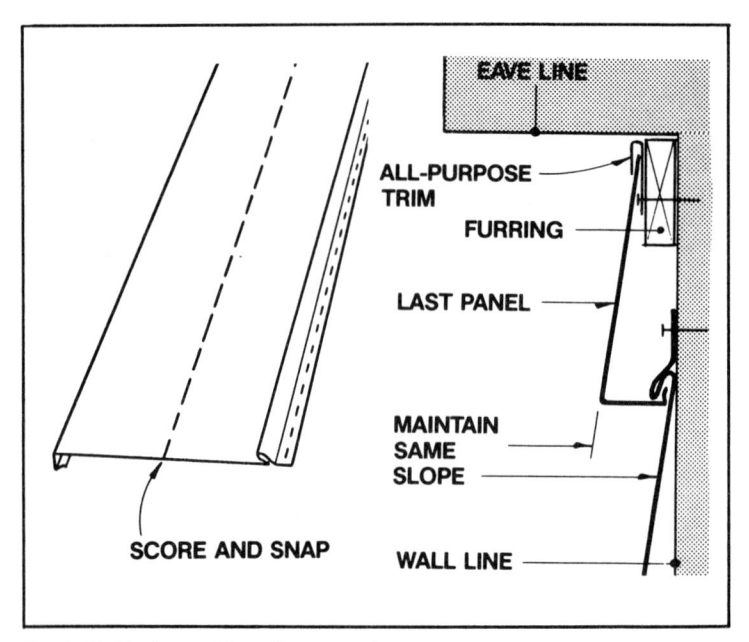

Fig. 8-40. Cutting and installing a panel.

Cutting. To determine the width of the cut required, measure from the bottom of the top lock to the eaves, subtract ¼ inch, and mark the panel for cutting. Take measurements at several points along the eaves to insure accuracy. Score the panel with the utility knife and bend until it snaps. See Fig. 8-40.

Installing. Apply gutterseal to the nail flange of the all-purpose trim. Slide the final panel into the all-purpose trim. Engage the interlock of the panel below. If required, lock can be flattened slightly using a hammer and a 2- or 3-foot piece of lumber before the final panel is installed so it will grip more securely. Press the panel into gutterseal adhesive. With this technique, fewer face nails will be required.

INSULATED SIDING

Due to the need for energy saving, more attention is being given to insulated siding. There are two types: *factory-laminated backer board* and separate *drop-in backer panels* installed on the job. Both laminated and drop-in types are available in wood fiber board (2 and 4 of Fig. 8-41) and polystyrene foam board (1 and 3 of Fig. 8-41). Some laminated-type insulated siding panels are available backed with aluminum reflective foil for increased insulation value.

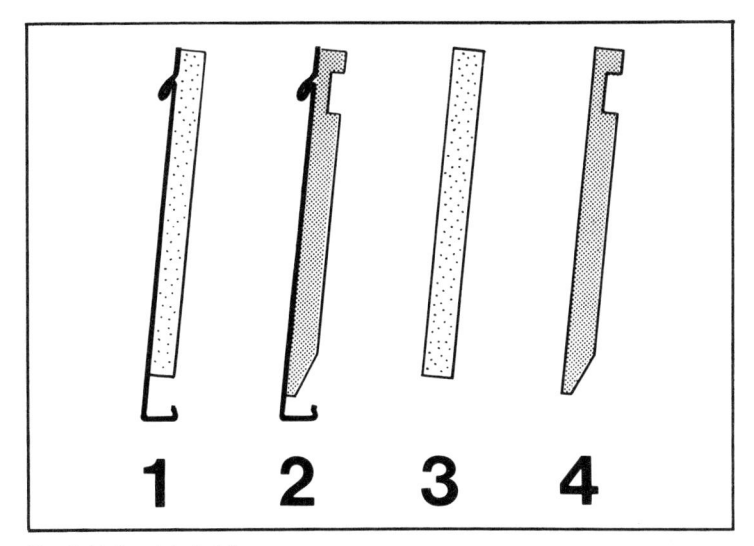

Fig. 8-41. Insulated siding.

Drop-In Backer. Drop-in backer in convenient lengths is installed on the job site. The pieces are progressively dropped in behind the siding panels after they are engaged in the interlocks. The panels are then nailed to the wall. Use longer aluminum nails.

Cutting. A power saw works best when cutting insulated siding panels. The backer must be cut back if tinsnips and a utility knife (A of Fig. 8-42) are used for cutting. Cut back approximately 1 inch to allow for overlaps.

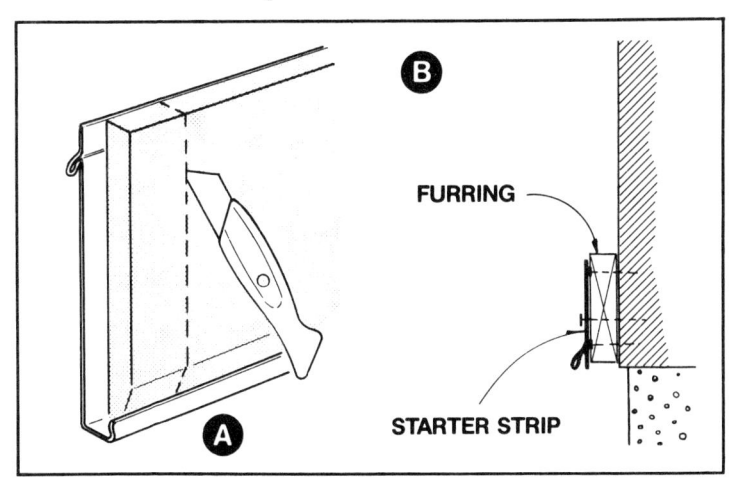

Fig. 8-42. Cutting and furring insulated siding.

309

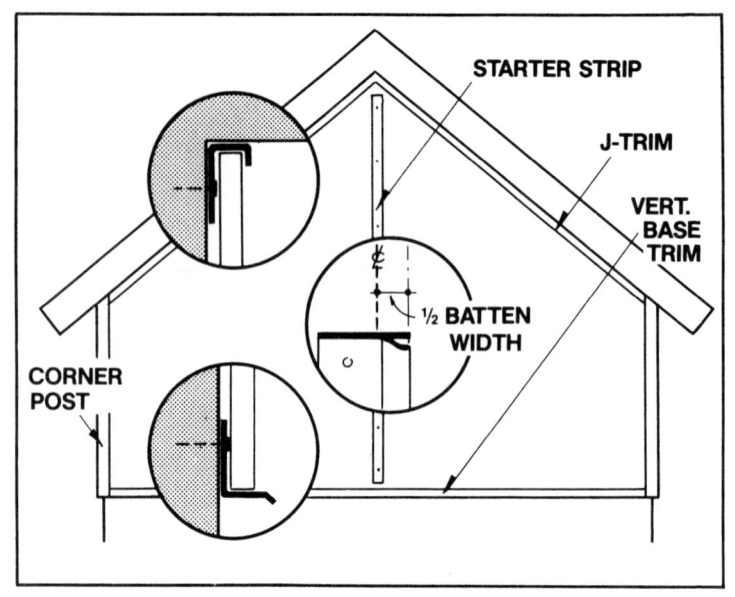

Fig. 8-43. Vertical siding application.

Furring. The starter strip should be furred out the thickness of the backer to maintain the same slope throughout the subsequent siding courses. See B of Fig. 8-42.

Application. Vertical siding is used both for an entire installation and as a contrast to horizontal siding, especially on gable ends. Most procedures outlined for horizontal siding are generally the same for vertical siding except that the starter strip is applied vertically and panels interlock in a vertical position. See Fig. 8-43.

Accessories and Starter Strip. Snap a chalk line, that is parallel to the eaves or the window heads, along the base of the house as a guide for applying vertical base flashing trim (or J-channel). Apply J-channels under the eaves. Add outside corner posts as required. Windows and doors are trimmed with J-channel on the sides and under sills, with vertical base flashing (or J-channel) being used at the window heads. To locate the starter strip, drop a plumb line from the gable peak off-center by one half the width of a vertical panel batten, and mark a chalk line. The starter strip bottom edge is nailed to this line (see Fig. 8-44). The raised batten will now be properly centered for best appearance.

First Panel. Measure and cut the first panel to correct length. Cut the batten edge off this panel. Slip the cut edge under the starter strip and nail panel through slotted nailing flange. Cut the other

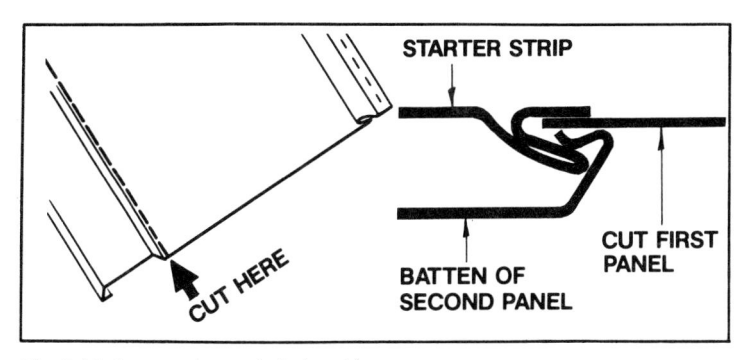

Fig. 8-44. Accessories and starter strip.

panel to correct length, and engage batten flange in starter strip and nail panel (see Fig. 8-45).

Remaining Panels. It will now be possible to continue the installation working in both left and right directions from these two initial center panels (Fig. 8-46). This makes for an even-spaced batten appearance when there is a gable. An alternative way to install the starter strip is to nail it plumb at the corner and install panels working from one direction.

VERTICAL SIDING

Doors and Windows. Fitting vertical panels around door and window trim is similar to that shown for horizontal siding. The cut edge of the vertical panel is capped with all-purpose trim and in-inserted into a J-channel (See A of Fig. 8-47). Furring out might be required depending on where the cut is made (for instance, if the cut is made in the batten portion of the panel). The procedure at inside and outside corners would be the same as for horizontal siding. The all-purpose trim must be nailed before installing the vertical panel (B

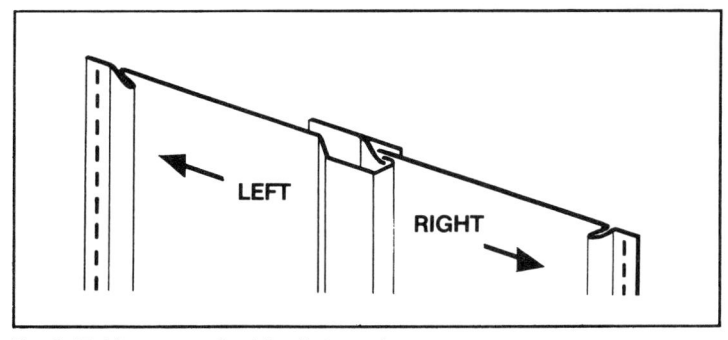

Fig. 8-45. Measure and cut the first panel.

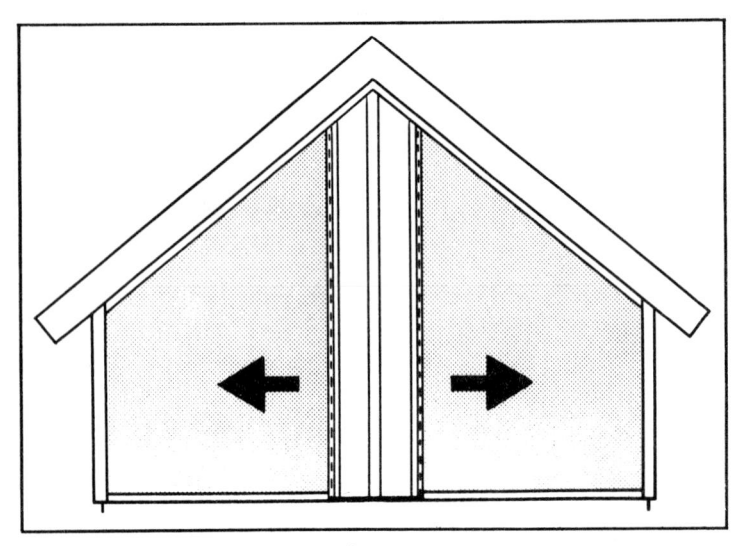

Fig. 8-46. Install the remaining panels.

of Fig. 8-47). It can be held in place with gutterseal mastic in the all-purpose trim (see section on fitting under the eaves).

Panel Bent Corners. At outside corners, a panel can be bent around the corner rather than using an outside corner post. Cut the panel to the proper length and lock it into the previous panel. Mark

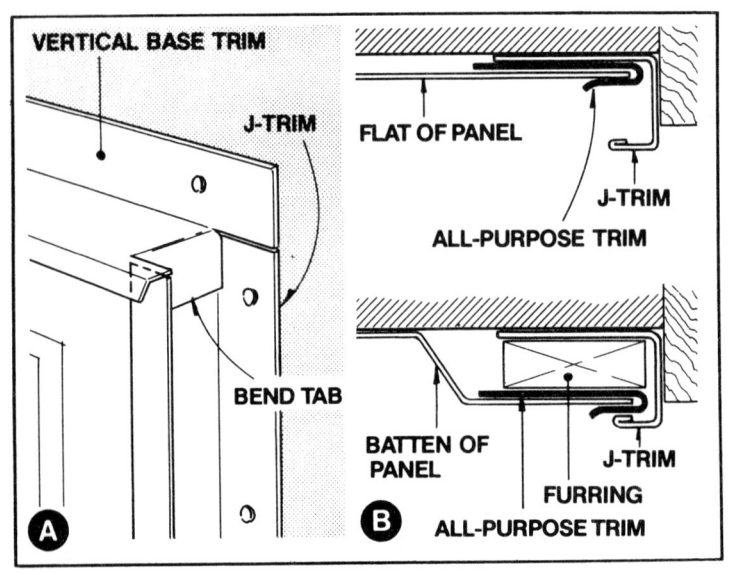

Fig. 8-47. Fitting vertical siding around doors and windows.

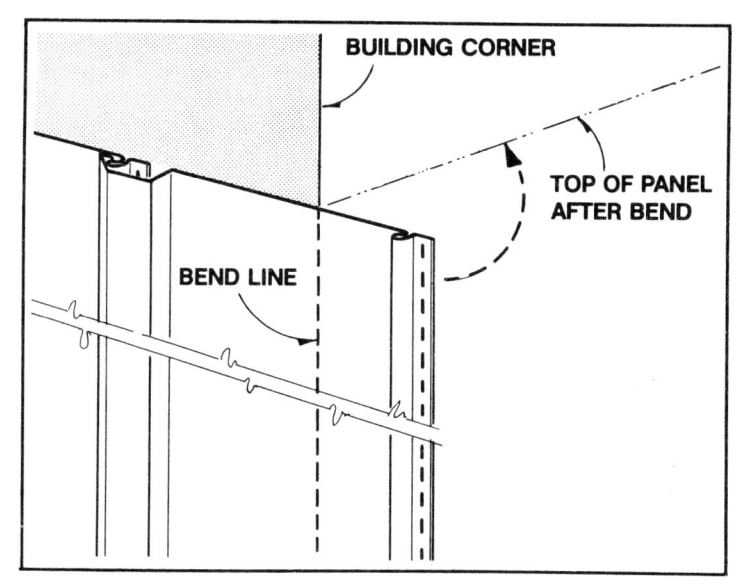

Fig. 8-48. Installing bent panels at corners.

where the panel should be bent around the corner and remove the panel (Fig. 8-48). Use a portable brake and bend the panel to form a right angle. Install the panel and nail it in place. Continue with the next vertical panel, as usual, on the adjoining wall.

Narrow Cut Panels. When panels are cut narrower to fit into corners, at the end of a run for example, the raw edge can be trimmed using all-purpose trim in combination with gutterseal mastic. See Fig. 8-49.

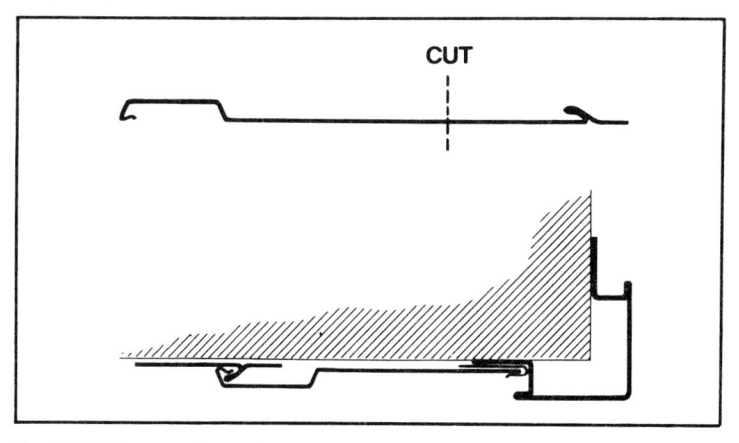

Fig. 8-49. Narrow-cut panels.

CAULKING AND CLEANUP

In general, caulking is done around doors, windows, and gables where metal meets wood and when metal meets metal (except where accessories are used to make caulking unnecessary). Caulking is also needed where metal meets brick or stone around chimneys and walls. Try not to use exposed caulking on top of siding panels. Surface caulking required at panel cut-outs around faucets, meter boxes, etc. must be done neatly.

It is important to get a deep caulking bead (¼ inch minimum), not just a wide bead. Cut the plastic tip of the caulking cartridge square to get this deeper bead. Move the gun evenly, and apply steady, even pressure on the trigger. Butyl caulking is preferred because it has greater flexibility. Most producers supply caulking in colors to match siding and accessories. Do not depend on caulking to fill large gaps (more than ⅛-inch wide) because expansion/contraction of the siding can cause cracking of the caulking.

Clean Up. Keep hands as clean as possible during application or use clean work gloves. To clean smudges, use a soft cloth or damp sponge dipped in mild detergent solution or in soap and water. Avoid rubbing too hard; this might create a glossy area on the finish surface. Never use harsh abrasive cleaners. For asphalt or grease stains, mineral spirits can be used with care. Thoroughly clean off any residue.

Job Site. Re-install all fixtures, brackets, downspouts, etc. that were removed. Many applicators paint accessories that weren't replaced (such as kitchen fan outlets or service cable) to match the new siding color. Most manufacturers have available touch-up paint, or matching paint formulas. These can be purchased at your local paint store.

All scrap pieces, cartons, nails, etc. should be removed each day. The jobsite should be left neat and clean.

SPECIAL SITUATIONS

Replacement of a Damaged Panel. Cut damaged panel just above center with utility knife for entire length of panel (1 of Fig. 8-50). Discard the bottom cut section of damaged panel. Do not nail remaining part of damaged panel, as this will not allow for expansion/contraction.

Remove top lock of a new panel by scoring with utility knife. Bend and snap off. Remove burrs on scored edge. Try small piece of siding panel to fit under old lock. If too tight, carefully open with wide putty knife (see 2 of Fig. 8-50).

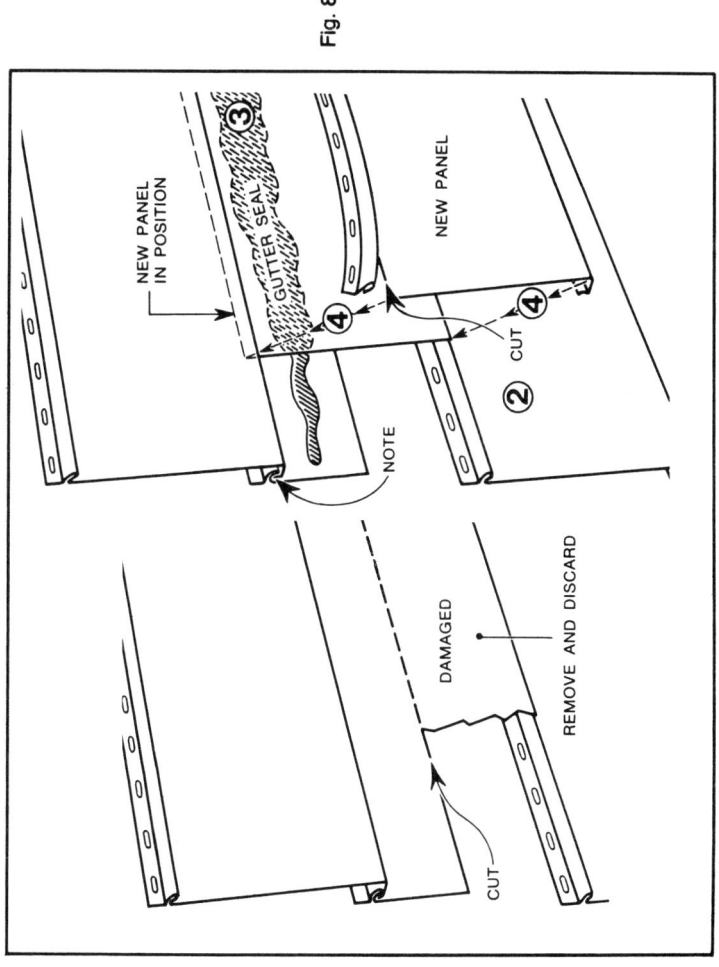

Fig. 8-50. Replacement of a damaged panel.

Fig. 8-51. Replacement of a damaged corner post.

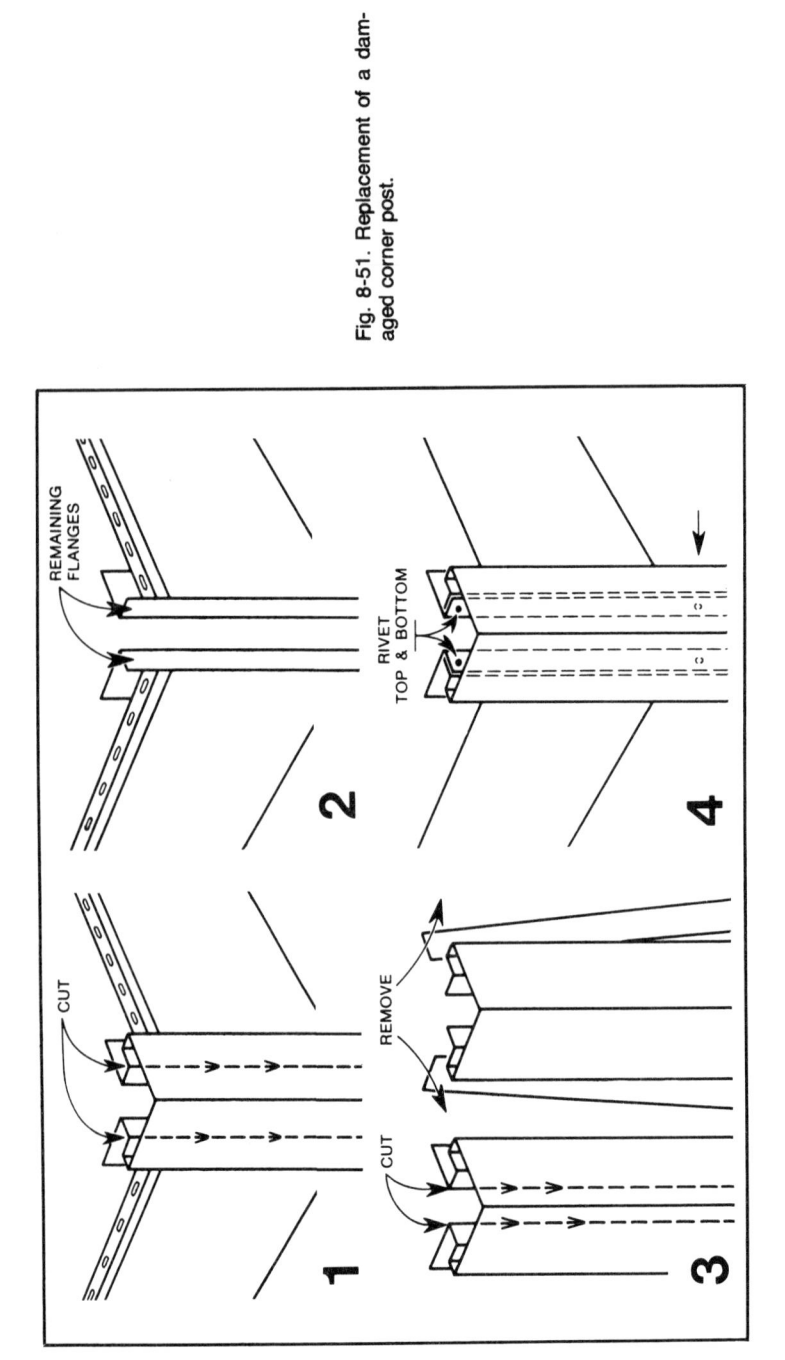

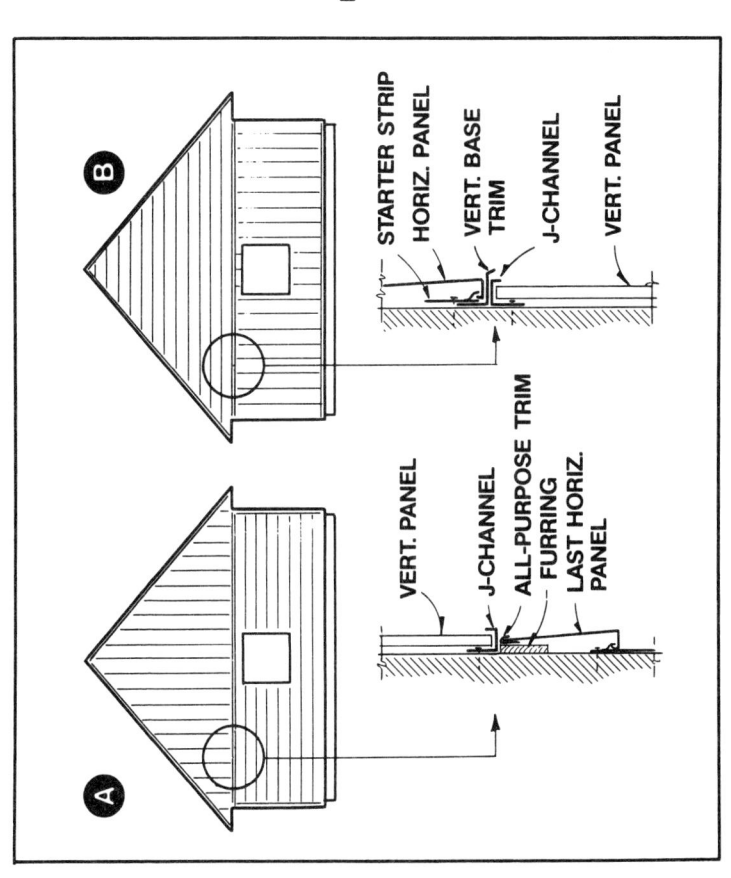

Fig. 8-52. Transitions.

Apply heavy bead of gutterseal full length of damaged panel at point shown in 3 of Fig. 8-50.

Install new panel carefully over gutterseal (4 of Fig. 8-50). Engage top and bottom of panel into respective locks. Be sure gutterseal makes contact with new panel. Apply pressure with palm of hand. Do not nail panel. Use this procedure on all siding.

Replacement of Damaged Corner Post. Cut the damaged corner post by scoring with utility knife at the two points marked in 1 of Fig. 8-51.

Use a pair of pliers, or other suitable tool to remove outside face of post, by bending back and forth. See 2 of Fig. 8-51.

Remove the nailing flanges of the new corner post by scoring and bending (3 of Fig. 8-51).

Hook new corner post on one side, overlapping the flanges, then spread the new post enough to overlap the flanges on the other side of the post. After the new post is in place, use pop rivets on both sides, under the butt edge of the siding, to hold new post in place. See 4 of Fig. 8-51.

Transitions: Vertical Over Horizontal. Cut the nailing flange and lock off last horizontal panel course and fur out if necessary. Use all-purpose trim to receive this cut piece. Apply drip-edge molding or J-channel over top of horizontal panel to receive vertical siding. Punch weep-holes in J-channel for water drainage. See A of Fig. 8-52.

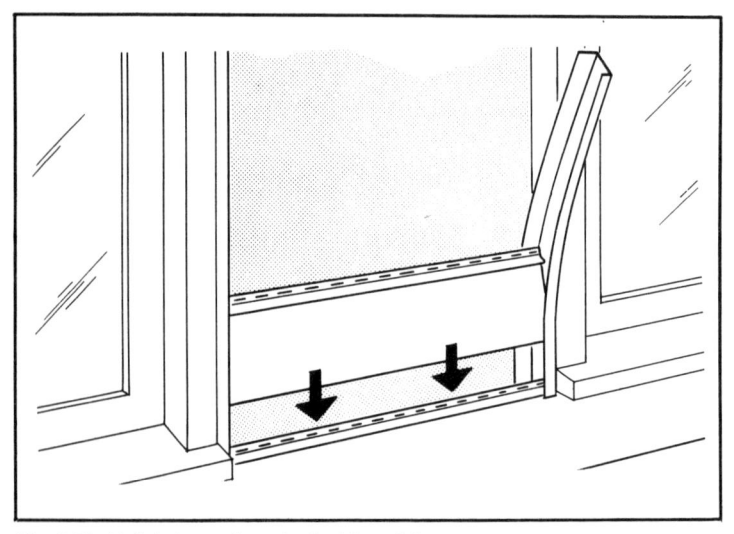

Fig. 8-53. Nail J-channels on both sides of the space.

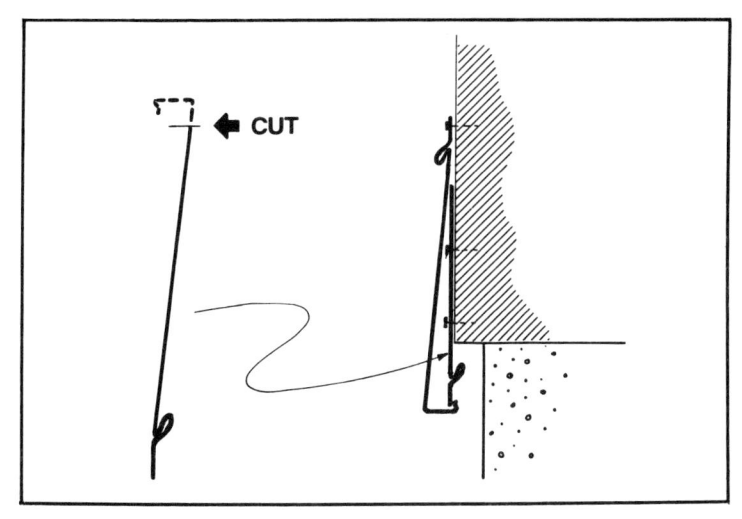

Fig. 8-54. Application of a difficult-condition starter strip.

Transitions: Horizontal Over Vertical. Use J-channel to cap off vertical. Then use vertical base trim and starter strip to start horizontal panels. See B of Fig. 8-52.

Short Panels Between Openings. For runs between windows, nail J-channels on both sides of the space (Fig. 8-53). Bow the siding to slip into channels. If the space is too narrow to allow the bowing of panels, one J-channel can be left unattached initially. This J-channel can be nailed in position as successive panels are nailed in place.

Difficult Condition Starter Strip Application. The procedure shown in Fig. 8-54 can be used where the conventional starter strip is too narrow to fit uneven base line, or where broken shingles or boards make installing the starter strip difficult or impossible. To solve the problem, cut the butt end from a siding panel and install it upside down, inside out, against the base line of the house. The first panel course is then engaged in a normal manner as shown.

Glossary

abrasive—Any of the coated papers (such as sandpaper), coarse fabrics or other materials (pumice and rottenstone), or steel wool that can be used for transforming a coarse surface into a smooth one.

adhesion—The capability of a paint or other clear coating to stick to a bare or previously painted surface.

airway—A space between roof insulation and roof boards for the movement of air.

air dry—The capability of a coating to dry at temperatures between 50 to 80 degrees Fahrenheit with a relative humidity between 40 to 60 percent.

albinoing—Removing all color pigments from a surface. The result of bleaching.

alkali—A substance such as lye, soda, or lime (often an additive to concrete), that is destructive to most paint coatings. It must be removed before painting.

alkaloid—A colorless, crystalline, organic substance that can be difficult to obtain, but it will speed paint application. The most useful form is $C_{17}H_{21}NO_{4}$.

aldyd—A synthetic resin added to various coatings to increase film forming capability. Properties imparted include hardness, gloss, and low penetration into substrate.

alligatoring—A common paint failure. Coarse checking pattern characterized by a slipping of the new paint coating over the old paint coating so that the old coating can be seen through the fissures.

architectural finishes—blistering

architectural finishes—Commercially applied finishes not readily available for nonprofessionals. Includes baked on finishes and bridge paint.

asphalt—Most native asphalt is a residue from evaporated petroleum. It is insoluble in water, but soluble in gasoline, and it melts when heated. Used widely in construction for waterproofing roof coverings.

attic ventilators—In houses, screened openings provided to ventilate an attic space. They are located in the soffit area as inlet ventilators and in the gable end or along the ridge as outlet ventilators. They can also consist of power-driven fans used as an exhaust system (see louver).

batten—Narrow strips of wood used to cover joints or as decorative vertical members over wide boards or plywood.

batter board—One of a pair of horizontal boards nailed to posts set at the corners of an excavation. Each is used to indicate the desired level, and also as a fastening for stretched strings to indicate outside lines of foundation walls.

beam—A structural member transversely supporting a load.

bearing partition—A partition that supports any vertical load in addition to its own weight.

bearing wall—A wall that supports any vertical load in addition to its own weight.

bed molding—A molding in an angle as between the overhanging cornice or eaves of a building and the sidewalls.

binder—The nonvolatile vehicle portion of a coating, such as linseed oil or acrylic emulsion, that binds pigment particles.

bleaching—Lightening of a surface either to remove stains leaving the natural tone or removing all traces of color pigment. The result is an albino effect.

bleeding—Seeping of resin or gum from lumber. This commonly occurs around knots in wood.

blind nailing—Nailing in such a way that the nailheads are not visible on the face of the work; usually at the tongue of matched boards.

blind stop—A rectangular molding, usually three-fourths of an inch by 1⅜ inches or more in width, used in the assembly of a window frame. Serves as a stop for storm and screen combination windows and to resist air infiltration.

blistering—A condition of paint failure most commonly caused when a coating is applied over a wet or hot surface.

blue stain—A bluish or grayish discoloration of the sapwood caused by the growth of certain mold-like fungi on the surface and in the interior of a piece. Made possible by the same conditions that favor the growth of other fungi.

body—A term used to describe the thickness or thinness of a paint coating.

bodied linseed oil—Linseed oil that has been thickened in viscosity by suitable processing with heat or chemicals. Bodied oils are obtainable in a great range of viscosity, from a little greater than that of raw oil to just short of a jellied state.

boiled linseed oil—Linseed oil in which enough lead, manganese, or cobalt salts have been incorporated to make the oil harden more rapidly when spread over a surface in thin layers or coatings.

bolster—A short horizontal timber or steel beam on top of a column to support and decrease the span of beams or girders.

Boston ridge—A method of applying asphalt shingles or wood shingles at the ridge or at the hips of a roof as a finish.

boxing—The process of mixing paints by pouring from one container into another several times to ensure complete mixing.

breathability—The capability of a coating film to permit the passage of moisture vapor without causing paint failure such as blistering.

brick veneer—A facing of brick laid against and fastened to the sheathing of a frame wall or tile wall construction.

brushability—The smoothness of a paint. If it can be brushed on with ease, it has brushability.

brush marks—Lines that remain in a coating after it has dried. Most commonly this is a result of spreading a paint coating too thin.

build—The thickness of a coating after drying. Some finishes are built onto a surface. Varnish is an example.

burnish—To make a surface shiny by rubbing or polishing.

butt joint—The junction at which the ends of two timbers or other members meet in a square cut joint.

cantilever—A projecting beam or joist, not supported at one end, used to support an extension of a structure such as a roof or deck.

cant strip—A triangular-shaped piece of lumber used at the junction of a flat deck and a wall to prevent cracking of the roofing applied over it.

cap—The upper member of a column, a pilaster, a door cornice, molding, and the like.

casement frames and sash—Frames of wood or metal, enclosing part or all of the sash, that can be opened by means of hinges affixed to the vertical edges.

casing—Molding of various widths and thicknesses used to trim door and window openings at the jambs.

catalyst—An additive that speeds up the drying process of a coating. Common in two-part epoxy coatings.

caulking compound—Any of the putty-like substances used for filling joints around windows, door, chimneys, etc.

cement base paint—A paint with a makeup of portland cement, lime, pigment and other ingredients. Most commonly sold in powder form and mixed with water before use.

chalking—The decomposition of a coating film into a loose powder on the film surface. Chalking capability is built into most paints to permit cleaning of the finish. Excess chalking must be removed before a new coating is applied.

checking—A paint failure similar to alligatoring.

checkrails—Meeting rails sufficiently thicker than a window to fill the opening between the top and bottom sash made by the parting stop in the frame of double-hung windows. Most commonly beveled.

clapboard—A long, thin board, thicker on one edge, overlapped and nailed on the exterior for siding. It is applied horizontally.

clear coating—Any topcoating that is transparent. Varnish and lacquer are examples.

close-grain woods—Commonly hardwoods that have small pores when dry. Examples include maple, birch, and cherry. These do not generally require filling before a finish coating is applied.

collar beam—Nominal 1-inch or 2-inch thick members connecting opposite roof rafters. They also serve to stiffen the roof structure.

color retention—The capability of a coating to show little or no color change when exposed to the elements.

column—In architecture, a perpendicular supporting member, circular or rectangular in section, usually consisting of a base, shaft, and capital. In engineering, a vertical structural compression member which supports loads acting in the direction of its longitudinal axis.

combination doors/windows—Combination doors or windows used over regular openings. They provide winter insulation and summer protection and often have self-storing or removable glass and screen inserts. This eliminates the need for handling a different unit each season.

concrete (plain)—Concrete without reinforcement or reinforced only for shrinkage or temperature changes.

condensation—In building, beads or drops of water (and frequently frost in extremely cold weather) that accumulates on the inside of the exterior siding of a building when warm, moisture-laden air from the interior reaches a point where the temperature no longer permits the air to sustain the moisture it holds. Use of louvers or attic ventilators will reduce moisture condensation in attics. A vapor barrier under the gypsum lath or drywall on exposed walls will reduce condensation in them.

construction (frame)—A type of construction in which the structural parts are wood or depend on a wooden frame for support. In codes, if masonry veneer is applied to the exterior walls, the classification of this type of construction is usually unchanged.

corbel out—To build out one or more courses of brick or stone from the face of a wall to form a support for timbers.

corner boards—Used as trim for the external corners of a house or other frame structure against which the ends of the siding are finished.

corner braces—Diagonal braces at the corners of a framed structure added to stiffen or strengthen the wall.

cornice—Overhang of a pitched roof at the eaves line. It usually consists of a facia board, a soffit for a closed cornice, and appropriate moldings.

cornice return—That portion of the cornice that returns on the gable end of a roof structure.

counterflashing—A flashing usually used on chimneys at the roofline to cover shingle flashing and to provide protection against moisture.

coverage—The amount of area a coating will spread over. This is most commonly expressed in square feet.

cracking—A coating failure used to generally describe breaks in the dried finish. Alligatoring is one example.

crawl space—A shallow space below the living quarters of a basementless house. It is normally enclosed within the foundation walls.

creosote—A liquid coating used as a wood preservative. Wood treated with creosote should not be painted.

cricket—A small drainage roof structure. A single slope or a double slope is placed at the junction of larger surfaces that meet at an angle such as above a chimney.

custom color—A nonstandard color produced by adding a predetermined amount of color pigment dyes to a base color.

decay—Disintegration of wood or other substances through the action of fungi.

deck paint—An enamel with a high degree of resistance to mechanical wear. It is designed for use on such surfaces as porch floors.

density—The mass of substance in a unit volume. When expressed in the metric system, it is numerically equal to the specific gravity of the same substance.

dewpoint—Temperature at which a vapor begins to deposit as a liquid. Applies especially to water in the atmosphere.

direct nailing—To nail perpendicular to the initial surface or to the junction of the pieces being joined. Also called *face nailing*.

dispersion—The stable suspension of pigment in which the individual pigment particles are present as separate entities and not as aggregates.

dispersion agent—A substance added to aid the stable suspension of pigments in the dispersed state.

dormer—An opening in a sloping roof, the framing of which projects out to form a vertical wall suitable for windows or other openings.

double glazing—An insulating windowpane formed of two thicknesses of glass with a sealed air space between the panes.

double-hung windows—Windows with an upper and lower sash. Each is supported by cords and weights.

downspout—A spout or pipe to carry rain water down from the roof to a cistern or to the ground by way of a roof or gutter.

downspout leader—A pipe for conducting rain water from the roof to a cistern or to the ground by way of a downspout.

downspout strap—A piece of metal that secures the downspout to the eaves or wall of a building.

dressed and matched (tongued-and-grooved)—Boards or planks machined in such a manner that there is a groove along one edge and a corresponding tongue on the other.

drier paint—Usually oil-soluble soaps of metals such as lead, manganese, or cobalt, which, in small proportions, hasten the oxidation and hardening (drying) of the drying oils in paints.

drip—(1) A member of a cornice or other horizontal exterior-finish course that has a projection beyond the other parts for throwing off water. (2) A groove in the underside of a sill or drip cap to cause water to drop off on the outer edge instead of drawing back and running down the face of the buildings exterior siding.

drip cap—A molding placed on the exterior top side of a door or window frame to cause water to drip beyond the exterior siding of a house.

dry rot—A building term used to describe various types of decay in woods.

earth pigments—Naturally occuring pigments such as umber, sienna, talc, etc. used for natural color tones in paint coatings.

eaves—The extension of a roof deck beyond the house walls.

efflorescence—A white residue left on the surface of masonry after water has evaporated (see *alkali*).

emulsion—Color finishes that contain a high varnish content. Most important characteristic is that enamels dry to a hard finish. They can be flat or high in gloss.

epoxy—Extremely hard and tough coating made from synthetic resins; most commonly a two part formulation.

erosion—The natural wearing away of a coating due to the actions of the elements.

etch—Surface preparation by chemical means (usually to masonry work to improve a surface so that a coating will have an adhesion base.

expansion joint—A bituminous fiber strip used to separate blocks or units of concrete to prevent cracking due to expansion as a result of temperature changes. Also used on concrete slabs.

extender—An inexpensive, inert pigment often added to coatings to increase the mass and lower the overall cost of the paint. Can be used to control certain properties in a coating such as gloss, viscosity, and sheen.

extractives—Naturally occuring, water-soluble chemicals generally associated with rustic woods such as cedar, cypress, and redwood.

facia (fascia)—A flat board, band, or face used sometimes by itself, but usually in combination with moldings. Often located at the outer face of the cornice.

fading—Loss of color due to exposure to the sun (see albinoing).

feathering—The blending of the edges of a finished coating. In sanding, when an edge and flat surface are leveled so the result cannot be seen or felt.

filler—Paste or liquid material used to fill pores in certain open grain woods, such as oak, before applying a topcoating or finish coat.

film—The dry coating on a surface.

fire resistive—In the absence of a specific ruling by the authority having jurisdiction, applies to materials for construction that are not combustible in the temperatures of ordinary fires and which will withstand such fires without serious impairment of usefulness for at least one hour.

fishplate—A wood or plywood piece used to fasten the ends of two members together at a butt joint with nails or bolts. Sometimes used at the junction of opposite rafters near the ridge line.

flaking—Coating deterioration or failure characterized by loose pieces of film (see *peeling*).

flame spread rate—The results obtained from a carefully conled test to determine the rate at which a dry coating will burn on various substrates such as plywood, asphalt shingles, etc.

flashing—Sheet metal or other material used in roof and wall construction to protect a building from water seepage.

flash point—The temperature at which a coating, solvent, or building material will ignite. The lower the flash point is the greater the fire hazard.

flow—The capability of a coating to level out and spread to a uniform film.

flue—The space or passage in a chimney through which smoke, gas, or fumes ascend called a flue.

fly rafters—End rafters of the gable overhang supported by roof sheathing and lookouts.

footing—A masonry section, usually concrete, in a rectangular form wider than the bottom of the foundation wall or the pier it supports.

foundation—The lower parts of walls on which a structure is built. Foundation walls of masonry or concrete are mainly below ground level.

force dry—Any means that speeds up the natural drying process of a paint coating (electric fan, hair dryer, etc.).

frieze—In house construction, a horizontal member connecting the top of the siding with the soffit of the cornice.

frostline—The depth of frost penetration in soil. This depth varies in different parts of the country. Footings should generally be placed below this depth to prevent movement.

fungi (wood)—Microscopic plants that live in damp wood and cause mold, stains, and decay.

fungicide—A chemical that is poisonous to fungi. It is a common paint additive.

gable—The triangular part of a wall under the inverted V of the roof line.

gable end—An end wall of a house having a gable.

girder—A large or principal beam of wood or steel used to support concentrated loads at isolated points along its length.

glazing—Any work that involves fitting glass into window or door frames.

gloss—The shininess of a coating or surface.

gloss enamel—A finish coating made of varnish and sufficient pigments to provide opacity and color, but little or no pigment of low opacity. Such enamel forms a hard coating with maximum smoothness and a high degree of gloss on the surface.

grain—The natural direction of fibers in wood.

grain, edge (vertical)—Edge grain lumber that has been sawn parallel to the pith of the log and approximately at right angles to the growth rings. The rings form an angle of 45 degrees or more with the surface of the piece.

grain, flat—Flat grain lumber that has been sawn parallel to the pith of the log and approximately tangent to the growth rings. The rings form an angle of less than 45 degrees with the surface of the piece.

grain, quartersawn—Another term for edge grain.

green lumber—Lumber that has been freshly cut or inadequately dried. It tends to warp or bleed resins.

grout—Mortar made of such consistency (by adding water or special liquids) that it will flow into the joints and cavities of the masonry work and fill them solid.

gusset—A flat wood, plywood, or similar type member used to provide a connection at an intersection of wood members. Most commonly used at joints of wood trusses. They are fastened with nails, screws, bolts, adhesives, or combinations of these.

gutter—A shallow channel or conduit of metal or wood set below and along the eaves of a house to catch and carry off rainwater from the roof.

hardness—The capability of a paint coating to dry to a state that resists dents, scratches, etc.

hardwood—The lumber from deciduous trees such as oak, and maple.

header—(1) A beam placed perpendicular to joists and to which joists are nailed in framing a chimney, stairway, skylight, etc. (2) A wood lintel.

heartwood—The wood extending from the pith to the sapwood. The cells of heartwood no longer participate in the life processes of the tree.

hiding power—The capability of a coating to completely cover a surface and hide the color beneath.

hip—The external angle formed by the meeting of two sloping sides of a roof.

hip roof—A roof that rises by inclined planes from all four sides of a building.

holidays—A term used to describe areas where a paint coating has not completely covered the surface. Also, those areas that the paint brush missed.

humidifier—A device designed to increase the humidity within a room or a house by means of the discharge of water vapor into the atmosphere of the area. Humidifiers are individual room size units or larger units attached to the heating plant to condition the entire house.

I-beam—A steel beam with a cross section resembling the letter I. It is used for long spans as basement beams or over wide openings, such as a double garage door, when wall and roof loads are imposed over and on the opening.

insulation board—A structural building board made of coarse wood or cane fiber in one-half and five-thirty-second inch thicknesses. It can be obtained in various sheet sizes, various densities, and with several treatments.

insulation, thermal—Any material high in resistance to heat transmission that, when placed in the walls, ceiling, or floors of a structure will reduce the rate of heat loss.

jack rafter—A rafter that spans the distance from the wall-plate to a hip, or from a valley to a ridge.

miter joint—orange peel

miter joint—The joint of two pieces at an angle that bisects the joining angle.

moisture content (of wood)—Weight of the water contained in the wood. Usually this is expressed as a percentage of the weight of the oven-dry wood.

molding—A wood strip having a curved or projecting surface used for decorative purposes, for both interior and exterior application.

mortise—A slot cut into a board, plank, or timber, usually edgewise, to receive a tenon of another board, plank, or timber to form a strong joint.

mullion—A vertical bar or divider in the frame between windows, doors, or other openings.

muntin—A small member that divides window glass.

multisolvent—A mixture of cleaning solvents.

nap—The length of fibers of a roller used in painting.

natural finish—A transparent finish that does not seriously alter the original color or grain of natural wood. Natural finishes are usually provided by sealers, oils, varnishes, water-repellent preservatives and other similar materials.

non-bearing wall—A wall supporting no other load than its own weight.

non-volatile vehicle—The portion of a paint coating that actually remains on the surface to bind the pigment portion to the surface after the vehicle has dried or evaporated. This can be linseed oil, latex emulsion, or others.

nosing—The projecting edge of a molding or drip. Usually applied to the projecting molding on the edge of a stairtread.

notch—A crosswise rabbet at the end of a board.

O.C., OC, and on center—The measurement of spacing for studs, joists, and the like in a building from the center of one member to the center of the next.

oil stains—Wood stains that are formed by mixing oil-soluble dyes in an oil. The term is often applied to pigmented wiping stains.

opaque—The opposite of transparent. Any coating that has unusual hiding power.

open-grain wood—Woods with large pores, such as oak or walnut.

orange peel—The irregular surface of a film; it resembles the dimpled skin of an orange. A paint failure (common when spraying paints) resulting from the failure of a coating to level.

outrigger—An extension of a rafter beyond the wall line. Usually a smaller member nailed to a larger rafter to form a cornice or roof overhang.

paint—A combination of pigments with suitable thinners or oils to provide decorative and protective cover.

paper, building—A general term for papers, felts, and similar sheet materials used in buildings without reference to their properties or uses.

paper, sheathing—A building material, generally paper or felt, that has been saturated with asphalt. It is used in wall construction and roof construction as protection against the passage of air and moisture.

parting stop (strip)—A small wood piece used in the side and head jambs of double-hung windows to separate upper and lower sash.

partition—A wall that subdivides spaces within any story of a building.

paste filler—Wood filler in paste form that must be thinned before it can be used.

peeling—Paint failure usually caused by moisture or a dirt undercoating. A common result of poor surface preparation.

penetrating finish—Any coating which, when applied, sinks into the surface while leaving almost nothing on the surface.

penny—As applied to nails, it originally indicated the price per hundred. The term now serves as a measure of nail length and is abbreviated by the letter d.

perm—A measure of water vapor movement through a material (grains per square foot per hour per inch of mercury difference in vapor pressure).

pier—A column of masonry, usually rectangular in horizontal cross section, used to support other structural members such as girders and joists.

pigment—The fine, solid particles used in the manufacture of a paint coating which impart color, opacity, and protective qualities to the film.

pitch—The incline slope of a roof or the ratio of the total rise to the total width of a house. For example, an 8-foot rise and 24-foot width is one-third pitch roof (or one in three). Roof slope is expressed in the inches of rise per foot of run.

pitch pocket—An opening extending parallel to the annual rings of growth that usually contains, or has contained, either solid or liquid pitch.

pith—The small, soft core at the original center of a tree around which wood formation takes place.

plate—Sill plate: a horizontal member anchored to a masonry wall. Sole plate: bottom horizontal member of a frame wall. Top plate: horizontal member of a frame wall supporting ceiling joists, rafters, trusses, etc.

plough—To cut lengthwise grooves in a board or plank.

plumb—Exactly perpendicular; vertical.

ply—The number of thicknesses or layers of roofing felt, veneer in plywood, or layers in built-up materials, or any finished piece of such material.

plywood—A piece of wood made of three or more layers of veneer, joined with glue, and usually laid with the grain of adjoining plies at right angles. Almost always an odd number of plies are used to provide balanced construction.

polyurethane—An oil-modified urethane varnish that dries to a hard and tough finish.

pores—Wood cells of comparatively large diameter that have open ends and are set one above the other to form continuous tubes or fibers. The openings of the vessels on the surface of a piece of wood are commonly referred to as pores.

preservative—Any substance that, for a reasonable length of time, will prevent the action of wood destroying fungi, borers of various kinds, and similar destructive agents when the wood has been properly coated or impregnated.

primer—The first coat of paint in a paint job that consists of two or more coats. The paint used for such a coat.

putty—A type of cement, usually made of whiting and boiled linseed oil, beaten and kneaded to the consistency of bread dough. It is used in sealing glass in a sash, filling small holes and crevices in wood, and similar purposes.

quarter round—A small molding that has the cross section of a quarter of a circle.

radiant heating—A method of heating that usually consists of a system of hot water with pipes placed in the floor, wall or ceiling, electrically heated panels, or a large mass (such as a brick wall) that is heated by the Sun.

rafter—One of a series of structural members of a roof designed to support roof loads. The rafters of a flat roof are sometimes called *roof joists*.

rafter, hip—A rafter that forms the intersection of an external roof angle.

rafter, valley—A rafter that forms the intersection of an internal roof angle. The valley rafter is normally made from double, 2-inch thick members.

rake—Trim members that run parallel to the roof slope and form the finish between the wall and a gable roof extension.

raw linseed oil—The crude product processed from flaxseed, and usually without much subsequent treatment.

reducer—Paint thinner used for reducing the viscosity of various finishes. There are different thinners for different coatings (lacquer thinner, mineral spirits).

reflective insulation—Sheet material with one or both sides of comparatively low heat emissivity such as aluminum foil. When used in building construction, the surfaces face air spaces and reduce the radiation across that air space.

reinforcing—Steel rods or metal fabric placed in concrete slabs, beams, or columns to increase their strength.

relative humidity—The amount of water vapor in the atmosphere expressed as a percentage of the maximum quantity that could be present at a given temperature. The actual amount of water vapor that can be held in space increases with the temperature.

resin—A natural resin is a non-volatile solid or semisolid exudation from pine trees or other plants such as rosin. Resins are also synthetically made.

resorcinol glue—A glue that is high in wet, strength and dry strength, and resistant to high temperatures. It is used for gluing lumber or assembly joints that must withstand severe service conditions.

ridge—The horizontal line at the junction of the top edges of two sloping roof surfaces.

ridge board—The board placed on edge at the ridge of the roof into which the upper ends of the rafters are fastened.

roll roofing—Roofing material, composed of fiber and saturated with asphalt, that is supplied in 36-inch wide rolls with 108 square feet of material per roll.

roof sheathing—The boards or sheet material fastened to the roof rafters on which shingles or other roof covering is laid.

rubber-emulsion paint—Paint that has rubber or synthetic rubber dispersed in fine droplets in water.

rust preventive—Paint or primer that inhibits rust.

saddle—Two sloping surfaces meeting in a horizontal ridge such as between the back side of a chimney, or other vertical surface, and a sloping roof.

sand-float finish—Lime mixed with sand. The result is a textured finish on concrete.

sapwood—The outer zone of wood that is next to the bark. In a living tree, it contains some living cells as well as dead and dying cells. In most species, it is lighter colored than the heartwood. In all species, it is lacking in decay resistance.

sash—A single frame containing one or more lites of window glass.

sash balance—A device, usually operated by a spring or tensioned weather stripping, designed to counterbalance a double-hung window sash.

satin finish—A semigloss coating.

saturated felt—A felt that has been impregnated with tar or asphalt.

scratch coat—The first coat of plaster or cement that is scratched to form a bond for the second coat.

scribing—Fitting woodwork to an irregular surface. In moldings, cutting the end of one piece to fit the molded face of the other at an interior angle to replace a miter joint.

scrubability—The capability of a coating to withstand scrubbing and cleaning with water, soap, and other cleaners.

sealer—A finishing material, either clear or pigmented, that is usually applied directly over uncoated wood to seal the surface.

seasoning—Removing moisture from green wood in order to improve its serviceability.

semigloss—A paint or enamel made with a slight insufficiency of non-volatile vehicle so that its coating, when dry, has some luster but it is not very glossy.

settling—A natural occurrence happening when the pigments in paints settle to the bottom of the container. The reason why coatings should be stirred before use.

shake—A thick, handsplit shingle, resawn to form two shakes. It is usually edge grained.

sheathing—The structural covering, usually wood boards or plywood, used to cover studs or rafters on the exterior of a

sheathing—soil cover (ground cover)

structure. Structural building board is normally used only as wall sheathing.

sheet-metal work—Components of a house employing sheet metal such as flashing, gutters, downspouts, etc.

shellac—A transparent coating made by dissolving in alcohol a resinous secretion of the lac bug (a scale insect that thrives in tropical countries).

shingles—Roof covering of asphalt, asbestos, wood, tile, slate, or other material cut to stock lengths, widths, and thicknesses.

shingles, siding—Various kinds of shingles such as wood, used over sheathing for exterior sidewall covering.

shutter—Lightweight louvered or flush wood or non-wood frames in the form of doors located on each side of a window. Some are made to close over the window for protection and others are fastened permanently to the exterior wall for decoration.

siding—The finish covering of the exterior wall of a frame building. It is made of horizontal weatherboards, vertical boards with battens, shingles, or other material.

siding, bevel (lap siding)—Wedge-shaped boards used as horizontal siding in a lapped pattern. This siding varies in butt thickness from one-half to three-fourth of an inch and in widths up to 12 inches. Normally used over some type of sheathing.

siding, Dolly Varden—Beveled wood siding that is rabbeted on the bottom edge and installed horizontally.

siding, drop—Usually three-fourth inch thick and 6 to 8 inches wide with tongued and grooved or shiplap edges. Often used as siding without sheathing on secondary buildings.

sill—The lowest member of the frame of a structure resting on the foundation and supporting the floor joists or the uprights of the wall. The member forming the lower side of an opening such as a door or window sill.

skin—A tough layer formed on the surface of a coating when left in an unsealed container and exposed to the air for some time. Skin is formed by oxidation or polymerization.

sleeper—A wood member embedded in concrete, as in a floor, which serves to support and fasten subfloor or flooring materials.

soffit—The underside of an overhanging cornice.

soil cover (ground cover)—A light covering of plastic film, roll roofing, or similar material used over the soil in crawl spaces of buildings to minimize moisture permeation of the area.

soil stack—The vertical main section of a system of soil, waste, or vent piping.

sole plate—See *plate*.

solid bridging— A solid member placed between adjacent floor joists near the center of the span to prevent the joists from twisting.

solvent—The volatile part of a paint. Also the part that evaporates.

span—The distance between structural supports such as walls, columns, piers, beams, girders and trusses.

spar varnish—A type of varnish intended for outdoor use. The life span of such a coating might only be one year.

splash block—A small masonry block laid with the top close to the ground surface to receive roof drainage from downspouts and to carry it away from the building.

spot prime—To apply primer only to those areas in need of additional protection such as areas scraped to bare wood and rusted areas that have been sanded.

square—A unit of measure—100 square feet—usually applied to roofing material. Sidewall coverings are sometimes packed to cover 100 square feet and are also sold on that basis.

stain, shingle—A form of oil paint, very thin in consistency, intended for coloring wood with rough surfaces such as shingles without forming a coating of significant thickness or gloss.

storm sash (Storm Window)—An extra window usually placed on the outside of an existing one as additional protection against cold weather.

story—That part of a building between any floor and the floor or roof above.

string (stringer) —A timber or other support for cross members in floors or ceilings. In stairs, the support on which the stair treads rest.

stucco—Most commonly refers to an outside plaster made with portland cement as its base.

stud—One of a series of slender wood or metal vertical structural members placed as supporting elements in walls and partitions.

substrate—The surface to which a coating is applied.

tack cloth—A piece of cloth, dampened with a combination of varnish and turpentine, and used to pick up dust particles prior to applying a clear finish.

tail beam—A relatively short beam or joist supported in a wall on one end and by a header at the other.

tenon—The projecting part cut on the end of a board, plank, or timber for insertion into a corresponding hole (see mortise) in another piece of lumber to form an attractive and strong joint.

termites—Insects that superficially resemble ants in size. Subterranean termites establish themselves in buildings not by being carried with lumber, but by entering from ground nests after the building has been constructed.

termite shield—A shield, usually of non-corrodible metal, placed in or on a foundation wall or other mass of masonry or around pipes to prevent the entrance of termites.

thinner—Any liquid that is used to thin a paint coating.

thixotropy—The property of a coating that allows it to undergo a transformation from a partially gelled state to a liquid flowable state, and then back to a partially gelled state due to agitation and subsequent rest. This property helps to create dripless coatings and it is commonly used in latex paints.

toenailing—To drive a nail at a slant with the initial surface in order to permit it to penetrate into a second member.

tongued-and-grooved—See *dressed and matched lumber.*

topcoat—The last coat applied.

touch up—Repairing a coating in spots without color or gloss difference.

trim—The finish materials in a building, such as moldings, applied around openings (window and door trim) or at the floor and ceilings of rooms (baseboard, cornice, etc.).

truss—A frame or jointed structure designed to act as a beam of long span. Each member is usually subjected to longitudinal stress only, either tension or compression.

turpentine—A volatile oil used as a thinner in paints and as a solvent in varnishes. Chemically, it is a mixture of terpenes. A product of softwood (conifers) trees.

ultraviolet light—Rays of the light spectrum lying outside the visible spectrum. One of the prime weathering elements of paint and clear coating degradation.

undercoat—A paint coating applied prior to the finish or top coats of a painting project. It can be the first of two or the second of three coats. In some usages of the word, it is synonymous with the priming coat.

under layment—A material placed under finish coverings, such as roof deck sheathing, to provide a smooth, even surface for applying the finish.

valley—The internal angle formed by the junction of two sloping sides of a roof.

vapor barrier—Material used to retard the movement of water vapor into walls and prevent condensation in them. Usually considered as having a perm value of less than 1.0. Applied separately over the warm side of exposed walls or as part of batt or blanket insulation.

varnish—A thickened preparation of drying oil, or drying oil and resin, suitable for spreading on surfaces to form continuous, transparent coatings or for mixing with pigments to make enamels.

venetian window—A window with one large fixed central pane and smaller panes around the perimeter.

vehicle—The liquid portion of a finishing material. It consists of the binder (non-volatile) and volatile thinners.

vent—A pipe or duct that allows the flow of air as an inlet or outlet.

vermiculite—A mineral closely related to mica. It has the faculty of expanding on heating to form lightweight material with insulation quality. Generally used as a poured-in (bulk) insulation for walls and ceilings.

viscosity—The thickness or thinness of a liquid.

volatile thinner—A liquid that evaporates readily and is used to thin or reduce the consistency of finishes without altering the relative volumes of pigments and non-volatile vehicles.

washability—The capability of a coating to be easily cleaned without damaging the coating itself.

water-repellent preservative—A liquid designed to penetrate into wood and impart water repellency and a moderate preservative protection. It is used for millwork, such as sashes and frames, and it is usually applied by dipping.

weathering—The wearing away of a film coating through the natural actions of wind, sun, rain, etc.

weather strip—Narrow or jamb width sections of thin metal or other material to prevent infiltration of air and moisture around windows and doors. Compression weather stripping prevents air infiltration, provides tension, and acts as a counterbalance.

wrinkling—Paint failure as evidenced by ridges and furrows on a dry paint film.

Index

A
Asphalt roofing cement	78
Asphalt shingles	32

B
Building materials	265

C
Caulking	170
application tips for	196
applying	176
around the eaves	192
latex-base	170
oil-base	170
silicone	171
sill joint	191
Cedar shakes	4
Cedar shingles	3
Chalking	123
Chimney flashing	61
Concealed-nail method	22
Concrete	269
estimating quantities of	231
large repairs	224
maintaining surfaces	213
Concrete patches	217
Condensation	239

D
Downspouts	65
rectangular	68
round	68
Downspout elbows	69
Downspout installation	66, 76
Downspout maintenance	69
Downspout straps	84
Drafts, plugging	169
Dry well	85, 89

E
Exposed-nail method	22

F
Fastenings	267
Flashing	42, 47
chimney	61
Flat roof	7

G
Gable roof	8
Gutters	65
cleaning out the	71
maintenance	69

H
Hardboard	266
Hip roof	39

I
Ice dams	260
Insulation	242, 249, 262
batt	257
blanket	257
fiberglass	176
loose fill	256

341

L

Ladder use	16
Leaks, plugging	169
Lumber	265
common	265
select	265

M

Masonry, repairs and maintenance of tools	205
Materials, building	265
Mildew	131

N

Nails	267
Nails, roofing	33

P

Paint, blistering	127
boxing	144
failures and solutions	164
latex	92
selection	91
paint varnish	96
Paint thinner	112
Paintbrushes	98
Painted surfaces, maintaining	165
Painting	91
concrete	157
exterior	138
metal	152
surface preparation for	119
Painting equipment	98
Painting tools	116
Plywood	266
grades and uses of	266
Putty	174, 188, 204

R

Rain barrels	85
Re-roofing	32
Rollers	106
Roof, estimating shingles for	39
Roof construction	6
Roof inspection	12
Roof trusses	10
Roofing	1
Roofing nails	33
Rool roofing	8

S

Sheathing	10
Shingle installation	48
Shingles, asphalt	32
climbing with	62
nailing caps	59
Siding	274, 275
accessories for	277
alternative methods of	292
backer tabs for	299
bottom cap for	290, 291
casing cover for	294
caulking of	294
chalk line for	289
coil stock for	293
corners of	278
cutting of	303, 309
cutting procedures for	296
difficult starter strip application of	319
equipment required for	281
estimating material for	282
expansion allowance for	290
expansion and contraction of	298
first course of	297
fitting at gable ends for	306
fitting under eaves for	307
furring for	307
gable ends	295
hanging	300
horizontal over vertical	319
improper staggers of	299
individual corner caps for	302
inside corner posts for	290
insulated	276, 308
J-channel for	277
lapping of	298
measuring and cutting of	304, 306
measuring for	303
nailing centers of	301
nailing of	291
nailing pointers for	300
nails for	300
narrow cut panels for	313
outside corner posts for	291
overlapping	298
panel bent corners for	312
panels at windows and doors for	303
proper staggering of	299
replacement of damaged corner for	318
replacement of damaged panel for	314
saving energy with	284
short panels between openings for	319
sill ends for	294
special situations for	314

starter strip for	277, 292	Splash block	85, 87
styles of	275	Spot prime	138
surface preparation for	286		
tools required for	279	**T**	
trim and fur for	304	Tile roof	5
trim for	279		
two-piece sill for	294	**V**	
using a power saw to cut	296	Valley	42, 49
vertical	277, 287, 292, 311	cleaning out the	70
vertical over horizontal	318	Vapor barriers	245, 258, 261
vinyl	272	Ventilation	239, 262
window head cover for	294	Ventilators	246
window and door trim for	294	Vinyl siding	272
wood furring for	286		
Siding installation	290, 297, 306	**W**	
Siding using tinsnips to cut	296	Weather stripping	173, 176, 263
Slate roof	5	foam	175, 203
Soleplate	10	Well, dry	85, 89

343